Hypnotherapy Handbook

Hypnosis and Mindbody Healing

Kevin Hogan

Contributors

Elizabeth J. Nahum	C. Devin Hastings
Mary Lee LaBay	Holly Sumner

Hypnotherapy Handbook:
Hypnosis and Mindbody Healing

Hogan, Kevin, 1961-
Hypnotherapy Handbook: Hypnosis and Mindbody   Healing in
the 21st Century

Bibliography
1. Hypnotherapy
2. Hypnosis
3. Psychotherapy

ISBN: 0-9635085-0-4

CIP Data:

RC497.H   615.851 2 - dc21

by Kevin Hogan, Ph.D.
Copyright 2000
All Rights Reserved

editor- Katie C. Hogan
editor- MaryLee LaBay

contributor- Holly Sumner
contributor- C. Devin Hastings
contributor- Elizabeth J. Nahum
contributor- MaryLee LaBay

Published by
Network 3000 Publishing
3432 Denmark #108
Eagan, MN 55123
Phone: 1-612-707-1898
Toll Free Phone: 1-800-398-4642
Toll Free Fax: 1-888-707-1896

Printed in the USA by

MORRIS PUBLISHING

3212 East Highway 30 • Kearney, NE 68847 • 1-800-650-7888

Table of Contents

Introduction

Healing with Hypnotherapy

Disclaimer: Throughout this book you will learn how *hypnotherapy is complementary to medicine.* It is your responsibility as a hypnotherapist to be certain that your clients are directed to the appropriate medical practitioner in the community. If you leave the medical, psychiatric and psychological professions out of treatment with your client, your client may be the one to lose. Please always be certain that your client receives a medical diagnosis from a competent medical practitioner. Thank you. KH.

This book is written for the hypnotherapist who wants to be able to help people who have suffered and experienced significant emotional and physical problems. It is a book for the hypnotherapist who wants to see his clients experience wellness and achieve the goals that are set by the hypnotherapist and the client.

You will learn the CARPeTS model of hypnotherapy. CARPeTS is an anacronym for Case Analysis, Regression Therapy, Parts Therapy, Time Track Therapy and Suggestive Therapy. This model appears to be the most effective paradigm for the hypnotherapist helping people who suffer from chronic illnesses of all kinds including fibromyalgia, chronic fatigue, environmental illnesses, multiple chemical sensitivity, impotence, tinnitus, hyperacusis and most pain related disorders.

In addition to learning how to help the millions of people who suffer from these severe difficulties, you will also learn how to do past life regression therapy from one of America's leading past life regression therapists. Although I personally remain very uncertain as to the veracity of the actual past life experience itself as being historically verifiable, I am convinced that the therapeutic modality presented in this book by contributor Elizabeth Nahum will change lives, just as you will read about in this book You will also learn about how to use hypnotic techniques in emergency and crisis situations.

As you read this book you will gain the confidence you need to help people heal and change their lives. You will read excerpts from actual sessions to confirm that you understand how to utilize these advanced techniques of hypnotherapy.

Making Tomorrow Better than Yesterday

The field of hypnosis, the use of self hypnosis and the practice of hypnotherapy have one theme in common, we want to make tomorrow better, in some way, than yesterday was, for our clients. Clients do not come to us to "stay the course" or "keep going." Clients come to us for a change. They want to feel better. They want to learn more, think faster, feel less pain, lose weight, stop nasty habits, change their emotional responses to the events of their lives and all sorts of other changes.

In 1999 less than 1% of all Americans sought the services of a hypnotherapist. By comparison, almost half of all adult Americans bought an herb of some kind for some health benefit. It is certainly true that some herbs can really help people's health, but it is doubtful that any herb can do for a client what effective hypnotherapy or even self hypnosis can do for them.

People come to see us because they know that if they don't do *something* their life will just continue to get worse. The person who seeks you out is likely to know that she must make some life changes and make them soon. What most of these people don't know is how they ended up in the boat they are in. Most people, for example, are unaware that they have the ability to have far more control over the direction of their life than they think they do. Even in the area of health care, most people can dramatically improve the quality of their health by interacting with a highly skilled hypnotherapist. They can improve many aspects of their well being by self hypnosis.

I'm always afraid of saying that hypnosis and hypnotherapy are a panacea, because no single modality of therapy or of change can accomplish everything a person needs or wants to change in their life. However, I will say that on average, hypnosis and the intentional use of the mind and brain will do more for someone than any other single self help or wellness "tool."

This book will take you through the basics of visualization through the most advanced techniques of the skilled hypnotherapist called hypnoanalysis.

1

Getting Well Again

I think we all agree that people are both mind and body integrated into a living and breathing being. If we accept this premise, then we are able to more readily be able understand how hypnotherapy can be effective in healing illness, emotional disturbances and bad habits.

The human being is constantly striving for an equilibrium in almost all facets of life; conscious and unconscious. When a negative force interferes with the equilibrium of the being, a counter-force normally occurs, creating a ridge of pain or emotional upset within the individual. The upset may manifest itself as illness and the person will likely remain ill until the ridge has been "taken apart" or collapsed through abreaction.

Most of our life is experienced at the unconscious level. It has been calculated by some psychologists that we can process about 126 bits of information (in our conscious mind) per second. Meanwhile our unconscious mind is processing over one million bits of information per second. That's pretty amazing but not all that surprising.

Generally speaking, we do not regulate our breathing at the conscious level. We do not regulate our pulse and heartbeat at the conscious level. We do not normally regulate the action of our brain functions, seeing, hearing, smelling or tasting at the conscious level. Most of our life experience is at the unconscious level.

Meanwhile, the conscious mind is attempting to deal with the internal and external forces in the environment that are out of equilibrium, in attempt to bring them to equilibrium. As the conscious and unconscious minds compensate for these stimuli, imbalances will and do occur. These imbalances cause illness with a wide variety of symptoms and manifestations.

These imbalances seem to manifest themselves at physical locations in the body where previous illness or injury have occurred. If someone had broken an arm many years ago and the person comes under great stress, there is a likelihood that the location of the previous injury will again become painful. On occasion, there is no easily identifiable link to previous injuries and illness with the current symptoms.

Another key consideration in learning how we become ill, is the fact that identical traumatic situations will affect different people in very different ways. The death of a parent may trigger depression in one child, anxiety in another and trigger no negative upsets in another child. It is normally not possible to discover why this specific stimulus triggered one set of symptoms in one person and not another, without the use of hypnosis. Once the cause has been un-covered, it is very possible the illness may be eliminated using hypnotherapy.

Many illness are the result of bacteriological infections and viruses. These forms of illness are best left to the medical doctor for diagnosis and treatment in most cases. Occasionally hypnotherapy will "clear" this kind of illness, but hypnotherapy is more likely to be beneficial in illness of a psychophysiological nature. Illness that is at least partially psychosomatic in nature is most often visualized with this formula:

Predisposition + stress = psychosomatic illness.

"Predisposition" can be understood to mean the individual's history of health, mental and emotional fitness, and environmental influences. "Stress" can be understood as a sum of fears, anxiety and worries, real or imagined. Environmental stresses include traumatio events immediately before the onset of illness. Death of a loved one, war, financial problems, relationship problems and the like, can all be stressors that ignite within the individual predisposed to illness.

Common psychosomatic (psychosomatic, in general, means that there are both psychological and physiological elements in an illness) illnesses seen at the dawn of the 21st century can include some forms of: panic attacks, fibromyalgia, chronic fatigue, chronic pain, anxiety disorders, depression, environmental illness and a host of symptoms and diseases with no apparent pathology. Using (some experiences but not all) depression as an example of psychosomatic illness, we find some common roots. Many clients have repressed guilt and/or hostility as the key to their depressive illness. In these instances, hypnotherapy can be used to create an equilibrium within the individual and the depression often disappears.

Symptoms and illness are the manifestations of the "ridges" noted above. (A ridge occurs when part of the person wants one thing and another part wants another thing. A ridge is like a fence where one person's yard "pushes up against" another person's yard and is held in place by the fence.) Many cases of headaches, stomach aches, tinnitus, environmental illness, panic, anxiety, depression, irritability, insomnia, and so on are caused by these ridges. On one side of a ridge you have the dynamics of the unconscious mind pushing toward the ridge. By eliminating the dynamics and pressures in the unconscious mind, the ridge collapses, and the illness disappears or becomes significantly less impairing.

Healing is the reduction of the emotional response to an illness. A cure is the actual physical remission of symptoms. A partial healing is a partial reduction of negative emotions. A partial cure is a partial reduction of physical somatics or symptoms. *It is common but not axiomatic that healing leads to a cure.* One significant element in helping an individual heal is simply allowing the person to have the insights that have been discussed here. When the client understands that his illness may have a psychophysiological component, and acknowledges this fact, healing can begin. Without the acceptance of this fact, healing is far less likely.

With this understanding, it is absolutely critical that the client pursue all possible physical pathologies to his illness for two reasons. First, if there is a physical pathology it should be medically treated. Second, when no pathology is found this will aid the client in being certain that his illness is psychophysiological in nature.

The next significant element in healing is for the client to understand the necessity of the therapist. It is very rare that an individual will experience healing through his own efforts. It is far more likely that hetero-hypnosis will be the most useful tool for healing mindbody illness and most experiences of pain. The reason is that it is difficult to self-regress and self-abreact. The individual's cause of illness is in the unconscious mind and not the conscious mind. Clients often believe that if something is psychophysiological in nature it should be easy to "get over it." This is simply not the case. People die every day from psychophysiological illness. Will power and intelligence are relatively insignificant in healing. Insight and motivation to improve are key factors.

Dr. James Watkins, the eminent hypnotherapist of war victims stated this axiom,

---

"The more resistance he (the client) naturally feels towards accepting a concept or idea, the more likely it is that the idea is approaching close to the true heart of his illness." (Hypnotherapy of War Neuroses)

As each layer of the cause of the illness is revealed, the person feels better and better. The hypnotherapist integrates each unconscious causal relationship into the conscious mind for the individual to experience insight. The insight of the specific cause of the client's illness becomes a significant piece of the healing puzzle. As the final layers of the cause are revealed, the individual typically reaches a significant level of healing.

Unfortunately, not everyone is completely healed with this hypnotherapeutic process. There are other factors at work that may preclude healing. One of them is called "secondary gain." Another factor in healing is "the desire of the person to get well."

Motivation and Secondary Gain

Secondary gain was first identified by hypnotherapists in World War II. A soldier, for example, may have in large part wanted to get well during the war, but to return to the shelling and the front lines with all of the blood, killing, and terror, was too much for the unconscious mind to bear. The soldier knew he was letting his comrades down every moment he was away. Meanwhile, deep within himself, he also wanted to go home, where there was no killing, where life was better and a loved one awaited. Whatever problem or injury the soldier might have, it may not get better, and indeed might get worse because of the blessing and curse of "secondary gain." If the soldier gets out of the war hospital in good health, it means he returns to the front lines that put him in the hospital in the first place. That would be an insane thing to do in the conscious and unconscious minds of many young men.

If the soldier did not get well, he would be returned to the states and those he loved. There would often be a deep psychological price to pay in this case, as well. The inner struggle of guilt could be agonizing and permanently debilitating in some respects. Returning to the front would be impossible for many.

Secondary gain is the gain an individual receives from being ill or injured. In fact, it may be true that in most, if not all illness, there is some important benefit derived by the patient from the illness. Sympathy, love, caring, nurturing, safety, security, peace, are all among the common secondary gains a person may receive from being ill. In the case of a wounded soldier in a MASH unit, the secondary gain of not getting well would be the ticket home. Even if he never got better; and he may not without hypnotherapy; he would not again face the trauma of killing. Unfortunately, the ridge created by the gain pushes against the forces of the conscious and unconscious mind to go back to the fighting and help his comrades. This ridge often replays itself in the individuals future as a form of post traumatic stress disorder.

This mix of values and emotions is the stuff of great Hollywood movies and chronically ill people. We clearly see deep-seated loyalties powerfully divided in the mind. God, country, the soldier's unit and the loved ones back home may meet head to head with the desire to stop killing and go home to be with those loved ones. Values of such a powerful nature collide head to head in many life situations and create powerful ridges of emotion which manifest as chronic illness of a psychological and/or physical nature.

The secondary gain refers to the benefit the individual receives from being ill. For some individuals the benefits of being ill is greater than the price to be paid for good health. The body stays ill. It should be noted however, that this is normally not a conscious decision or choice that is made by someone. In fact, most people who are ill, don't give much thought at all to the benefits of being ill whether physically or emotionally. Most people simply want to feel better and assume they will deal with the future, in the future.

The unconscious mind makes other plans. The desire for sympathy or safety, love or security, peace or comfort, often easily exceed and overcome the conscious minds meager desire to get well. The unconscious mind (or the part of it that is fighting) will "win" if it is not shown that a compromise can be reached that will still assure the survival of the self. People literally have become paralyzed because of secondary gain issues. People have gone blind, deaf and mute because of secondary gain. People's lives are often destroyed because of secondary gain issues, and yes, people do die because of secondary gain issues.

When working with a client, you should know that he will not stay well if there is a significant secondary gain issue that has been neglected. It is common that brief symptomatic relief is gained with numerous types of therapy but long term healing or cure will likely be experienced only if secondary gain issues have been eliminated

A Christian Scientist will not want to seek healing from a practitioner of hypnosis. He will in all likelihood feel guilty or greatly uncomfortable if he does come to see you because he may have a belief that he honors God if he shows his faith in the wake of illness. The secondary gain is the conscious and the unconscious mind's certainty that he is pleasing God by taking the stand that his faith will save him. His lack of faith will destroy him. Pleasing God is quite a powerful secondary gain issue and a very real one. Simply put, many people will not pursue hypnotherapy because they believe, knowing no better, that it is evil. Therefore the secondary gain they receive from their illness is the comfort they have in pleasing God.

The key value of a skilled hypnotherapist is often his ability to discover the cause of a specific illness or challenge the client is experiencing. With insight, the client will see the forest and the trees. Right now, the client often sees only one or the other. Once you, as a therapist have identified a cause you then will gently and patiently help the client see the cause. The client will normally not be able to do this on his own.

The discovery process as accomplished within the team of therapist/client however is one that in all sincerity must take place in the clients own time and be a personal cognition or "AHA" experience. When a hypnotherapist makes the mistake of telling a client that an illness is psychosomatic, the therapist is normally rejected completely or in large part by the client. Clients often will "fight for" a physical cause for a problem they are experiencing because they do not want to think that anything is wrong with their mind. This is where the axiom, "people are not broken," can be useful to adopt as a client and a therapist. The client has ridges that are supported by at least two powerful viewpoints for each problem the client is experiencing. They do not necessarily need to be considered opposite view points on a compass. Sometimes they are only 90 degrees apart instead of 180 degrees apart.

People often believe they can figure out the cause of psychosomatic illness on their own. This can result in nothing more than a recursive loop and time wasted. It *may* be possible to discover the specific sensitizing event, the cause, but more often the client will at best come up with a secondary , or later event on a chain of similar events. Reducing the negative emotion of later events that triggered the emotions and somatic pains or illnesses of the initial event, can certainly be temporarily relieving. It often appears that the person is healed or improved. The symptoms normally come back in a short period of time if the incident is not the initial incident or at least one of the initial incidents we are looking for. Neurobiologically, this experience has an explanation and this will be considered in a later chapter.

Speaking from my personal experience alone, I have observed that most clients presenting significant illnesses or emotional problems tend to be very intelligent and/or very successful from a financial standpoint. The person with high intelligence and/or level of success normally reach such success through personal effort. They have discovered that when they set out to accomplish a task, it gets done. This mindset, paradoxically does not work as well in the therapeutic process. Insights are rare when the client is attempting to direct instead of being led to insight. Quite often there is a "part" of the individual that is responsible for the stubbornness of wanting to figure out the cause and healing aspects of his illness, on his own. This part has served well in achievement and assumes it will serve well in healing. Unfortunately this is not normally the case.

Dr. Watkins had this to say about this kind of phenomenon,

18

> *"An intellligent patient will make rapid strides forward, however, if he can be made to see that the more resistance he naturally feels towards accepting a concept or idea, the more likely it is that the idea is approaching close to the true heart of his illness. It is commonly noted that a person who is teased about a weakness he does not have is not much disturbed. But toss a verbal dart in the direction of a true flaw in his make up and watch him bristle up and protest."*
>
> *(Hypnotherapy and War Neuroses)*

In effect, when the client begins to fight you as a hypnotherapist, it is then that you know that the possible healing is just around the corner! When you are at the core, the cause, the dynamic of the illness, the cure is there. The last step is often the most difficult of course, for this very reason! The complete release of illness, if it is psychosomatic in nature, will occur when the final layer of the onion is peeled and the cognition is made by the client.

As the hypnotherapist, your job is to be certain that the cause is accepted by the client. This is the moment of release. This *should* heal the individuals psychosomatic illness but it often does not. Something else is in the way. It is secondary gain of course.

There is a part or parts that are in opposition to the symptomatic release or cure that keep the psychosomatic illness in place. There is a part or parts of the individual that are gaining more benefit by maintaining the illness than allowing it to be released. In the case of an unconscious "part," the client is unaware of why he is still stick. At the conscious level, the client is probably aware of why he doesn't want to get better and normally he will readily admit to this.

There are very few clients that I have seen that truly enjoy having psychosomatic illness. When the benefits of being well are not considered useful to the survival of the being by some parts in the individual, the individual will not improve.

2

The Fundamentals
of
Healing with Hypnotherapy

When your client comes to see you they are probably, in part, afraid that their future will be similar or worse than their recent past has been. Many people dread the future. Some fear it. Your job is to help propel your client into the future in a logical and directed fashion. You are helping your client design a future that will be dramatically better than what they are just now emerging from. When people come to see you they should be able to tell you what they would like in their future and what they do not want in their future. They should be able to tell you what they are moving toward and away from. If they can't do this, then you will want to help them discover this for them.

Looking ahead to a brighter future is something that will give your client hope to continue working with you while they deal with the sticky and very difficult issues they are experiencing and that you will learn about over the next several sessions. Always remember that although most clients will come to you and "present" one issue (depression, for example) for help, the reality is that they have numerous issues that likely need to be dealt with to get them on the right track.

Sometimes it is necessary to take two steps backward in order to take three or more steps forward. In fact, this is true with almost every client you will ever see. Helping your client see how his life has been shaped by the events of his past will help her change for the future. There are several insights a client needs to have about her past before you can help her jettison into the future.

1) The client needs to realize that some events that happened to them were beyond their control and they changed them just by being at the wrong place at the wrong time. (They may have been molested as a tiny child, they may have been raped, they may have been in a tragic accident. Someone they loved may have died prematurely.) These events changed the way they lived and maybe even where and how they lived.

2) The client must see that their interpretation of past events and experiences has shaped their current experience as individuals, with others, and even their health. Whether people are currently pessimists or optimists changes their experience of day to day life. The client is not to be told they are wrong. However, it may be constructive for the therapist to help the client to see life experiences from other points of view.

3) The client must see that all of their decisions and choices in life have changed them and to have made other decisions and choices would not necessarily have been better or worse but it would have been different.

4) The client needs to be able to look at their past as a mature adult and re-evaluate the childhood

and immature experiences that have shaped their life and give them a chance to re-evaluate their life.

Almost everyone carries around emotional baggage that influences their everyday life. The balance of this chapter will be dedicated to the notion of "clearing" the emotional baggage, past trauma, pain, and negative emotional events that are holding your client back from achieving their life goals.

At various times in our life and especially in early childhood, there occurred what we call, imprints. We are going to define imprints broadly as significant emotional events. These imprints bind our clients to their past emotional traumas and make it difficult and sometimes impossible for them to go forward in life without first cutting the rubber band holding them back. Once the rubber bands are cut, then they will be able to propel themselves forward in the direction of the realization of their goals and maximize their potential for wellness. Learning how to specifically "cut" the rubber bands will be covered in detail in the next chapter and then in more complex issues, throughout the rest of this book.

A few common imprints that often have powerful negative emotions connected with them are noted below.

Death of a loved one
Loss of loved one by other means (divorce, abandonment, etc.)
Physical trauma
Illness
Abuse (sexual, child, severe verbal)
Humiliation

These negative imprints affect different people in different ways. Some individuals take incidents like these more or less "in stride," because they had resources available to them at the time of the imprint. Other people's lives are nearly destroyed by these kinds of events. As time goes by, the emotions experienced within these imprints can haunt individuals. Clearing the negative emotions is the critical element in creating change and enhancing the possibilities for wellness.

Clearing negative emotions is often a simple process that comes under a kind of hypnotherapy that we will call "regression therapy" throughout this work. This specific element of regression therapy utilizes both a process of desensitization and an element of insight. Desensitization neutralizes negative feelings or emotions toward specific stimuli. Insight in this context means that the client experiences an "aha!" experience or gains some insight into what has been holding her back. Clearing releases the hold that the past has on the individual.

Recovering and retaining the memories of events is part of this elementary process. Allowing the conscious mind to see that given the necessary resources, this event or series of events would not have happened, or could have been dealt with differently is often a key component of improvement.

One reason for the variety of responses among individuals in traumatic experiences is the lack of plentitude of resources that were available to the individual at the time of the imprint. A resource is anything that could have or still can be used to make coping with negative events easier. A resource that could be used against a rapist would be a gun or a can of mace, for example. In the clearing process, a resource is anything that helps bring greater understanding, or alternative choices to a situation. Wisdom, knowledge, physical strength, better or different decisions are all examples of resources.

Resources

Some common resources that people do not have as a child when many imprints first are experienced are noted below. There are literally hundreds that could be listed but here are a few.

Knowledge
Ability to Fight Back
Coping Mechanisms
Support of Others
Successful Role Models
Age of Individual at Time of Imprint
Previous Negative Emotional Events (number of or intensity of)
Other Intangibles that made the Imprint an Overwhelming Experience

The Imprint

An imprint is normally composed of the following elements:

1) A physical or emotionally painful event.
2) A (perceived or real) threat to the individuals life, psyche, or potential survival.
3) A lessening of conscious awareness or complete dissociation from the event.

It is not surprising that many powerful imprints are not easily brought to conscious awareness. In fact, generally the more powerful the imprint, the more difficult to recover the entire memory. ⁁ The unconscious mind is roughly composed of all that we are not aware of at this moment. The unconscious mind could be called the storage house of long term memory. It is the part of the mind that is not being manipulated at the present moment. It is the large storehouse of information that has been recorded through an individual's life that is not currently being used for analytical purposes. The unconscious mind accepts incoming information in a largely literal and uncritical fashion. It believes what it sees. It is the part of the mind that many believe is able to merge with the collective unconscious that Carl Jung wrote of. The unconscious mind is the part of the mind where repressed memories are located. (By definition, repressed memory is memory that is currently inaccessible to conscious awareness.) Once a memory is retrieved it is no longer repressed and is able to be experienced in consciousness.

Parts of the unconscious mind (ego states) attempt to repress some memories as these various ego states perceive the memory as real, irrationally or not. The term "repress," is used here to connote the action of the various parts of the unconscious to lock away those memories of events that the individual being was not prepared to handle or cope with. Parts of the unconscious mind repress certain memories to keep the person "safe and secure" from the threats "within." The intention of these parts, often dysfunctional, is typically positive. Unfortunately by burying these negative events, later in life the individual will be unable to cope with similar situations as there have been no references or resources developed to cope with the new challenges! It is generally necessary to bring these events into conscious awareness in order to eliminate the hold they have over a person's life, and it can be very difficult.

Imagine that someone is physically abused by a parent. A child is beaten and verbally taunted. "You're worthless, you're disgusting, and you don't deserve to live."

This memory is perfectly encoded in the unconscious mind and then is quite often "buried," especially if the person who is abused has no resources or references for coping with the kind of abuse. When a memory is buried or repressed, it still can have substantial impact on a person's life. Simply "forgetting" about something bad doesn't make the problem go away. In fact, it normally makes the problem get worse. This is why "clearing" emotions tied to these overwhelming traumas and negative events is necessary for your client.

In our example, the mind has linked these elements neurologically, in a semi-permanent manner. (They are permanent until they are detached.) As a hypnotherapist our goal is to detach the negative emotions from the imprints. By doing so, the re-stimulating effect of the memories is drained.

The abused child will experience pain similar to that pain he had when and where he was struck, when he hears the words, "You're worthless or "you're disgusting." Similarly, if he is struck in a similar manner to how he was abused, the message that he is worthless and disgusting will be brightly lit in his mind. These are called psychophysiological or psychosomatic responses. Psychosomatic responses

27

are often diagnosed as an illness, disorder or disease that in large part is caused or notably influenced by emotional factors. The sense of self worth (A) is anchored to cruel words (B), which is anchored to the pain of being struck. (C)

Because the unconscious mind generally accepts information literally in imprint experiences, we can conclude that the unconscious equates all these experiences with each other. Therefore:

A=B=C

Phobias are normally "one trial learnings." (Phobias are irrational fears or aversions to objects or something for which someone would normally not fear.) They can also be life-altering in nature. Imagine if you will that a person goes into a store and falls and hits their head, rendering them momentarily unconscious or dazed. Someone says, "Get an ambulance, she hit that hard...she'll never come here again." Someone else says, I'll find a pillow so she can lie down."

The individual's unconscious mind records all of this information unwittingly. It is always there. The next time the person is asked to go to the store, the person may develop a headache and need to go lie down. In other individuals, depending on other imprints the person has in effect, the hurt person may not want to go out of the house at all for a reason that is unclear to the conscious mind. All she knows is that wanting to go shopping creates fear and headaches and that she really shouldn't go shopping again.

A=B=C

Understanding that everything that occurs in an imprint experience generally is equated with everything else, is very helpful. In "clearing" the imprint, we do not want to erase the actual memory of the event, only the limiting emotions that are equated with the event. When the emotion is drained from an event, the re-stimulating effect is neutralized. In the above example, the person hurt in the store will no longer be subject to headaches or irrational fears of leaving the home as the event has become cleared of the unconscious emotional distress.

Re-stimulation occurs when we mentally touch a memory that has pain of any kind attached to it. We re-stimulate that pain along with the emotional impact the memory has. The negative impact can be desensitized with regression therapy and other hypnoanalytic techniques.

Examples of re-stimulated imprints would include some of the problems that typically go undiagnosed by your medical doctor. Again, there are literally hundreds of symptoms of psychosomatic illnesses. These are just a few. (Remember to put the word "some" in front of each of these items!)

1) Chronic Pain
2) Tinnitus
3) Visual Hallucinations
4) Auditory Hallucinations
5) Warts
6) Skin Disorders
7) Lung Disorders
8) Psychological Disorders
9) Neuroses
10) Psychoses

When physical cause for these types of symptoms and disorders have been ruled out, it is often reasonable to conclude that the unconscious mind is at work. We will discuss this in great detail throughout this work.

Regression Benefits and Risks?

Repressed Memory became the battle cry for psychological turf wars in the 1990's. It's a shame that recovering repressed memory received so much negative press because much of what was argued about the phenomenon was correct on both sides, but the arguments ultimately led to the challenge of the validity of these memories in lawsuits and not the benefits of the memories in the therapeutic context. The argument was made that there was no such thing as a repressed memory. The reason generally given was that psychologists implanted false memory into the minds of clients. Whether or not psychologists did this is certainly an important issue. However, to attempt to make a mockery of one of the most important areas of therapeutic healing is foolishness. Repressed memory is a proven phenomenon, and has been since the days of Sigmund Freud.

Freud clearly noted that the repressed memories of patients influenced their behavior. Freud is often maligned for his work, when in fact he was a genius. Freud did not have the benefit of nearly 100 years of psychotherapy and hypnotherapy research to fall back on. He was blazing new trails. Some were controversial, others completely inaccurate, while still others are solid science to this day.

When an individual decides to take control of their life and make the decision to see a hypnotherapist, they have decided they want a better future than they have had in the recent past. It is important for the hypnotherapist to eradicate those imprints of the past that have unconsciously influenced the individual for the worse. That is why we must go back...for the client's future.

There are numerous methodologies for eradicating the emotional impact of traumatic memories and repressed memories. In this chapter, we will touch on two methods that have stood the test of time in this area. Then, later in the book we will detail even more advanced methods.

The most elementary method for clearing negative emotions is the use of regression as described below. This will not take care of every problem or illness you are presented but it offers you an easy to learn tool while working your way through the more complex work of this book later. A brief discussion of the concept of regression is in order before we begin.

It has been proven that the memory of many adults can easily reach back to the pre-school age. It has also been shown that in many cases, an individual can remember events from the first year of life. On occasion I have worked with clients who have had remembered birth experiences that were later verified through records and research.

Research completed in 1995 revealed that children who were taken from the womb with the aid of forceps were far more prone to violent behavior than children born without the doctor needing forceps. The research was statistically significant, and confirmed the case studies and anecdotal case histories that reveal children born with excess trauma or via c-section often have powerful imprints that need clearing from the birth experience. To introduce you to the concept of regression, you may continue with the following self hypnosis regression. (Regression to the cause of a problem should not be done in self hypnosis, but regression to positive experiences act as resources and positive references for you and your clients and therefore is a very ecological process!)

A Simple Regression Outline

Recall a time in your past when you were given something and you felt very appreciative.

When you have thought of such an event, close your eyes and take a deep relaxing breath in and then slowly out.

Return to the day, in your mind's eye, to what you were doing just before someone gave you something that you felt very appreciative for.

Make sure you aren't "in" yourself (associated) and not looking at yourself as if you were watching a movie. (dissociated) You want to re-experience the event exactly as it happened in the past. Just like watching video or movie through your own eyes.

Listen to what you are saying. Listen to what the person who gave you something is saying and any other sounds that are going on in the background.

Notice what you see. What colors do you see? What colors are there in the environment? When the person gives you something, notice it's color.

What sensations do you feel? Notice your breathing and your heart rate. Notice how it feels when the person gives you the special something.

Continue to run this movie, this experience, this event all the way to when you say "thank you," or to where you express appreciation for the gift.

After you have run through the movie once, return to the beginning of the event and notice additional information that you didn't see, hear, and feel before. If it helps to verbalize everything, please do.

Once you have run the movie to the end a second time, run it again for a third and final time being careful to notice additional images, sounds and feelings within the event.

When you are ready, you can open your eyes and feel wide aware and refreshed.

(Run this event only three times. Notice how the event becomes clearer each time you went through it. Notice how you heard more sounds, and felt more sensations and feelings the third time. Notice how you visually saw things the third time through that you did not the first and second time.)

One of the biggest advantages of regression is the ability to reconstruct events in a fairly accurate fashion. It is precisely this ability which allows us to help our clients return to those unpleasant events that have been keeping our client pinned down for years. This mental ability allows anyone to safely and carefully detach negative emotions from the traumatic events of the past which still hold sway over the person many years after the event has been forgotten by others.

There is one caveat however. It is not easy to get to a truly repressed memory. Uncovering emotional imprints takes a great deal of skill and often takes a great deal of time by a truly artful hypnotherapist. As you read further in this book you will learn the techniques you need to access the original imprint that is so elusive.

When we are doing regression therapy, we often have no idea where the client will take us to. We know it will go backward in time and we know we will run into clusters of similar memories tied together by various negative emotions. For example, if a certain phrase that someone says upsets you, we will not look for the needle in a haystack that started the negative feelings. Instead we will look for the earliest experience available to the mind and run this event first. (Sometimes we take a recent event to help the client experience a greater level of security.) Then we will ask the unconscious mind to go to a previous event that is similar that it is willing to let us look at. As the unconscious mind discovers that "we" mean it no harm, it will allow us to get closer and closer to the original imprint that caused the bad feelings or emotional/physical problems. This cluster of events tied together by emotions can be called a gestalt.

Regression Therapy Template

1) "Close your eyes and take a deep breath in, then slowly release it."

2) "Think of a time recently when you felt (the presenting problem)."

3) "Once you have the event clearly in mind, return to the beginning of the event in your mind's eye."

4) "Run the event forward like a movie and tell me everything that you see, hear and feel. Tell me everything you experience."

5) Once they reach the end of the movie, then have them begin the event again and notice additional sights, sounds and sensations.

6) As they re-experience the event time after time determine whether this is the original event. If so have the client repeat the event until they experience an emotional release. If not then instruct them as follows:

7) "Return to an earlier similar event where you felt _____."

[If the client is experiencing a physical somatic such as pain or tinnitus, then the client will follow a somatic "bridge" back to the past, stopping off at numerous events where the somatic was particularly bad each time. If the client is experiencing a negative emotion such as depression, anger, anxiety, fear, panic, or grief, then you follow the affect (emotional) bridge, slowly back to the causal event or events.]

8) Cycle back through this process until the client has experienced the initial imprint. If time does not permit (allowing two hours per session) finish one event then pick up where you left off in the next session.

Of course you will never leave the client in the middle of an imprinting experience in trance just because time is up for the day. Whatever experience you have the client dealing with must be dealt with in completion before emerging the client from trance and sending them home.

The Regression Therapy Template is what you really want to become accustomed to utilizing.

Broadening the Scope: What Is Hypnotherapy?

Hypnotherapy is best defined as an interpersonal relationship that is marked by a significant degree of dissociation and focusing on the part of the subject and the moving and changing of the subjects "energies" with the assistance of the hypnotherapist (or other source).

The most advanced formulation of hypnotherapy is that of hypnoanalysis. Hypnoanalysis is to hypnosis as calculus is to mathematics and surgery is to medicine. Hypnoanalysis is the advanced utilization of a practitioner's skills and talents as a hypnotherapist to facilitate physical, emotional and or mental health in individuals who fail to respond to other therapeutic interventions. Hypnoanalysis focuses on the causes and effects of symptoms. Hypnoanalysis unravels the mysteries of the cause of physical and emotional and in many cases then helps us reduce or eliminate those symptoms.

Healing (defined in this text as the reduction or elimination of the emotional response to symptoms) certainly can and does occur from the careful application of *hypnosis* and/or hypnoanalysis. How is healing accomplished? What techniques and applications are successful in the healing process? What specifically is it that really heals the individual?

Hypnotic applications and techniques can be used to heal, improve general health, and reduce pain in most people. The model that seems to best stimulate healing is that of regression. In regression therapy (a fundamental experience in facilitating hypnoanalysis), the hypnotherapist returns a client, while in a trance state (2), to the initial cause of an event at which time the client will re-experience, in a vivid fashion, the circumstances that caused an illness. (Learning how to know if you have an initial cause or a secondary cause will be discussed later in this book.) The critical event is then examined in detail to bring into account as many seemingly insignificant elements as is humanly possible. The event is described by the client as it is happening, in a careful step by step method until the event is completed. The emotional and/or physical pain that was experienced is revisited.

Regression is very important to hypnoanalysis and a simple example of regression will be discussed as an example of how hypnoanalysis can heal clients through desensitization. This form of regression therapy is only one therapeutic intervention available to the hypnoanalyst. Because of it's simplicity and ease of understanding, this module will focus on desensitization via regression.

Upon the conclusion of the first re-running of the event, in regression, the client may then be told to return to the beginning of the event again and take in all the additional details of the event that were left out on the first running. The client is not given any suggestions as to what might be present or felt. The therapists job is to help the client re-create a complete and vivid account of the event causing the presenting symptoms. This complete revivification will allow the client to experience all of the possible triggers of the presenting symptoms. This can be something as seemingly insignificant as a child's toy, the color of a carpet, the intensity of light in a room, the sounds that are in the memory.

The first time an event is run through, there will typically be a great deal of emotional and often physical pain re-experienced by the individual. If you have a true initial cause of a present time symptom, you will have a great deal of emotional display on the part of the client. Each time a causal event is run through, you will notice changes in the client on a number of levels.

The first level is the actual representation of the event. The first time through an event is normally the least accurate description of the event. However, each additional re-experiencing of the event normally enhances the memory, simply by the new information being recalled through association. It should not be assumed that this memory is exactly what occurred in reality, but the clients reality. A smell recalled in the first memory can easily trigger other associated elements of the original event. This continues until the event includes a consistent description of the event on two continuous revivifications with at least four of the five senses represented.

The second level is the emotional tone of the client. The client that is truly re-living the experience, will re-experience some or all of the original pain. Emotional and physical sensations will be re-experienced. This will be obvious by the tears and strained tone of voice of the client going through the event, in the case of an event with grief. The second time through an event is normally equally as emotionally and physically painful. As each re-running of the event is accomplished, the emotions observed tend to change from deep sadness, grief, and tears to that of a bored state. The continual re-running eventually becomes boring for the individual. This is an acceptable place to cease the revivifications. (If the emotional impact does not reduce after several tellings of an experience, you need to go further back on the client's time line and discover the earlier, similar event.)

The bored state can be very important to the healing of the individual for reasons you may have already guessed. The old stimuli and triggers of the current symptomology are no longer triggers of fear, anxiety and illness. Now these triggers have either been eliminated or trigger a bored response. Triggers for many illnesses, phobias, and pains now trigger only a bored response. The symptomology often completely disappears because the cause has become irrelevant.

In a sense, what we have done is taken our memory of the cause of illness or pain complete with the frame of anxiety, depression, frustration and other negative emotions, and we have re-framed the entire memory in a complete sense to one of neutrality, much like a memory of yesterday's breakfast. At this point the illness, pain, phobia is said to have been abreacted. Abreaction is the elimination of the psychogenic cause of an undesirable symptomology that includes an emotional release. What was a stimulus for illness is now erased. All of the components of the stimulus have been eradicated so the client has an opportunity to enjoy the maximum health potential possible, both physical and mental. This is a presupposition of hypnoanalysis and many variables in health and healing are involved in actual session work.

A session to eliminate one psychosomatic response can take several hours. The returning to, and re-telling of a single event seven or eight times can be very time consuming. The benefits of the release are obvious. When the person is returned to the present time, they feel tired, exhausted, but normally much, much better, if not largely healed from the abreaction.

Discovering the initial cause, however, is not as easy as might be expected. Later in this module, we will discuss how to discover the original cause of any specific symptom. We will discuss how to determine whether you are re-running secondary events. You will learn how to differentiate between an accurate representation of an actual event and that of an imaginary event. You will also know when not to use regression therapy with clients. There are many instances when regression can do more harm than good.

Discovery of Cause
(...and the careful avoidance of induced memories)

The notion of "regression to cause" is certainly not a new one. My (KH) personal hypnotherapeutic theorem is "when you discover the specific cause(s) of a problem (physical, mental, spiritual, emotional), you often then heal the problem." The reason you want to get to the root cause of an illness or a problem is that causes are like dandelions. If you don't pull the whole root up, the problem will re-appear at a later date. By extracting the entire dandelion from the earth, the weed will not return.

Unfortunately, many therapists attempt to guess or predict just what the cause of a presenting problem is. This is often seen in session when a therapist begins to vocalize his judgments during trance. For example:

"...and did your mother ever sexually abuse you? fondle you? touch you in
ways that made you feel uncomfortable?"

This line of questioning during trance can easily create a "therapist induced memory." A useful distinction in definitions is best considered here:

1. An Induced Memory is one that is created by another person, group, or form of media in an individual.

2. A Therapist Induced Memory, is one that is created in a client by a therapist.

3. A False Memory, is a memory that an individual remembers but in reality is fallacious. Some false memories are induced memories. At an extreme we could argue that all memory is false memory in that all information that is perceived is distorted and generalized by our mental and physical faculties. A false memory is more often a mis-remembering on the part of the client, often in the form of a gestalt, i.e.., multiple memories collapsed into one memory.

4. A Memory, is a specific or general recall of events as it is encoded in the brain by an individual.

An irresponsible therapist may load questions, knowingly or unknowingly, during trance, for his/her clients as noted above. By asking a client during trance, if he has been abused, you may begin to install the theme into the client even if it is not true. It certainly is possible for the unconscious to reject the idea, but it is equally as likely that the client will unconsciously search for a time when such an event may have occurred. Not finding precisely what has been requested, the client's unconscious mind may take a real memory that has the potential story line for the memory and combine it with the therapist's suggestion, creating a gestalt. In this case, the gestalt will be a therapist induced memory.

Corporate America takes full advantage of this phenomenon in it's advertising and marketing of products to people of all ages and ideologies. Induced memory is not a "mental health practitioner only" phenomenon. Anyone who bypasses the judgmental portions of the brain will be capable of creating induced memory and suggestions for future activity.

Bypassing the critical factor or critical judgement of your client happens when you have complete rapport and trust with your client and when they experience no fear from you as a therapist.

How then, does the therapist discover the cause of a problem or illness without inducing any form of false memory?

The therapist begins by having the client fully *associate* to his current problem or illness. The client experiences the problem that he wishes to have eradicated, in trance.

(To *associate* to a memory is to re-live the memory through your own eyes, not seeing yourself in the memory, but actually perceiving the events as they were.)

Example: If the client has migraine headaches and wishes healing, the therapist asks the client to experience the sensations of a migraine.

Associating to pain, is a kinesthetic activity. It is normal that people who are chronically ill or in great pain will actually dis-associate from their pain or illness regularly. This person doesn't always seem to "be here." For this client, having the client see memories through his own eyes is not an easy task. Emotions and somatic sensations become very powerful. The therapist may have to associate the client to positive or enjoyable experiences before he has the client return to an earlier time when the symptoms of illness or the experiences of pain were powerful. Once the client knows it is safe to return to associated states, you can return the client more easily to states that were less than pleasant.

"Now, return to an incident when you experienced these sensations."

The client describes everything in a specific event where he has chosen to return to. The therapist wants to know what the client sees, hears, feels, smells and tastes. Temperature, ambiance, pressure, internal sensations and other sensory perceptions are all described to the therapist.

"Describe what you feel, see, hear, smell and taste in this event. Fully associate to the event. Be 'in

43

yourself', re-experiencing the event as you describe it to me. "

It is unlikely that this first specific event is the cause of a person's illness or problem. The client presented you with this incident, however, and therefore you are wise to listen to the event. Visiting subsequent events on a chain of incidents, like this one, will not likely yield any significant long term benefits for the client. The client will normally be almost as emotionally distressed after the fourth telling as he was after the first telling, in the case of subsequent events. After running through the event two or three times, the emotional "charge" of the event will begin to dissipate if it is the initial event. Sometimes the client will have a difficult time detailing the event after the client has previously contacted the entire event for you. The client will normally become bored or amused by the entire event if it is the initial event. What was painful to face is now boring or amusing. The emotional charge is drained and removed from the emotional cause of the illness. In actual session experience the client intuitively knows when he has touched on the original cause of his symptoms whether physical, mental or emotional or all three. You will clearly see the difference in the descriptive nature of the clients language and the emotional changes in the descriptive process.

If the client contacts a subsequent event, it will be necessary to continue your back-tracking to the causal event with this firm but polite command to the unconscious mind:

"Return to an earlier similar incident, now."

The procedure is repeated until the causal event has been un-covered.

Is This Event A Causal Event?

A causal event (there can be several for any one problem a client experiences, though we normally look for one key event) is normally indicated by the following criteria:

1) A drastic alteration in the emotional tone of the client with each re-telling of the event. The client should move from mild emotions to negative emotional displays then toward neutral or positive emotions with each re-telling.

2) The client sometimes begins to blank out details with third, fourth and more re-tellings of the event, when they previously had told you what had happened.

3) The client is no longer attached to the event in a negative fashion.

4) The client feels significantly better at the end of the session.

It is common that the session will come to a point that it seems to be stalled. There may be no earlier incidents yet the person is not feeling better. Another common experience in session is that the client is not improving as far as his emotional tone as he details events which he may believe are the initial cause. There are several excellent strategies for uncovering the cause and facilitating healing in stalled sessions and these will be dealt with in a later chapter.

Time Track Alteration Intervention

Normally the best course of action after doing a thorough case analysis with your client is to begin regression therapy. There are always exceptions to every rule. Typically when I work with clients who suffer from post traumatic stress disorder I begin with ego state therapy (sometimes beginning with ideomotor signals) then move to regression therapy. On occasion these interventions will not be appropriate and the Time Track Alteration Intervention will be most appropriate.

This intervention is very effective at removing the negative emotional impact from traumatic events. This method allows us to bring resources back to the events that have happened in the past and use those resources to give our clients a different perspective on what would have been necessary to have avoided the trauma.

Example: Think of a time when you were a child that you got yelled at by an adult for something you simply didn't do. You attempted to clarify the issue by telling the adult of your innocence but the adult didn't listen. Instead the adult told you to shut up and not question adults...and don't ever do it again. (Whatever it was!)

What resources did the child need in this scenario? (Resources can include how you have handled similar situations since this event, or determine how others successfully deal with similar situations and what the difference is with what they do and with what you did. A resource can also be something straight from the imagination. In the example cited above, a special resource would have been a video camera strapped to the side of the child all day, so the child could prove his innocence. Typically I shy away from these kind of resources as they are not as "real" to the unconscious mind and insights are not so obvious when we use this type of resource. But, it is a special, if not very unusual resource.)

What resources did the adult need in the scenario?

What would have happened in the incident had the adult had the resources that they needed, and you as a child had the resources you needed? Be specific and detailed in your thought process because this is what you will be discerning for your clients.

Recently I worked with a teenage boy whose mother had yelled at him for participating in something he wasn't involved in. The resources he needed to give his mother in trance were, trust, understanding and the willingness to listen. The resources he needed to give himself included the ability to discuss the issue in a non-defensive attitude, a point of view that brought into account the adult's fear of the teenagers' involvement in the event and the understanding of the parent's past experience with the teenager where the teen *did participate* in similar notorious events.

Upon giving the resources to the younger self and the parent, the teen was able to see that it was these additional resources that made the difference in interpreting the event from the view point of both participants. There never would have been an incident in the first place.

Had the event been the younger self witnessing the murder of an innocent person, the resources involved could be very different. Sometimes a resource can be physical in nature. Sometimes the person was too small to be effective against an abusive child or parent.

By returning to these events with new resources we can literally alter our current perceptions by changing what happened on our time track. By giving our younger self resources, we can then have our older self experience different memories than we have had for years. By altering the originating event, we can alter the domino effect similar events up until the present, literally changing our perceptions of others. What follows is an outline of how to do Time Track Alteration.

Time Track Alteration Outline

1) "Close your eyes, take a deep breath and release. Good. Now tell me, what is the specific feeling you are having that you would not like to?"

2) "Return to the earliest time you can remember feeling this way."

3) "What beliefs did you form about yourself, life or others during or after this experience?"

4) "I want you to float up out of your body now and imagine that you are watching this happen as if

you were sitting in a movie theater. You should be seeing yourself on screen."

5) "As you look at this event that created these negative emotions, what was the positive intention of the other person in the event? If you don't know please guess."

6) "What was the benefit of feeling as you did during or after the event occurred?"

7) "What resources did you and the other person in the event need then that neither of you had then but that *you do now*? (As they begin to tell you these resources affirm each resource as being correct if it is so.)

8) "Give those resources that you mentioned that the other person needed to them and you take the resources that you needed and instill them into the you on the movie screen."

9) "Now, float up out of your movie theater seat and go into the other person in the event (or if there is more than one person, then do this the appropriate amount of times). Run the movie through from their point of view and see how the events change when they have the resources you decided to give them."

10) "Now you go through the imprinting event with your new resources with you. Make sure you are seeing this through your own eyes as the younger self."

11) Continue running the new imprint until it is convincingly positive as the original imprint was negative. This may take several runnings of the movie.

12) "What changes in your beliefs about yourself or this event do you have now that you didn't have before?" (If the beliefs have dramatically changed this is the goal. If not, run the positive imprinting again a few more times.)

13) "Now, I want you to come forward in time to the present and as you come forward through time the events on your time track will alter where necessary to take into account the new learnings you have gained today."

14) "When you have completed this in your mind, you may open your eyes feeling wide aware and refreshed." (Allow for a slightly dazed look when the person's eyes open, then smile and shortly go on with another subject.) Don't discuss the work you have just done with the client as it needs time to settle in.

It should now be evident as to why it is necessary to often go back and remove the negative emotions from imprint events. Once the rubber band has been removed we truly can propel our client into the future with hope and optimism. Without the removal of the rubber band, the past scars would constantly resurface over and over again. Now, they will never have the power to haunt again as they have been cleared. As each area is cleared, a greater sense of freedom, awareness and "beingness" is experienced by the individual. There is some time and effort involved in this work. It can be emotionally draining for the therapist but it is invigorating for the client as they watch themselves grow and feel better week after week.

Guiding the Client to Wholeness and Wellness

The client often wants to get well, while an unconscious part or parts have clearly decided that it is not in the best interests of the individual to improve their health or change behavior. Returning to the wounded soldier that we considered, earlier,   it certainly seems reasonable, that a part of the soldier's unconscious mind would rebel against returning to the front lines and therefore do whatever is necessary to keep the individual from going back to his unit.   It makes complete sense to the hypnotherapist who has worked with people over the years and it makes sense to the individual when he can experience these dual views of reality.

If we (as the hypnotherapist) decide for the client that he must go back to the front lines or we create goals for the client, then the part will not likely yield the grip it has on the client. However, if we let the client decide for himself what goals he needs and wants to aspire to, then he will in all likelihood eventually be released from the pain or suffering that he is experiencing. (At least in the emotional aspect, if not the physical)

Many therapists do not like the idea of having the client re-experience past pain and suffering that he experienced.   They believe that symptomatic remission can occur without discovering cause and/or without discovering what various parts of the mind are dynamically working for and against a healing. In one sense, the therapist with this belief structure is correct.

You can obtain immediate case gain, and dramatic gain at that, with simple tools that do not address these issues. Unfortunately, in most cases these gains are temporary and become re-stimulated at a later date and the therapist never becomes aware of his failure.

The process of healing for many individuals is that of :

> *(Insight) (Motivation to Improve)* = *Healing*

The motivation to improve as mentioned above will often provide seemingly miraculous healings which occasionally persist. More often than not however, the healing proves temporary and the illness returns because of the lack of personal insight. Having discussed the dynamics of insight previously we will only remind the reader of the critical importance of insight and move on to the motivations for improvement.

If a client is chronically ill from psychosomatic illness, he is receiving some kind of secondary gain. Often it is manifested in the sympathy received by the client from those who love the client. Sympathy certainly is an expression of emotion that we do not want to squelch in people. We all want attention. When we are sick, people often are more gentle and concerned about us which is often believed by the client to be an experience that will change upon getting well again.

As a therapist we can encourage the client to conclude that upon getting well people will like us and approve of us all the more. While living with psychosomatically induced chronic illness the client is not likely to improve if he continues to receive sympathy from his therapist or from his friends, family and peers. By joining the local support group created to create support for the specific psychosomatically induced chronic illness we also create a huge roadblock to healing. The illness receives constant validation and bonds between sufferers often encourage the suffering and in fact, *guilt,* when an individual begins to improve.

Therefore, when joining any support group, it is important to be certain that the group's focus is specifically on improving the health of the individuals and not a validation of the illness itself. Having someone to talk to that is ill with a similar illness that a client has is very important and having the group support can lessen the suffering. However, the effectiveness of the group lessens over time for most individuals and the individual in most cases should seek advice as to whether to discontinue attending meetings after some period of time. The emotional impact of most psychosomatic illnesses can be lessened in most cases by a competent hypnotherapist and the contact with the group can be lessened as the emotional impact is lessened unless there is a specific benefit that is encouraging healing for the client. We will discuss group dynamics in psychosomatic illnesses later in another chapter. (Where the group tends to encourage wellness and not the illness most will improve with insight. The opposite is true of course if the group's focus is on the illness and permeating the illness.)

NOTE: It is here that the difference between the experienced and unaware therapist makes a critical difference in the healing of a client. If a client is made out to be ill with a psychosomatic illness and is in fact suffering from a pathological illness or disease (cancer for example) the client will in all likelihood get worse. In general, this serves as a reminder to always have a person seek medical diagnosis before taking them on as a client.

Insight

1) Educate the client to the process of psychosomatic illness.

2) Educate the client that psychosomatic illness is not something for which we are normally personally responsible for. The dynamics of his illness are almost certainly caused by experiences that had created great internal conflict within him and that the creation was largely accomplished at an unconscious level. He needs to know that an illness is an illness. Whether its most significant cause was organic or emotional needs to be irrelevant to society and the client both. If the client or group is attempting to prove the illness is organic when it is not, the illness then becomes further installed into the client and the healing process becomes more difficult to participate in.

3) Educate the client that it is in his best interests for healing to accept the fact that specific events and experiences created specific pains and sufferings which he is experiencing and that upon acceptance of this fact, he will be catapulted in the direction of healing. Once a general intellectual understanding of the cause of his illness is intact, then it is even more important for the client to accomplish

the true cognition of the specific cause of his illness versus the illnesses held by others with like symptoms. Once the dynamics of illness are thoroughly understood and honored, the healing begins. The energy of the emotional impact of the illness begins to reduce. It no longer becomes necessary to complain about the pain experienced on a daily or hourly basis. The need to acquire sympathy is reduced. The need to increase symptoms to increase the amount of sympathy is reduced. All of these types of internal response are dramatically altered by something as simple as insight and indeed this is one of the most powerful reasons for the necessity of the return to cause.

Once the client sees and re-experiences precisely how he became ill, he then discovers how to become well again. Healing is normally not a one session phenomenon.

It is through the processes discussed in this book by which clients with psychosomatic illnesses will improve. However, because of the caveat offered by Watkins, I would not recommend the use of these techniques by untrained and un-experienced therapists. Alternatively, once having been trained in these techniques, and, having had time to apprentice with an excellent practicing therapist, your skill and client results will expand dramatically.

Hypnotherapy Handbook

3

Before the Client Comes to Your Office

The Therapeutic Alliance

If you have been working with clients for any length of time you no doubt know that the alliance between the therapist and client is the central point at which therapy begins.

> *Without rapport and a sense of affinity between the therapist and client, it is rare that significant changes will take place.*

The therapeutic alliance is built when the client sees that the therapist really cares about the client and wants the client to get well or achieve whatever goal that the client has set for herself. Whether hitting a baseball or experiencing symptomatic reduction of something like chronic fatigue syndrome, the clients needs are our focal point.

We come together in harmony with our client to attempt to overcome problems, reduce pain, eliminate psychosomatic illnesses and achieve peak performance. Very few if any of these things can happen without a strong therapeutic alliance.

Does the client feel as if you are on their side?

Do you listen to the client carefully?

Are you politely inquisitive and sincerely curious about your client and the difficulties he/she is facing?

Do you know about the experience the client is sharing with you? In other words, have you researched the difficulty that your client is experiencing before they come to your office?

Answer "yes" to these and you are winning the first battle for your client. Your client will intuitively know these things and will feel comfortable with you! Your client comes to you because in all likelihood many other things failed! The client who seeks out a hypnotherapist has usually attempted numerous other therapies and therapists and found nothing that "worked." What will open your relationship with your client is the rapport and trust that you build with your client. It's hard to fake true concern and interest. Either you care or you don't and if you do, you have a chance to be effective in your work.

Hypnotherapy in large part, is about bypassing the critical faculty of the human mind to facilitate healing. Essentially, this means that the client absolutely and completely trusts the hypnotherapist to the point where there is almost a surrender on the part of the client to the therapist. Someone who reads a script or some "canned" set of responses to a client when they should be doing therapy will rarely if ever experience the bypassing of the critical faculty. This is because part of the mind is always looking for what is "nonsense" or "bogus," not only in therapy, but in every part of life. This part of the mind is tired of being taken advantage of and being ripped off.

> ***Before learning any technique or tool in hypnotherapy, you must become an expert at building your credibility and complete trustworthiness in the mind and the heart of the client. There is no other way to create long term change, improvement in symptoms and miracles.***

Before The Client Comes to Your Office

Every client I see must type a long history letter to me before they ever come to my office. They must include in this very thorough document the following:

1. The presenting problems they are experiencing. (Tinnitus, bulimia, CFIDS, impotence, fibromyalgia, depression, frigidity, etc.)

2. They must write out the history of the problem including when the problem started, how it has progressed, and what the preceding 18 months to the onset of the problem(s) were like emotionally and physically for the client.

3. The client must write their desired outcomes from therapy. What do they realistically expect the end result of therapy should be.

4. What are the current major stressors, worries, fears, upsets in life. Everything they can think of.

This process accomplishes several things. First the client becomes aware of the emotional link to his problems. The rule of thumb I use is that almost all idiopathic illnesses are "psychosomatic."

Psychosomatic simply means that there is a "psyche" (soul/mind) component to the person's illness or problem in addition to the physical component.

If a person has lost a limb for example and is trying to regain confidence in their life, there is no psychosomatic component in a lost limb or nerve deafness, for example, but there is a great deal we can do to help these people re-orient their life to the world and cope effectively. There are exceptions, but not many. This doesn't mean that hypnotherapy can "cure" all of their maladies but it does mean that by working with the mind we can make major changes in their life IF we have the critical faculty bypassed, and trust is established.

We bypass the critical faculty in part by what happens before the client comes to the office. We bypass the critical faculty by our perception in the public, in the eyes of the world, in the mind of the individual.

If the client is put to work on thinking about how they got to where they are, and they know that you want to know this information, it prepares them for opening up in greater depth when they are in your office. In addition, the very act of doing this task puts you "in charge." They are complying with an instruction you have given them. It is the first of many important instructions you will give them. It certainly is an important instruction.

Before the client comes to your office, make sure that you have read the client's history that they have faxed or mailed to you. It will give you an appreciation for the client that very few other practitioners have ever had for them, or they wouldn't be seeing YOU!

The client comes to your office with a curious mystery surrounding you in their mind. They come with hope but certainly not a sense of trust if you don't build it with them before the session. The client doesn't know what to expect when they come to see you but whatever they are thinking it is unlikely to be extremely positive. You are considered a "might as well try it," or "worth a shot," or "what have I got to lose." You must get past this point of neutral or negative expectations to a sense of caring and professionalism. You must be the person they have always wanted to come and see because this is the beginning of their miracle if they are to have one!

Be Prepared to Explain Our Language to Your Client

We must be able to explain the language and vocabulary that we use to the client. Each field of study or discipline has it's own vocabulary and ours is no different. Hypnosis and Hypnotherapy should really be distinguished from each other. They are only tangentially related although the root word is similar in both!

Some people who teach hypnosis believe that hypnosis is the offering of suggestions by the "therapist" to the "client" once a certain "level" or "depth" of trance has been achieved. I call these people "hypnotists." A hypnotist is someone who almost exclusively "talks" while the client "listens." This kind of intervention can be useful for creating changes in habits like procrastination and finger nail biting, and later in this book I will address how to do just that rapidly and permanently! This kind of "therapy" is called "suggestive therapy" as it focuses on suggestions that are given by one person to another.

Suggestive therapy activates the mind/body response with many people. This response is in large part (though not completely) also known as the placebo effect. Let's say that one more time, this response is in large part, though *not* completely, the placebo effect. I will discuss the placebo effect in the next section and describe how it differs from suggestive therapeutics and hypnotherapy. For now, let's return to defining some terms, including hypnosis, hypnotist, hypnotherapy, and psychology.

Psychology is literally the study (ology) of the soul (psyche). However, a psychologist is not one who studies the soul as the name would imply! My doctorate degree is in psychology and I can assure you that psychologists for the most part do not study the soul!

Most professions are defined by their titles. A geologist is one who studies minerals. A biologist is one who studies life and life forces. Psychologists and hypnotherapists however have the unwelcome distinction of being people who do not study what their title implies! A hypnotherapist literally, would be someone who does therapy with one who sleeps! A hypnotist would be one who induces sleep! None of these of course are true. Psychologists do not study the soul, they study the actions and behaviors of animals (including humans). Some psychologists attempt to alter the behavior and actions of animals (including humans). Many other psychologists focus their attention on changing the internal experiences of animals (again including humans).

Hypnotherapy is a process and interactive experience that helps people improve their health, reverse the course of illness, achieve a more emotionally stable life and increase performance in areas as diverse as learning, memory, sports, and even sexuality. Hypnotherapy is a therapy unlike all others in that it allows the client to release the negative "energy" that is often "stored" in the unconscious mind and replace negative memory with new patterns of thought that create remarkable change within people. Although the experience often feels "magical," I must confess it is not. It is experienced because of a strong therapeutic alliance and the ability of the hypnotherapist to find causes and effects, blocks and repressions and create a safe emotional release, then help the client create new experiences that will fill the voids left behind.

Hypnosis can be defined as both a field of study in one sense and as an individual state of significant dissociation and focused attention. Some people define hypnosis to be a synonym of trance. I do not. I do not say that you have entered into hypnosis because there is no place that is called hypnosis. I do not like the term "hypnotized" because it is a misnomer. I do like the word "trance." Trance indicates that state of dissociation or focused attention (different things to be sure). In this book, the word "trance" will be used where you might have heard "hypnotized" or hypnosis in another book or class.

Hypnosis has been defined as the bypassing of the critical faculty of the mind. This is a good definition but is difficult to measure. The idea of this definition is that when the critical faculty of the mind is bypassed the unconscious mind readily accepts suggestions without critical consideration or examination. I like this definition but it is only a working definition and is not really "true" in all cases. The critical faculty which is made up of "ego states" is rarely a team of completely dis-interested parties. The definition is well intended and accurate for those who have 500 hours of experience with clients but awfully hard to share with those who are not experienced.

Hypnosis is of course, difficult to define in part because of it's history! Hypnosis originally meant sleep and of course in real life hypnosis has nothing to do with sleep. Trance has nothing to do with sleep. People can fall asleep from a trance state as they can from any state they are in but really sleep and hypnosis are not synonyms and are really closer to antonyms.

What then, shall we do? How do we proceed where there is no agreement of definitions? We must create a structure to communicate with that makes sense and is easy to understand. Here then are the definitions that will be used.

Hypnosis is first and foremost a field of study of changing behaviors and interpretations of experiences using the mind/brain. It is not a state of mind, or an experience.

Hypnosis can also be defined as an event whereby one person or "thing" (television, audiocassette, movie) bypassing the critical factor of the mind of another creating a sense of trust and expectancy.

A hypnotist is *someone who talks* to a client after bypassing the critical faculty of the mind to offer suggestions in the hopes that the suggestions will be accepted and acted upon.

A hypnoanalyst is *someone who listens* to a client after bypassing the critical faculty of the mind (gaining complete trust and confidence) and is allowed to find the causes of the client's presenting problems and symptoms. The hypnoanalyst then utilizes hypnoanalysis to create change and foster healing in the individual.

A hypnotherapist is someone who does not have the skills and experience of the hypnoanalyst but has more experience and skills than a hypnotist. The hypnotherapist is one who helps others create change through behavioral modification strategies after bypassing the critical faculty of the mind.

Hypnotherapy is a relationship between two people where one person focuses all of their attention toward making actual and lasting shifts and changes within another person toward or away from various experiences at the request of the person needing help.

The **critical faculty** of the mind is the sum of the parts of the mind that "protect" the mind from that which it knows to be untrue or that which it judges to be "bad." The critical faculty is a largely permeable barrier between the conscious and the unconscious parts of the mind. The critical faculty usually consists of several ego states that act as the guardians to the mind. The critical faculty is formed in each person usually around the age a child started kindergarten so you can know that whatever the critical faculty "believes" it believes with a fervor and is not easily persuaded otherwise.

Trance is an experience on the part of an individual that can be either one of very highly focused attention or that of a dissociated experience that seems to create a distance from the "self." These two experiences are not opposites but they are very different experiences.

Repression refers to a memory or set of experiences that for some reason is not currently available to "you" or your client at this moment. Some people have years of their life completely repressed. They currently have no memory for periods or people or both. This however can and does change using various techniques and strategies. "Lifting repressions" can provide miraculous changes within individuals.

A **psychologist** is one who uses behavioral modification techniques to create change or self understanding in others without the benefit of trance. A **licensed psychologist** is a person who can professionally (for pay) test individuals for emotional disorders, professionally evaluate personality profiles, and can use psychological techniques and strategies which are often shared with hypnotherapists but rarely hypnoanalysts.

Numerous other definitions will be given throughout this book but this will suffice for the purpose of familiarizing our client with our vocabulary.

4

Your First Session With A Client

Earlier, we discussed how the mind, body and brain develop and the relationship of this development to hypnoanalytic theory. We learned that our genes and our environment help mold who we are, how we think and much of our mental, physical and emotional health. In module two it is now necessary to meet and learn about the client as an individual. The amount of time that we will spend with a client is dependent upon the degree of the illness, disorder, distress or difficulty the client is experiencing. This entire course focuses on hypnoanalysis which is the crown jewel of hypnosis. An underlying assumption of this course is that a client that is in need of hypnoanalysis is not a client that you will see one time. In my (KH) personal experience, a client in need of hypnoanalysis is in need of an average of 12-15 hours of total session work. Approximately 60% of that time is spent in hypnoanalysis. Not every client you see will need hypnoanalysis.

Clients who you can help with hypnoanalysis are those who have challenges that have often been passed onto the hypnotherapist by a medical doctor that has little or no time to spend with the client. This client often presents issues that are not readily treatable by traditional medicine. Many clients that I see have chronic (ongoing) illnesses that they have endured for decades. On occasion the illnesses the client experiences may yield to hypnoanalysis after just 8-10 hours of session work. Sometimes we experience a reduction in symptoms. It is rare that we will experience no change in the clients condition.

Hypnoanalysis is the hypnotic process that involves the search for the cause, effects, reduction or elimination of symptoms that a client experiences. This book will guide you through all of the accepted and effective modes of hypnoanalysis. Hypnoanalysis should not be confused with psychoanalysis which tends to focus on root causes that are often sexual in nature. Using hypnoanalysis by definition means we have no predicted cause of a disorder or set of symptoms. There do appear to be some patterns of cause and effect relationships that are somewhat predictable but it is not the purpose of this course to turn you into an illness handicapper, but that of a sleuth. In other words, certain genetic pre-dispositions seem to be correlated with certain anxieties and depression symptoms. Certain parenting behaviors, disciplines, abuses, neglects and other environmental stimuli often correlate positively to certain symptoms. However, correlation's are not certainties, they simply are tendencies and patterns of relationship.

Your clients must be treated as individuals, as unique and as important as you are. With this in mind, it is my policy to take a complete case analysis with every client I work with. It is also my policy to then discuss what hypnosis and hypnoanalysis are and then I normally utilize a special induction called, The Dave Elman Induction to elicit a brief (10-20 minute) trance experience for the client. With this accomplished, we set a date for our first session of hypnoanalysis to begin. In your next module, I will help you explore other inductions that you can utilize in your practice to facilitate trance and hypnoanalysis.

The client should be comfortably seated upon arrival to your office and some physical distance should be maintained between you and your client. He or she may be apprehensive about the thought of hypnosis or possibly the substance of what is about to transpire. It is your job to help the client be as relaxed as possible. I begin by introducing myself and briefly stating my experience and background in the field of hypnosis. After a few minutes of pleasantries I have the client fill out and sign the necessary paperwork and legal documents required by my state. In the State of Minnesota, in the United States, we have specific disclosure that must be placed on a disclosure statement and given to each client. That language is offered verbatim in the example below. In Minnesota we also must disclose personal credentials, education, theory of practice and training received. Laws vary from state to state and country to country. It is your responsibility to obey the laws of your municipality. (In the state of Minnesota hypnotherapists fall into the realm of legally practicing unlicensed mental health practitioners. Other states have laws on the books completely outlawing such practice. Other states have no mention of hypnotherapy in their laws at all!)

Upon the completion of the paper work and filling out the client information chart (see below) I inform the client that because insurance is not paying for his session, that his chart remains completely private between the client and me. If insurance were paying the fee, the insurance company would have a right to the chart, case history, and all information that transpired. The company the client works for may also have rights to the information as might future companies the individual may work for. However, because the client is not relying on insurance what transpires between us is 100% confidential and private. That is something licensed professionals are normally unable to promise a client. Only a court order can access a clients file without the clients permission in Minnesota. This is powerful incentive for a client to work with me instead of other practitioners.

The discussion of confidentiality creates a nice bridge to beginning my general case analysis with the client. In clients presenting numerous symptoms I often utilize a second case analysis process that is quite detailed and will discuss this secondary analysis later in this module. To begin my analysis, I view the clients medical charts that they have brought to me or those that have been faxed to me. (Working with clients with hearing disorders and tinnitus for example, means I must view audiograms for an understanding of the clients internal experience.) After I understand the information the client has given on the Confidential Client Information chart, **I want to know exactly why the client has come today and what experience they would prefer.** *We discuss in great detail the history of their current symptoms and previous medical/mental health experiences and I take extensive notes often numbering 5-10 pages. **I then continue my case analysis with the analysis grid.***

The purpose of the analysis grid is to rapidly isolate key individuals that we will likely be referring to in hypnoanalysis. This chart has provided me with years of good use in identifying the people who seem to have stimulated, caused or re-stimulated the client's symptoms. What follows is the protocol for utilizing the analysis grid:

Explain to your client in a fashion similar to this: "Some of the questions I ask may seem a little funny or unusual in nature. The reason is simple. It is my objective to understand and feel what it is like to live as you with all of the pain and suffering that has transpired recently and in your life. Without actually re-living your entire life, there are key issues that come up regularly with clients and that is exactly why sometimes these questions are so intriguing. Okay, let's begin. Here's a question no one has likely ever asked you before,..."

1. "...In the past, who demanded, at some time, that you (the client) love them. In other words who seemed to want to force you to love them? (Write the answers in the upper left side of the grid. There are often several people to answer each question so make sure you get everyone. If they cannot think of someone, let it go and come back to it, one time, later.)
After you have looked at the past, consider the present. The key issue here is not who wants the client to love them but who may be demanding or forcing the clients love.

If love is a word that the client feels uncomfortable with, "cared for" or "affection" can easily be substituted. Many times a friend will be a key element in a client's illness and not someone who the client loves, like a parent, child, or spouse.

2. "...In the past, who, at some time, simply demanded that you talk or communicate with them? Maybe they made you feel bad if you didn't." (Write the answers to

these questions in the upper right hand quadrant of the grid below.) Then ask for people in the present.

3. "...In the past, at some time, who refused or didn't want to love (care for/show affection) for you?" (Write the names in the lower left quadrant of the grid, then elicit anyone in the present that is indicated.)

4. "...In the past, at some time, who refused or didn't want to communicate or talk to you?" (Write the names in the lower right quadrant of the grid, then elicit anyone in the present that is indicated.)

Immediately you begin to view patterns in the person's life that will likely come up during hypnoanalysis. Some of the names of people elicited will be irrelevant to your work. However, it is the norm that one or two or more of the people noted in the grid below will become significant in the client's illness or challenge they are facing. The analysis grid allows you to be on a first name basis with most of the people you will meet in regression hypnotherapy. Another benefit here is that you don't have to ask for names and relationships while the person is in trance. It allows the client to be more fully associated to her experience instead of explaining that "Mums" is how she refers to Mom or Mother. Knowing how a person refers to the important figures in their life is important. Getting an idea of the problems they experienced before you get back to various causes is a big added bonus. Now, look at the grid and to give you an idea as to it's workings. Fill in the blanks for yourself before going on in the book. This self exercise will help you understand what you are asking of your client.

Analysis Grid

Present and Past:

Love
(Affection)
(Cared For)

Communicate
(Agree)

Enforced:
(Demanded)

Refused to:
(Denied)

The grid is now complete. Sometimes the grid is full of names. Sometimes one name continues to be highlighted over and over. A person exhibiting either of these two patterns will exhibit patterns that are quite important to hypnoanalysis.

A person who has dozens of names to offer for the grid often has illnesses relating to maintaining relationships. There may be a root cause as to why this is, and hypnoanalysis will uncover such a cause. One name repeated in two or three of the quadrants, is often very significant to the clients symptoms. (It is not certain, but is something to be aware of as you interview.) The information you have just obtained is more often than not critical to the rest of your case analysis.

There is an un-ending number of cases where a client exhibits a symptom that another person he or she loves (or sometimes hates) experienced or experiences. Therefore, we want to immediately be aware of and consider the issue of "identification." Clients often develop symptoms of these people in much the same way medical students develop symptoms in med school. A focus of attention on symptoms can psychosomatically bring about such symptoms. Be aware that people die every day from psychosomatic illnesses. The simple fact that a virus or bacterial infection is not the cause of an illness does not make it less threatening. Suicide is often the final action of people with severe psychosomatic disorders. Psychosomatic illness is just as real and important as pathological illness. It is at this point in the case analysis that I ask the client who has died that really mattered in a person's life, not long before the illness started. This list should then be extended back to childhood. Create a separate list of people who died that really mattered since the onset of the clients illness or problem, as these deaths may have significantly affected the client.

"Who died that really mattered before onset?"

"Since the onset of your ____ who has died that was really important to you?"

Later we return to this issue, but for now, we want to eliminate this line of questioning from the conscious mind of the client by opening another door. Now I want to know what person or people they can be around and still have them affect the client in a negative manner long after the other person has gone home or left. It is the answer to this inquiry that will often yield the stimulus for increased or exacerbated symptoms. Sometimes there will be a number of people in response to this inquiry. Uncover them all.

"Who affects you negatively after you leave them?" ("In other words, who is it that sometimes gives you such bad vibes its tough to shake them even after they are gone?")

I leave the door open again and continue immediately with the client's physical symptoms. I do not simply wish to know what the client is presenting to me today, but everything that the client is experiencing that causes them pain or discomfort. Therefore, I ask about each area of the body so we miss nothing and note every significant ongoing chronic pain or problem that the person experiences.

It is very common that people will come to you suffering with several problems but they only present one to you as a therapist. In the spirit of professionalism we discover all other somatic and emotional experiences the person will share.

"Do you experience pain, discomfort, or disorder of some kind in or around the,..."

Head
TMJ
Eyes
Ears
Nose
Mouth
Gums and Teeth
Lips
Neck
Shoulders
Spine
Upper Back
Chest
Lungs
Lower Back
Arms
Hands
Skin
Rectum (including hemorrhoids, urinary difficulties, etc.)
Sexual Arousal (including, PMS, menopause related issues, etc.)
Thighs
Calves
Feet
Viruses like HIV or Hepatitis?
Diagnosed diseases like Diabetes or Cancer?
What have I missed?

As your experience as a hypnoanalyst widens, you will be aware that most people who come to see you will have numerous somatic difficulties. Often you will spend 20 or 30 minutes simply discussing the pains and difficulties. Be delicate when asking questions about the genital area. However, it is necessary to do so. If a woman is suffering from PMS that may be the cause of her headaches. If a man is unable to maintain an erection, that could be the cause of numerous other difficulties. Be gentle. Do not pry, simply ask the question mechanistically and proceed. Our beliefs about our sexuality can greatly influence our behavior and our health. Therefore the information is important and also means it is more likely to be protected from exposure.

Our next mission is to consider possible identification sources to each of the somatics. You will go down the list of each symptom and ask who had this same symptom before your onset, including loved or hated pets.

"Who had (each of these things)?" (Include pets)

Upon completion of possible identifications with other people and pets you ask about each person that is listed above this question:

"When did you want to be like them?"

Often the person will say "never." However, that may or may not be the case. It is possible that the person hated their mother but wanted the amount of freedom or control she had. Make sure you do not ask such a leading question, but frame your question in such a way that the person understands that they may have wanted the power or some other quality of the person and not just be known as being like (similar) to the person. Once we have established both positive and negative identifications, we want to know if there was a time when the client sincerely wished he could have helped the other person with their symptom or life. We ask:

"When did you decide you wanted to help each of these people?"

If the person was successful in helping a person, then there probably would be no identification symptomatically. However, if guilt or shame from not being able to help the person is an issue, they failed. Sometimes the realization is shortly after the failure, which is often the time of the identified persons death. Regardless of what you think, ask the client:

"When did you realize you failed to help them?"

There are some cases where the answer to this question is crucial and will be close in time to when the person's own symptoms began. Occasionally this realization will cause a spontaneous abreaction. Allow the person to cry, be angry and literally, "get it all out." If such an abreaction does not occur, and it only does in about 1 in 10 cases, continue with your case analysis. When a spontaneous abreaction does occur let it all come out. You will be instructed later in this course how specifically to continue when such an experience happens.

People often tend to evaluate themselves inaccurately whether describing their intelligence, income, status or behavior. However, without knowing how a client perceives their own emotional state, it becomes difficult to know what changes if any need to take place. If someone perceives themselves to almost always be enthusiastic and cheerful, then one must wonder why they are in your office. A relatively effective method of discovering how a client views their emotional states is to ask your client to evaluate each emotion listed below with the response, often, sometimes, seldom, or rarely. Occasionally you will hear "never." The emotions are listed in an order that would be preferable to the vast majority of people. Emotions at the top of the list are preferable to the long term emotional health of your client.

How often do you experience each of these emotions?

Enthusiasm
Cheerfulness
Boredom
Anger
Antagonism
Hostility
Fear
Embarrassment
Shame
Grief
Apathy

Generally speaking, I am optimistic about a client who can be angry or displays anger. People with these emotions still "care" about something. They have life left in them to fight. Hostility on the other hand is different than anger in that hostility is emotion with internal intent to harm. Anger is a response to a set of circumstances. Apathy is among the least desirable states of mind, as this is the point of having given up, they don't care anymore. People experiencing grief in a "grief situation" are considered normal. People experiencing grief in a situation where no grief is warranted can use your assistance in getting back on track.

After an evaluation of emotional states, I want to know what people are not doing around the office, in the family, or in a relationship. What have they given up doing that they should be doing? Most psychosomatic illnesses seem to have an element of secondary gain involved where the client will feel uncomfortable or incapable of doing certain work or fulfilling certain obligations. This is what we are looking for when we ask the question:

"What responsibilities are you neglecting?"

Having considered a person's responsibilities and obligations you are now ready to seriously ask a person about their self esteem. However, I avoid using the term self esteem because it is something we are all told should be high. So I like to ask a more subtle question:

"What do you think of yourself? Why?"

Now that we have considered an individual's evaluation of their self esteem, we will find it useful to discover who they are trying to blame in life for their illness, problems etc. Again the question is left intentionally ambiguous and vague.

"Who are you trying to blame? Why?"

Fear is the final key issue I discuss with the client before proceeding to a de-briefing about the clients experience and mis-experience with hypnosis. When you know what a client is afraid of, you discover a great deal about the direction your hypnoanalysis may take you. First ask your client to tell you about five fears he has in the present, then, ask for five fears he has in the future. Do not comment on the clients fears as he tells them to you. Your objective is to remain empathetic without judgment. Sharing these fears and everything in the case analysis involves a great deal of faith on the part of the client. Never violate that honesty and open-ness.

Five fears in the present:
1
2
3
4
5

Five fears in the future:
1
2
3
4
5

This concludes the general case analysis. This analysis should take about 90 minutes on average.

Sometimes it will be necessary to delve into greater detail because of lack of responsiveness on the part of the client or because of an understatement of difficulty on the part of the client. It is interesting that many clients will come to your office and then put on a front that everything is really going "OK." The following questions comprise the Secondary Case Analysis which will assist you in helping you learn more about how you can help your client.

Secondary Case Analysis

"If you were free from this (symptom/problem) how would your life be different?"

"If you had a magic wand and could make this X go away, how would you know when you woke up in the morning, that it really had vanished?"

"Tell me what you need and want from me. Tell me how you want life to be."

"What is your most common emotion?"

"How do you feel about life?"

"Who is hurting you? Who has hurt you?"

"Who said they were your friend or loved one but you later found out they really weren't?"

"Who made you see things their way?"

"Who wouldn't show you the affection you needed?"

"Who refused to communicate with you?"

"What phrase or words best describe your attitude toward life?"

"Who did you hear that phrase from? Who else?"

"When did you tell yourself that phrase the first time?"

"What are you trying to hide and keep secret in the present time? What else?"

"Do you flinch at motions? Why do you think that is?" (If yes)

"Do you like your work? Why?"

"Is your sex life excellent?"

"Do you feel secure?"

"Do you feel self confident?"

(Self confidence and security are analogous so examine differences carefully!)

Hypnosis De-Briefing

At this point you know why the client has come to see you, and have a fairly complete knowledge of the clients symptomology and emotional status. It is best now to de-brief the client on their past experiences with hypnosis, good and bad. It is important to discover all the client's beliefs and attitudes about hypnosis. Many times a client will mention that "hypnosis didn't work for me...". When I hear this from someone, I share with them that hypnosis can be thought of is a relationship between two people and what didn't work in one relationship might work well in another relationship. Do not state that previous practitioners were unskilled but let the client know that many practitioners operate on less than 30 hours of hypnosis training. It takes hundreds of hours of training and experience in hypnosis to begin to gain competence in the field. Few therapists have any understanding of hypnoanalysis which is really the crown jewel and most important process in the field of hypnosis.

Discover what their previous hypnotherapists may have done. Did they only offer suggestions after eye closure? If so that is not an effective procedure for dealing with challenges and health issues. Ask the client what kind of case analysis was given before the therapist began his work. If the case analysis was too brief or neglected completely then no positive therapy is likely to have transpired. You are different because you have been trained to be thorough. Your number one priority is to help the client improve. The way you do that is by acting carefully, methodically and in the clients best interest. You are not attempting to race to see how fast you can change the client. You want the client to feel better. Period.

Ask the client if they have ever been hypnotized. What happened? What was it like? What do they remember? All of this information is critical to understand before you begin to do your session work. If the client has had bad experiences you can help address those experiences now. If the client has good experiences, utilize those experiences and find what was particularly important to the client about those experiences.

Finally, ask what experiences the person has had in viewing stage hypnosis. If there are negative experiences here, be certain that you create distance between the stage performer and the therapeutic practitioner.

A thorough case analysis and hypnosis de-briefing will prepare you for an effective relationship with your client. After helping your client experience a brief induction, you may send your client home and set your first appointment.

Inducing Trance

The purpose of any induction is to assist a client in shifting from one state of mind to another state of mind. In hypnotherapy we often refer to this as trance. In England practitioners may actually refer to a trance state by the term "hypnosis." Learning the "Dave Elman Induction" is much more involved than simply reading words off of a piece of paper. Inductions involve and demand the awareness on the practitioners part of all of the physiological responses of the client. Dave Elman was a famous hypnotherapist who practiced in the 1950's and 60's. This induction is representative of one of his fine contributions to hypnosis.

Now. Take a long deep breath and hold it for a few seconds. As you exhale this breath, allow your eyes to close and let go of the surface tension in your body. Just let your body relax as much as possible....now....

...Now...place your awareness on your eye muscles and relax the muscles around your eyes to the point where your eyelids just won't work. When you are sure that they're so relaxed... that as long as you hold the relaxation, they just won't work, hold onto that relaxation and test them to make sure the eye lids stay closed ...good....

...Now...this relaxation you have in your eyes is the same quality of relaxation that I want you to have throughout your whole body. So, just let this quality of relaxation flow thorough your whole body from the top of your head to the tips of your toes.

...Now, we can deepen this relaxation much more. In a moment, I'm going to have you open and close your eyes. When you close your eyes that's your signal to let this feeling of relaxation become 10 times deeper. All you have to do is want it to happen and you can make it happen very easily. OK, now, open your eyes...now close your eyes and feel that relaxation flowing through your entire body, taking you much deeper. Use your wonderful imagination and imagine your whole body is covered and wrapped in a warm blanket of relaxation.

....Now, we can deepen this relaxation much more. In a moment, I'm going to have you open and

close your eyes one more time. Again, when you close your eyes, double the relaxation you now have. Make it become twice as deep. OK, now once more, open your eyes...close your eyes and double your relaxation...good. Let every muscle in your body become so relaxed that as long as you hold on to this quality of relaxation, every muscle of your will be deeply relaxed.

...In a moment, I'm going to have you open and close your eyes one more time. Again, when you close your eyes, double your relaxation you now have. Make it become twice as deep. OK, now, once more, open your eyes...close your eyes and double your relaxation...good. Let every muscle in your body become so relaxed that as long as you hold on to this quality of relaxation, every muscle of your body will be deeply relaxed.

In a moment, I'm going to lift your (right or left) hand by the wrist, just a few inches, and drop it. If you have followed my instructions up to this point, that hand will be so relaxed it will be just as loose and limp as a wet dish cloth, and will simply plop down. Now don't try to help me, you have to let your arm be simply calm and limp. Let me do all the lifting so that when I release it, it just plops down and you'll allow yourself to go much deeper.

(If subject helps to lift hand say:) "No let me do all the lifting, don't help me. Let it be heavy. Don't help me. You'll feel it when you have it."

Now that's complete physical relaxation. I want you to know that there are two ways a person can relax.

You can relax physically and you can relax mentally. You already proved that you can relax physically, now let me show how to relax mentally. In a moment, Ill ask you to begin slowly counting backward, out loud, from 100. Now, here's the secret to mental relaxation, with each number you say, double your mental relaxation. With each number you say, let your mind become twice as relaxed. Now if you do this, by the time you reach the number 98, or maybe even sooner, your mind will have become so relaxed, you will have actually relaxed all the rest of the numbers that would have come after 98, right out of your mind, there just won't be any more numbers. Now, you have to do this, I can't do it for you. Those numbers will leave if you will them away. Now start with the idea that you will make that happen and you can easily dispel them from your mind.

Hypnotherapist: Now, say the first number, 100 and say deeper relaxed.
Client: 100
Hypnotherapist: Now double that mental relaxation, let those numbers already start to fade.
Client: 99
Hypnotherapist: Double your mental relaxation. Start to make those numbers leave. They'll fade like sand from the hand now...
Client: 98
Hypnotherapist: Now, they'll be gone. They fade into black and they go far far away. Now listen carefully...

The client will have made the numbers disappear. You can now begin your hypnoanalysis or briefly explain how hypnoanalysis works to your client and send him home if this is his first trance experience. The Dave Elman Induction has the benefit of regularly producing a somnambulistic state in a fairly short amount of time.

The Six Pillars of Hypnoanalysis

The last section concluded with your client being in trance. Now what do we do next? There are six pillars of hypnoanalysis and all of them lead to therapeutic interventions. In most cases you will begin with regression therapy, but this is not always the case. Here are the six pillars of hypnoanalysis to help you discern what comes next!

1) Transference- Transference is the common experience of the client (or a part of the client) viewing the therapist as someone in his or her past. The therapist could be perceived as father-like, mother-like, etc. This can be useful if the therapist is doing so with a strategic purpose in mind. For examplo, if the therapist is attempting to gain access to an ego state, then it can be useful to briefly allow transference to take place for a few moments. However, once the ego state identified the therapist with a past significant other (father, mother, boss, brother, sexual abuser) the distinction needs to be quickly made that the therapist is NOT that person, nor is he anything like that person or people who have so negatively effected the client's life. This moment is referred to as a "transference interpretation."

It is at this point that the therapist gently but firmly challenges the ego state to realize that he has been reacting to all authority figures, or whatever group the therapist is now "falling into," as he did when he was, say a child, responding to Mom. This moment creates an "aha!" experience that allows the client to gain personal insight into his behavior. This previously unconscious behavior is now a conscious experience that allows the client to create intentional change.

Warning: It is very easy for a therapist to take on the role of significant others both "good and bad" without knowing it. Countertransference is very common in hypnotherapy and must be guarded against at all costs. It is probably safe to say that all hypnoanalysts have at one time or another fallen prey to the seduction of a client's unconscious mind and ego states. When we treat the client as a child, a lover, a parent, or anything other than a client, we have allowed countertransference to take place. This must be rapidly corrected or the therapeutic relationship should be terminated. **All hypnotherapists should solve their own transference issues with the assistance of other therapists as these transferences become obvious. Every therapist needs a therapist.**

Watkins (1997) has a general rule of thumb in dealing with clients: "Don't do what the parents, or whoever reared the patient early in life, did wrong in the eyes of the patient, whether it is ignoring or abusing."

Clients who have been sexually abused will sometimes (but certainly not always) act seductively toward the therapist. Be very aware of this common phenomenon. It could destroy your practice and harm the therapeutic relationship. You will find a common pattern in clients who report abuse. They tend to have been abused more than once. Rape victims are often victimized later in life. Molestation victims often are molested by other individuals than the first offender. Abuse victims are often abused by individuals other than the first offender. Bringing this pattern to the conscious mind of the client, at the appropriate time, aids in the healing process. *Without proper ego strength an assignation of self-blame might take place and ruin the therapeutic process.*

2) Regression and Revivification- Once in trance, the client can be returned to the initial sensitizing event (ISE) using regression techniques. *Once a client has been returned to the ISE, he can see how his ego states have shaped his behavior and make a conscious decision to change.* In Dianetic therapy, (which borrows heavily from Watkin's hypnoanalytic work) this incident is called an "engram" and through the years I have found that term to be accurate and useful. When I say that someone is "in an engram," I specifically mean that his ego state that developed at the ISE is unconsciously driving the individuals reactionary behavior. It is therefore critical to the therapist to return to this event so the ego state can be contacted and dealt with in an appropriate manner. We will briefly consider the key techniques here to return to that ISE.

a) The Somatic Bridge- The somatic bridge is a technique that was developed to let a somatic (a pain or unpleasant internal phenomenon like tinnitus or vertigo) speak for itself. Allow the somatic to come into consciousness and state it's purpose, goals, and/or objectives.

b) The Affect Bridge- This technique was defined in 1971 by Watkins. The objective of this technique is to track the feeling or affect component of a person's experience back to the ISE while in trance. This allows the client to see that the feeling belongs to an earlier experience and no longer needs to be experienced in the present time.

In session, I might say something to the effect of, "Your tinnitus is loud and it is frustrating you. It is causing you great annoyance. Take me with you back to a recent time when you felt depressed by it." Then as each event on the briedge is dealt with ultimately can tell the client, Take me with you back to the event that most likely was the cause (or a cause) of your tinnitus so we can experience what caused this noise to turn on." Sometimes the onset was a physical, external event like a gunshot or a rock concert. In cases like this the tinnitus eventually will be reduced in volume but normally will not remit entirely. In cases where the ISE is an emotional event, we normally are able to get an eventual remission although it may take months or years. In cases of pain, the remission often begins within minutes, hours or days!

3) Acceptance of the Client and His Ego States- It is not our job to judge our client. It is our job to facilitate healing. By accepting the client and his parts in a virtually unconditional manner, rapport is built rapidly. Rapport hinges on trust. Once the client and/or specific ego states trust the therapist, it is easier to access the ego states that are creating difficulties in the client's present time life.

4) Contacting Ego States- Once in trance, the simple question, "Would the part or parts that are helping Jim feel this pain be willing to come out and discuss the benefits and reasons for this experience?" *Do not interrogate the ego state. You are not a police officer.* Your tone of voice should be empathetic, appreciative and understanding. Your goal is to discover the age of the ego state (when it developed), what it's intention is or wants for the whole self and under what circumstances would the ego state be willing to accept a new job or create a new experience that would be in the best interest of the ego state and the whole person.

5) Create an environment of safe negotiation between ego states. Allow the various parts to all feel comfortable with the outcome of the therapy and communication. (In NLP this process is called Reframing.)

6) Abreaction Therapy- There is no question as to the value of abreaction or catharsis when working with clients. One significant cause of physical and emotional illness is the lack of emotional release (usually in the form of tears and/or grieving) from traumatic events. When the client is in trance, you can allow an ego state to abreact, or, the whole self as seems appropriate. Experience is the best guide and you will gain skill as you become more experienced in hypnoanalysis. The key point to remember is that the repressed feelings of grief, guilt, shame or anger have caused emotional or physical illness and we must allow the individual or his ego state(s) to experience the release of these "negative" emotions once and for all.

The client should be allowed to get ALL of his emotional repression vented. Once the tears have flowed, the anger has been vented and the repression has been lifted the ego state that has been influencing present time health often re-integrates with other parts and healing begins. The client must learn that the victimization he experiences was not of his own doing. He was a victim, plain and simple.

As the client re-experiences these traumatic events he begins to release the negative emotions. As the events are re-examined a desensitization to the event and the experience begins to occur draining the negative emotional energy from the ISE or engram.

5

Ego State Therapy
Understanding Dissociation

Ego State Therapy is also known as "Parts Therapy."

Imagine that you are going to purchase a car and part of you wants to and part of you doesn't. The job of the hypnotherapist is to find out what is in the true best interest of the client as a whole and then help negotiate a settlement between the disagreeing parts so they will buy a car, or not, and then go on in peace without further distress.

I typically address these "parts" in the following fashion. "Would the part of you that wants to buy the car come and talk to me. I am very much in line with your thinking and would like to talk just with you."

Then whatever I learn is carefully noted and I thank the part for it's honesty. Then I call out the next part. "Would the part that doesn't want to buy a car come out and talk to me. Is there something bad about what the other part wants to do here?"

This part then comes out and talks to me. This part might say that it costs too much money or it might

97

say that the client always wrecks nice things. It might say anything. Whatever the part says, I respect, acknowledge and carefully write down everything the part says.

Then of course we have to check and make sure there are no other parts that want to communicate about this issue. If there are, we ask them to speak up and be willing to share their thoughts. This works very much like family therapy. (The works of Virginia Satir are strongly recommended in gaining valuable background in this type of therapy.)

Degrees of Dissociation and Parts Therapy

In 1984 I lived in Southern California. It was at this time that the infamous "Hillside Strangler" committed his murders. One night I watched the evening news to hear the good news that Kenneth Bianchi had been apprehended and incarcerated. It turned out that Bianchi was diagnosed with multiple personality disorder (MPD) by John G. Watkins, arguably the most important hypnotherapist in the 20th century. (Watkins, as I have noted during my tenor as a staff writer for the Journal of Hypnotism was the originator of hypnoanalysis in World War II and it was his pioneering work that influenced Dave Elman and the future of hypnosis.)

It was not the "Ken" personality that claimed "credit" for the murders he committed. His alter personality, "Steve" offered no regrets however. "Steve," did the killing in Bellingham and Los Angeles. MPD is the most severe form of dissociation. In the case of MPD, the various ego states (parts) within an individual form distinct boundaries and do not communicate with each other as ego states do within a normal person who develops relatively normally in his life.

When we speak of dissociative disorders, we are talking about a continuum of states of mind that include everything from anxiety, unwanted out of body experiences, and depression to multiple personality disorder and psychoses. For the record, I have never worked with a person experiencing MPD and I have no reason to ever do so. I would urge you to do likewise. (I have unwittingly taken on psychotic patients only to refer them out immediately upon discovery of the psychoses. Please accept my strongest encouragement to refer out clients who cannot distinguish objective reality from their own subjective reality.)

There are many emotional, mental and physical disorders that a well trained and experienced hypnotherapist can assist with on a client's road to wellness. These disorders rarely yield to suggestive therapy, metaphor or non-analytical forms of hypnotherapy. Conversely, these disorders tend to significantly diminish in magnitude when worked through with an experienced hypnotherapist utilizing the three key pillars of hypnoanalysis, regression therapy, ego state therapy (similar to parts therapy) and transference.

I have discussed in some detail the benefits of regression therapy, which is usually the first line of therapy after a thorough case analysis and ego strengthening from the hypnotherapist. In this section, I would like to discuss in some detail the definitions, experience, and results of the second line of hypnoanalysis, which is ego state therapy (very similar but not identical to "parts therapy").

When faced with dissociative disorders like post-traumatic disorders (including abuse cases), anxiety, depression, chronic and acute pain, hypnoanalysis is indicated for clinical hypnotherapy.

Ego States- Important "Parts" that Create an Integrated Self

"Part of me wants to buy the house and part of me says, 'no way!'" This is representative of a normal person's typical internal conflicts and accurately describes a normal person's internal process of thinking and decision making. These are two separate (but overlapping) ego states that are working in the best interest of the self. Each part has "it's" reasons for supporting a different point of view. These parts are what we will call ego states throughout the remainder of this course.

An ego state (Watkins 1997) can be defined as "an organized system of behavior and experience whose elements are bound together by some common principle, and which is separated from other such states by a boundary that is more or less permeable... Ego states are generally experienced in normal people as normal mood changes. "

Ego states are organized in a few different and typical ways. Sometimes we find these states as a pattern of behavior resulting from similar stimuli. This is called "normal differentiation." Ego states that are formed by introjection of significant others are those where the person develops clusters of behaviors around his perception of a significant other like a

100

parent or teacher. In cases of abuse, this state may begin to "identify" with the significant other and act similarly to that person. Other states are formed around periods of time, like childhood. Still other ego states emerge as defense mechanisms from facing traumatic situations like rape, child abuse and other traumatic distresses. The "core ego" is the state that is most indicative of the normal self, the self that is conscious most of the time. This is also called the "executive ego."

Ego states are not simply a discovery made by great minds like Freud, Federn and Watson. It was Ernest Hilgard (1977) that actually proved the existence of ego states, although he called his discovery, "the hidden observer." Hilgard's experiments prove that there is a "part" of an individual, for example, that is "conscious" and able to feel pain or hear sound even when the individual's core ego is ablated in hypnosis.

In a healthy and normal individual there are many ego states that operate consciously and unconsciously. In a psychotic individual, or someone with MPD, the ego states are separated from each other within the self by non-permeable boundaries. On the other end of the spectrum from MPD divisions, we occasionally find people who have no ego state boundaries. They have few or no parts to speak of. These people view everything as the same in the world and are not very functional.

Human personality, according to Watkins, "develops through two basic processes, integration and differentiation. By integration a child learns to put concepts together, such as cow and horse, and thus to build more complex units called animals. By differentiation he separates general concepts into more specific meanings, such as discriminating between a cat and a rabbit. Both processes are normal and adaptive." (Watkins, 1997)

Ego states tend to describe themselves as "me" or "I" and discuss other ego states within the person, in the second person, "she" and "he." It should also be noted that in numerous instances in therapeutic work with my clients, ego states have represented other ego states as "it."

Differentiation vs. Dissociation

Differentiation and dissociation both involve the psychological separating of two "entities," but differentiation is of a lesser degree, and is normal adaptation. On the other hand dissociation is pathological because it is maladaptive, decreasing or eliminating internal communication at the conscious and unconscious level of the self, between parts.

Just What is Ego State Therapy Then?

The therapeutic goal of the hypnotherapist is NOT to fuse all parts together into one ego but to integrate them so they continue to be valuable to the survival of the individual and work in tandem for the mental and physical health of the whole person.

"Ego state therapy is the utilization of individual, family, and group therapy techniques for the resolution of conflicts between the different ego states that constitute a 'family of self' within a single individual." (Watkins, 1997)

Virginia Satir, arguably the most skilled family therapist of the 20th century, wrote and taught extensively about effective family therapy. Her work is completely applicable to working with individual clients in hypnosis. Hypnoanalysis utilizing ego state therapy hinges on a few key pillars for healing emotional, mental and physical difficulties.

Ego State Success

I first met "Rick" in 1995. He didn't come to see me because he couldn't leave his house. He suffered from two disorders, tinnitus and hyperacusis. Tinnitus is sound that is heard from within a person, often sounding like it comes from the ears, often sounding like it is "in the head somewhere." Hyperacusis is severe sensitivity to certain types of sounds or levels of sound.

Rick was unable to function normally because the volume of his tinnitus was extremely loud and his sensitivity to sound was so significant that he was sent into terrors by simply hearing the refrigerator or walking on grass and leaves.

Rick enjoyed his "old" life of 37 years working as a stage director in major theatrical productions all across the United States. Then one day, we found out in regression therapy, he fell on his head and neck skiing and got his "bell rung." The noise started there. A few weeks later he began to experience a severe sensitivity to the sounds at his work. Eventually he was forced to quit his job and go home. The tinnitus and hyperacusis were so severe he was literally immobilized. He was unable to talk or listen on the telephone.

I went to Rick's home and began two years of therapy with Rick there. Having suffered from tinnitus myself from 1993-1995, I was very sympathetic to Rick's traumatic experience.

Rick's severely impaired life reminded me of my own experience. The symptoms led Rick to severe depression and anxiety. He was desperate for help. We linked him up with other professional assistance which is necessary in these kinds of cases. (An MRI has to be done with a tinnitus sufferer to rule out a tumor, for example)

After weeks and weeks of regression therapy we finally found the causes of the tinnitus and only one of the causes was because of hearing loss which was moderate but not significant enough to cause the volume of tinnitus he was experiencing and certainly not relevant to his hyperacusis. The regressions helped us desensitize the severe anxiety and depression to mild anxiety and depression after many months of work. He had lived with tinnitus for a little over one year when I first met him. Our weekly work was seemingly endless.

Finally we had run out of time tracks to regress and we were making progress. It was now time for ego state therapy. I had Rick "bring out" the part of him that was keeping his tinnitus and hyperacusis in place.

KH: What is the purpose of having Rick experience such loud tinnitus and extreme hyperacusis such that it keeps him from working? The whole self is suffering greatly.

R: That's the point. He has to stop working. Jane (Rick's wife) doesn't want him working on the road all the time. He needs to get a job closer to home so the marriage really can work.

KH: I thought Jane said it was OK for Rick to work.

R: Sure, she *said* that but she didn't mean that.

KH: What leads you to believe that?

R: She will say whatever it takes to make Rick feel better, but the fact is she wants Rick to not be on the road.

KH: Is it because she is jealous?

R: No. It's because she wants him home at night with her.

KH: So you're holding the tinnitus in place to get Rick's attention and get him to stay home?

R: It worked didn't it?

KH: It did. You're doing a great job, but Rick is considering suicide on occasion and I'm nervous about that. I propose that you need to win your point here and allow the tinnitus and hyperacusis to not bother Rick so much.

R: How?

KH: I suggest that you allow the volume of the tinnitus and the sensitivity to sound be more tolerant so Rick can get a job locally and get off workers comp. Then he would be home almost all the hours that Jane is home.

R: What if he goes back on the road?

KH: You're still in control of the volume switch. You can turn the volume up again if Rick gets out of line and thinks about heading out on the road again. What do you think?

R: I think that might work. But what if he gets a job in theater?

KH: I expect that is fine. The idea is just to have him home most of the time right? It doesn't matter if he gets home after working locally does it?

R: No that's fine. Jane just doesn't want him going on the road.

KH: OK, then let's do this. Let's say that you reduce the tinnitus volume and the noise sensitivity and then Rick will not go back on the road. If he ever does, you will turn up the volume again as a signal to get him back home. Deal?

R: Sure.

KH: Thanks. Now, I'd like to talk to the part of Rick, that wants the noise to go away and sensitivity to sound to be lifted. Would you talk to me?

R: OK.

KH: Well, you heard all of that, what do you think? Can you go back to work without going on the road?

R: Absolutely. That's no problem. I've wanted to go back to work for a long time. I can work locally and that will be fine. What do I have to do?

KH: Nothing, just go ahead and go back to work as soon as you feel comfortable. Fair enough?

R: Sure.

KH: Great. Now, Rick, I want you to extend your left hand and allow the part of you that wants to signal you to stay home to rest there.

R: OK.

KH: Now, take that hand and bring it slowly into your chest and allow that part to merge back into your self becoming a part of your self and integrating back into your whole being....Now, take that part of you that wants to go back to work and let it rest in your right hand. Slowly bring that part back into you into your chest and allow it to integrate back into yourself fully and completely.

R: OK.

KH: Now, allow your hands to slowly bring your hands back to your knees and allow yourself to feel whole and complete with all of your being working together to meet the needs of the whole self....When you feel ready, you can open your eyes and feel complete, whole and refreshed.

Several weeks later, Rick applied for a local theater job, on faith that his tinnitus and hyperacusis would improve (it hadn't yet) and he was accepted after being interviewed. Within a few months the tinnitus and hyperacusis were still there but neither was significant enough in intensity to continue therapy. Rick's experience with hypnotherapy was a fantastic one allowing him to return to health and work. Hypnotherapy was an adjunct to medications and osteopathic intervention in Rick's case, and a successful one. Rick's total investment in client sessions was almost two years and he is very thankful.

6

Time Track Therapy

Our first session with our client is one where we will do a complete case analysis and possibly have the client experience positive regression to build ego strength as discussed earlier. Our second, third and probably fourth session with a chronically ill client will most certainly be invested in regression therapy. Our fifth session will likely be one filled with ego state therapy. (Sometimes ego state therapy is combined with regression therapy depending on the presenting issues.) Other times as in cases of post traumatic stress disorder, ego state therapy will be indicated in the second session.

In most clients by the time the sixth session has arrived they have purged the negative emotions that have held them in their illness for so long and they are probably ready for Time Track Therapy. **Regardless of what number session this is, it is normally best to utilize Time Track Therapy after Regression and Ego State Therapy.**

Hypnoanalysis helps the client gain insight and help the client purge emotions of anxiety, depression, anger, frustration, hostility and so on. Hypnoanalysis also helps the client re-align her internal sense of self to a more unified and focused self. To do any other form of hypnotherapy before these experiences have been accomplished, is really irresponsible. Once the client has experienced the ability to understand their experience and all internal "parts" or "ego states" are in alignment for what is best for the self, the client is ready for Time Track Therapy and the suggestive therapies we have discussed in this book.

Time Track Therapy is a synthesis of other therapeutic approaches and techniques that I have developed over the past several years.

The underlying principle of Time Track Therapy is this: After having experienced the purging of the emotions of anxiety, depression and other debilitating feelings, the client now has a right to experience the reality that in his past he did not always suffer from his current problem (at least in some form) and that it is reasonably possible or maybe probable that he will not experience the problem in the future. It is at this point that we will begin one session of Time Track Therapy. This is also the only session of hypnotherapy that I ever tape for the client because it is a session of suggestive therapeutics that are utilized in such a way that long term listening this kind of experience is really quite beneficial.

Without the purging of negative emotions and rooting out the cause of the illness, you are doing little more than giving a client an aspirin to feel better with this or any other suggestive therapy. However, Time

Track Therapy is a wonderful new pillar of excellent hypnotherapy.

Time Track Therapy allows us to create optimism and hope in the mind and heart of our clients. Here is a sample session of Time Track Therapy. This session is not to be used for chronic illnesses but for behavioral issues instead. The difference is that in a behavior we can see specific changes and be relatively certain they are within our control. Therefore this session is fairly "concrete" in it's orientation. With chronic problems like pain, tinnitus, and extended illnesses which are not likely to remit in their entirety we will discuss the protocol for that after this entire session (brief as it is) has been completed.

For habitual change we may not need to go to point four which is the far future in a person's physical life to confirm the change has taken place. However, when working with chronically ill people this is absolutely critical to experience.

Time Track Therapy Template

Habits and Performance Issues
(not Chronic Pain and Illness)

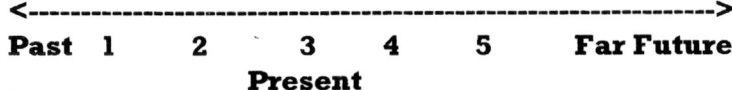

<--->
Past   1   2   3   4   5   Far Future
                       Present

(There is no need to induce formal trance before Time Track Therapy. You have almost certainly established excellent rapport with your client and simply asking them to close their eyes should be sufficient.)

Present:

I'd like you to sit back, or lay back,
take a long breath in and hold it and exhale.
Take another deep breath in and hold it, hold
it and exhale. Take another deep breath in
right now, and hold, hold, hold, and exhale.
Good. And now, I want you to close your
eyes and allow yourself to relax. Pay attention
to your breathing as you think about the reason
you are listening to my voice.

You've come here with a reason and
I want you to think about what that reason is
right now. If you have a goal or a purpose for
listening to my voice right now, think of it in your
mind's eye and imagine it right now.

You know, there was a time when this
problem existed in your life and there was a time
when the problem didn't exist in your life. In the
future there is a time where this problem exists in
your life and in the future there is a time when this
problem will no longer exist in your mind, in your
life, in your body, in your being.

I want you to listen to the music and my
voice and go with me on a journey into your life.
I want you to imagine yourself sitting right
where you are, and I want you to float up
out of yourself while still remaining in the room
you are in and look down on yourself and see

*yourself sitting there, relaxing, being calm, feeling
at peace, watching you watch your breathing,
and there is something about that that makes you
feel good inside even though you don't quite
know what it is.*

*As you float up, above yourself you go
through the ceiling, till you see the sky, till you float
through the sky, high into the sky, through the clouds,
straight up, you never thought it would be like this,
and through the light part of the sky, through the dark
part of the sky...and as you get to the dark part of the
sky where all there are is little dots, stars that light up
the sky, you see a line, like train tracks and they are
approaching. It is golden and go forever in both
directions. Like a magical time track. Six feet wide.*

*As you come closer to this golden
translucent line...and you've already come so far...
you ascend through the time line, and you look and
see the straight line that goes in both directions for
what seems forever. The ends of the line seems
to come together. You begin to realize that from
where you are now, hovering above the line, you
see there is a little marker that indicates what
day, time and year today is. You realize that this is
indeed a time track.*

Point Two, Near Past

*As you look back to what you know to
be the past because you see a marker indicating
last year, you decide that you will go back into
the past. You soar above the line and you begin
to fly into the past, above your time track, past*

last year, past 1997, past 1996, back to a time
when this problem was not as bad. You see that
year marked on the line. You see that the line,
the track, is still translucent. It's like water, but
you could walk on it if you landed on it or you
could descend right through it toward the planet
earth if you decided to and that is what you will do.

You begin your descent through the
line through the year you want to, through the
dark part of the sky, looking up seeing your
line firmly in place in the universe, going still
further down toward the earth.

It's bright sunshine, you go through
puffy white clouds, descending and landing
gently on our planet on a place that is familiar
to you and you see you outside. You see you,
enjoying your day, having a good day, doing
something you like to do, looking in pretty
good shape, all things considered and you feel
good about what you see.

You tap the younger you on the shoulder
and the younger you says, "hey how did you get
here?, hey, you're me."

"I know. I have this way to go back in
time and I wanted to come and see what it was
like to be me at this time, because I have a
problem that I'm in control of and if I can just
step into myself, to you, of this time, I know I'll
be able to not have this problem in the future.
I'll do the things the way I did and this time the
problem will get better."

114

*The younger you looks at you and wonders
what you just said.*

"You want to step inside of me?"

*The older you the you of today says,
"No, I want to step inside of me."*

*The older you gives the younger you a
hug and it feels very nice and the younger you
merges into you and you feel whole and well
and comforted by this experience. You look
around and see all the things you were doing
at this time and you realize that life was a little
different then, now.*

*You look to the sky as you see
nothing new around you. No one to talk to.
You feel quite good as you begin to ascend
from the earth, through the clouds, through
the light part of the sky, through the dark
part of the sky, until you look up and see
your time line. You see the track come into
view. That thin band that runs through the
universe that has no apparent end to either
end of the line and you come through it feeling
refreshed and comforted, and you decide that
if you can go to the past you can go to the future.*

Point Four- Near Future:

*You soar high above the time track,
looking at the time marker, flying above the*

115

track, flying high above the line toward the future. Past all the years you came through to get to where you were now flying forward toward the present and the future. You love this flying. You fly past 1997, 1998, 1999, to a time in the very near future where you see the year on the time marker, marking the time and the date and you go through the timeline descending right through, descending through the dark part of the sky and the light part of the sky, through the clouds, landing on the planet earth and all you see around you is you in a couple of years from now.

You look in better shape than you are now. You appear to be having quite a nice day. There is a sense of deja vu that permeates your body as you walk up to your older self, the you of tomorrow who is facing away from you. Just as you are about to touch the shoulder of the older you, the older you turns around, smiles, giving you a big grin, and says, "I've been waiting, what took you so long?"

"How did you know I was coming? I just decided to come..." and of course you realize that because this is the future the future you has already been here. You ask the older you, "How did you do it?"

The older you says, "When we made the decision, we had the plan and I just did what I said I was going to do."

"Was it easy?"

*The older you smiled and says,
"It's never easy." But it was simple. I
just did what I said I was going to do."*

*The older you puts an arm around
you, to give you advice and the older you
feels good next to you. The older you faces
you and gives you a firm strong hug and as
you hug your older self, your older self
comes into you and merges with you and
it feels good. So good. and as you look
around this space and time in the future,
you feel comforted knowing, what you
have done, and will do, and that the
process is doable and you begin to ascend
off the ground.*

*As you rise off the ground you look
down and see your older self there. She/he
looks up and gives you a wink and a wave.
You see the sun gleam warmly, ascending
high into the sky through the clouds, through
the light part of the sky and through the dark
part of the sky until you look up and see your
time track. The golden translucent line of time.*

*You ascend right through the center
of this year and moment you have just come
from and time and go through the time track,
ascending high above the time track, feeling
energized and enthusiastic about your life....
Then it strikes you. What would happen if
you went far into the past and found yourself as a little child. What would that be like?*

Imagine what you could tell yourself. Imagine what you could share with yourself that you know now but didn't know then. There are possibilities.

Before you think and dwell too much on this, you begin to go back in time, ascending, arms outspread, flying backward in time....past 2000, past the 1990's, past the 1980's....all the way back to the year you were six or five or four or seven years old.

Point One- Childhood:

You descend through the line of time at just the right point where you know you will find yourself on a good day and you descend through the dark part of the sky and the light part of the sky and through the clouds until you finally come to a rest back on the planet in a place that looks oh so familiar and you feel...young again.

It's a sunny day when you find a child playing by themself, Maybe riding a bike. The child sees you but he's not astonished.

The child says "Hello!"

You say, "Hi."

The child says, "What's your name?"

You tell the child and he/she says, "Hey, that's my name too!"

and you say "I know."

"How do you know my name?"

"Just because I know."

"Do you want to play a game with me?"

"Yeah. Yeah, I do."

"What would you like to play?"

The child tells you and of course your mind isn't on the game but on the child. The child plays the game with you and against. You smile at the beauty of the child before you. You feel so good inside. Oh so good. At the end of the game, the child tells you that "you play pretty good."

"I know," you say, "I used to play alot when I was your age."

The child's parent calls....or some adult sounding like a parent.

"Honey, it's time to come home," and the child attentively gets up and says, "I have to go." The child gets up and doesn't even hug you! "See you tomorrow if you come back OK?!" You don't know what to say to that and the child runs off saying, "Mommy, Mommy, guess who I just met?" The child runs in the house and you hear the child say, "I met a man/woman with the same name as me!"

Then all goes silent as the door closes behind the child.

Silence fills your mind as you realize that you have just met yourself as a child and you have never felt so good!

You begin to ascend from the earth, through the clouds, through the light part of the sky, through the dark part of the sky, until you look up and see the line of time hung so firmly in the universe. It comes clear and you go through the line representing where you were in time and you realize that there is just one more thing that you want to really do now. You want to go to the far future.

Point Five- Far Future

You go through your past, heading toward the present, through the 1970's and the 1980's, the 1990's, past when you saw yourself a couple of years from now, past the 2010 mark, past the 2020 mark farther into the future farther and farther. At some point the markers disappear but the line continues and you wonder what is different.

Then you realize that you have come to the future! You have come to the future! Not just the future, you have come to what you thought always was. You have come to what it is like in the future where there are no time markers.

As you look off it gets brighter and brighter. There is almost a quality of crystal and a tinge of gold. There are shades of colors you have only dreamed of.. There are clouds and mists so that as you look into the future you see the line merge with the clouds and the mist into one unified something that you understand but is not so easy to describe.

You realize that it was as if you had always known that it would be like this. You were right.

What an extraordinary gift to be able to see.

Then you realize that the problem at hand back in the present all those years ago, while a challenge at the time is nothing that you can't handle when you realize that this is your future. Your destiny.

As you ponder that briefly you realize that time is short. You've had your opportunity and chance. You now must go back to the present. You race back and you go back as you ascend and fly faster.

There is one.

There is another and you go past the 2030'a and the 2020's and the 2010's and the 2000's all the way back to the time that is today in the present and it is clearly

*marked on the line for you to know exactly
where you arrived here from.*

*You descend through the line,
through the dark part of the sky, through
the light part of the sky, through the clouds,
through the ceiling of the office you are in,
right back into yourself sitting in the chair
that you are in.*

*You feel refreshed and renewed
with a new sense of optimism and excitement
about ....everything! Everything!*

*Now, when I say one you will open
your eyes.*

*3. Become aware of the surroundings
around you.*

*2. Realize you are sitting in a chair in
my office.*

*1. When you feel ready,
open your eyes, wide aware and refreshed
with a feeling of newness and optimism.*

This presentation of Time Track Therapy is ideal for weight loss, habitual change and performance issues. When you have something more complex like a chronic illness you must use different phrasing. The reason is simple. In the above presentation you notice that the changes are fairly concrete. However, with people who suffer from illnesses that may or may not improve you must change your themes for the future.

People who are suffering know in their mind that getting well is unlikely (even if you think it is possible or even probable.) Therefore in order to maintain belief in the process we must change our languaging and juggle the way we manipulate time.

Changes for Time Track Therapy

Helping People Who Suffer
from
Chronic Pain and Illnesses

We do not mention the problems of the pain, the chronic fatigue, the fibromyalgia, the tinnitus, the hyperacusis by name when we are doing Time Track Therapy for these experiences and in fact the focus is changed to the emotional state of mind rather than the specific healing of the illness or symptoms. Your client has been with you now for 5-7 sessions before this intervention begins. They understand that getting well or getting better is a process and probably won't happen overnight. They understand that healing can be like a rollercoaster ride. Here is language I like to use when I work with the chronically ill.

*When you soar above your time track and
begin to head to the future you notice that
there are places where the line is clear as
crystal, translucent, and there are other
places where there are large dark spots
taking up virtually the entire space of the
line in the current year you are looking
down at.*

*As you look back to your past you see
the last year has had many large dark spots
often filling up almost every portion of the
time line. It has been a difficult year. As you
look to the near future you see a bit of a
clearing of the spots. They aren't as dark
although they still take up a large amount
of space. What's interesting is that as you
fly further above the line and further into
the future, the line begins to clear and the
spots begin to shrink. Some parts of the
line in fact have only little dots on them...
almost invisible. The message is clear....*

Throughout our presentation of the past and the
future with chronically ill people we use the
references to dark spots taking up most of the line to
represent the most difficult of times and we represent
the better times with very few spots or darkness on the
line. The client needs to experience the idea that
although dark spots are a part of the life line they do
change a great deal in their intensity and duration.

When working with people with chronic pains
and illnesses begin at point 3 which is the present.
(There is nowhere else to begin!) Then take the client
back to a time in the last week when they were

experiencing their symptoms in a very bad way. Be brief with this as this is really an exercise of joy and happiness, but the reminder of how bad it WAS compared to how it IS even today, just a few days later is very important.

Unlike the presentation for habits and performance where we took people to point 2, a point in the near past when the person felt fine or was doing well, the very next time we take a person to is to a time in the near future when they are "feeling better than they could have imagined." **This is very important: Allow the client to have an experience in the reasonably near future where they feel "better."**

When the client meets his older self at point four, the older self must not state anything unreasonable. I like the sentence, "I haven't felt this good in years." That is believable, it doesn't say the person is healed but leaves ample room for interpretation and optimism. In addition to the optimism, it gives the client a resource to share with his younger self that he will now go visit at point 2.

Take the client to point 2 at this time. Now, as you speak for the client, the client can share with the younger self of a few years ago, who is currently not in major pain or experiencing substantial suffering, that he WILL go through some difficult times over the coming months or years, BUT that things will get BETTER. The rest of the procedure at step two is similar to that which you read about in the presentation on the preceding pages.

The other key factor of working at point two is the **confidence and certainty** of your voice as you describe both the difficulties and the time of improvement.

*"The times you experience over the
coming years will be incredibly difficult.
There will be times when you wonder if
it is all worthwhile to even be here. (If
this is what they have expressed to you.)
But then there comes a time when you
begin to feel better and better. Although
there are times when it is clear there are
dark spots on the line, most of the time
you clearly feel better and have a new
appreciation for your health and happiness."*

Having experienced this slightly younger you
before the onset of the chronic illness, it is now time to
go to the advanced future to re-confirm the stability of
the individual's well being in the long run. Up until this
point in our session with the chronically ill client, he
has now experienced the near future where he feels
"so much better." He has been reminded that the
problem was not always as bad as it is now. What this
means is that he has temporarily experienced a very
difficult time. It has been better and will get better.

Point Four- The Far Future

Now it is time to go to the farther future. Take
the person to their seventies or eighties in
chronological age, to some time when they can
reasonably be expected to still be in good physical
condition and to where it might be reasonable to
assume they would even be healthier than they are
now, but not so old that they are ready for a nursing
home. We didn't take the person who needed a

change in habits to this point. It wasn't necessary, but with people in pain or those who are chronically ill, it is necessary. The person needs assurance that they can feel better, be alive and experiencing good times when they are significantly older!

"Now as you leave this time when you are a little younger than your present self you float up above the earth, through the clouds, through the light part of the sky, through the dark part of the sky, ascending ever so high, feeling great and looking up you see the line, the track of time suspended in the universe. You ascend through the line at the time from which you just came and soar high above the line. You decide it is time to go too the future and see what life will be like as you get older.

"You fly past the 1990's and the 2000's and the 2010's and all the way into the future when you are much older than you are now today, in the year 2000 (or whatever year this is) and you come to a point when you decide to descend through your line at a point where it is almost completely clear with just a few dark spots in the line.

"It is here that you descend through your line through the dark part of the sky and the light part of the sky, through the clouds and landing on earth. You land in a place that looks very

comforting...you're outside and you
see a much older (man/woman) walking
outside, looking at the beautiful spacious
surroundings and you begin to approach
 the (man/woman). He/she turns with a smile."

"I know, you knew I was coming right?"

The older you laughs and grins.

"You're learning."

"How are you doing?"

"It's been a good life and there still is
plenty to go. I'm probably in better
shape now than I was fifteen years ago.
You have a great deal to look forward to.
Take a walk with me."

The older you puts his arm around you
and paces the walking. You actually tire
a bit keeping up with the older you. The
walk is long, it is beautiful and you realize
that you have a time ahead of you in your
life when you are surrounded by beauty
and much better health. The older you
gives you great support, comfort and
wisdom and you feel tremendous in the
presence of this very special person.

Finally the older you stops, looks
around at the spacious environment
and then looks at you with a smile.

*"Now, go, you have a good life to live,
so much to look forward to. So many
people to share your life with."*

*And with that the older you hugs you and
merges into you and you feel ...whole....
and you look around one last time,
impressed and thrilled. You slowly ascend
off the earth, and as you look down you
see the older you standing there then
beginning to walk as he looks up at you
with a grin and a wink....*

*You ascend through the clouds, and the
light part of the sky and the dark part of
the sky and looking up you see your track
suspended in the sky and you realize that
there is just one thing left to do. You decide
to see how far out you can go into the future.*

*You fly above your line through the future
past all the time markers and past the point
where the time markers just disappear but
the line continues and you wonder what is
different.*

*Then you realize that you have come
to the future! You have come to the future!
Not just the future, you have come to what
you thought always was. You have come to
what it is like in the future where there are no
time markers.*

As you look off it gets brighter and

brighter. There is almost a quality of crystal and a tinge of gold. There are shades of colors you have only dreamed of.. There are clouds and mists so that as you look into the future you see the line merge with the clouds and the mist into one unified something that you understand but is not so easy to describe.

You realize that it was as if you had always known that it would be like this. You were right.

What an extraordinary gift to be able to see.

Then you realize that the problem at hand back in the present all those years ago, while a challenge at the time is nothing that you can't handle when you realize that this is your future. Your destiny.

As you ponder that briefly you realize that time is short. You've had your opportunity and chance. You now must go back to the present. You race back and you go back as you ascend and fly faster.

There is one.

There is another and you go past the 2030's and the 2020's and the 2010's and the 2000's all the way back to the time that is today in the present and it is clearly marked on the line for you to know exactly where you arrived here from.

*You descend through the line,
through the dark part of the sky, through
the light part of the sky, through the clouds,
through the ceiling of the office you are in,
right back into yourself sitting in the chair
that you are in.*

*You feel refreshed and renewed
with a new sense of optimism and excitement
about ....everything! Everything!*

*Now, when I say one you will open
your eyes.*

*3. Become aware of the surroundings
around you.*

*2. Realize you are sitting in a chair in
my office.*

*and 1. When you feel ready,
open your eyes, wide aware and refreshed
with a feeling of newness and optimism.*

Time Track Therapy is a wonderful intervention for virtually everyone. Remember that it is not a therapy all by itself. It is the culmination of many weeks of work and an opportunity for you to give the client a believable future based upon his current situation and past experience.

131

7

Suggestion and Expectation: Powers that Heal

There is a line that always must be drawn before "offering up the placebo" and *promising* healing of a disease or symptom. On the one hand we know that a very significant number of people suffering from various ailments will get better with just suggestions, faith, or positive expectations on the part of the therapist and client. On the other hand, we know that most people with various ailments and symptoms will not improve just because they expect that they will. How do we maximize the mind/body response without creating delusions and lies with our clients? How indeed. It is a very difficult course to maneuver. Understanding the body/mind response will help us in communicating with our clients.

Harnessing the powers of both suggestion and expectation are very important before beginning hypnotherapy and hypnoanalysis. First, let's look at expectation.

The placebo response is the body/mind response. This response is the response of an individual to the absolute certainty that some expected effect will take place due to taking some action. The placebo response can also be noted as a response of expectancy.

> *The placebo response, this mind/body healing response is one of the best friends a therapist has.*

When someone truly believes with absolute certainty that an effect of some kind will occur because of some action taken, the body/mind often responds in amazing ways. Although we will be sharing a few key therapeutic ideas in this book I wanted to share with you a non-therapeutic response of expectancy so you can consider the broad range of possibilities involved in the placebo response.

In the early 1970's an interesting study was proposed and performed in New York. In brief, a well known psychologist approached a school to utilize two teachers and two groups of students. Group 1, teacher A was told was a group of superior students. All the students have very high IQ's he is told. Do not tell the students or any other teachers. We (the principal and psychologist) expect you to have a great year. Exit teacher A.

Teacher B enters and is shared the following news (again I paraphrase): We have some news for you. The students you have (Group 2) are students that are students who are not doing so well. They have very low IQ's. Do not tell the students or any other teachers. Do your best. Exit teacher B.

Eight months into the study the research project is stopped because the students in group 1 almost to a student have an "A" average. The students in Group 2 are averaging a "D" grade. The punchline? The students were randomly assigned to the groups. There was NO difference in the average IQ of the students! The study was immediately stopped and has never been conducted again.

Expectancy is a powerful element that is difficult to measure but it DOES play a crucial role in behavior as it does in healing. The two teachers believed that they had superior and inferior students, respectively and they said nothing verbally to the effect during their eight months of teaching their students. Their non-verbal communication clearly gave their expectant attitudes a neon sign of certainty to the students of what was going to happen. It is this very same neon sign that a good therapist wants to wear.

Before going on let us note that the students that were expected to do well did not all get A+'s and the students expected to do poorly did not get all failure grades. It is important to understand and forever realize that the expectation of an individual is powerful but it is not the sole determining factor in change, success, good grades or healing for all people!

A good hypnotherapist will never say, "Absolutely, your tinnitus will disappear." We will never say, "You will lose 100 pounds and it will stay gone forever." But based on a superior understanding of how the expectant response of the body/mind can work, we can congruently say, "I really like your chances."

What are those chances by the way? Let's look at the spectrum of possibilities.

A recent study reported in JAMA (Journal of the American Medical Association) showed that over 7 in 10 people with asthma given an inhaler filled with water had their asthma attacks stopped. The people with asthma didn't know that the inhaler had water of course. They were certain it was the same medicine they had been using for years. To treat asthma with hypnosis/hypnotherapy alone, however would be unethical and possibly deadly to the client as we never know which 70% will respond favorably! This is the great reminder that hypnotherapy is an adjunct and complementary therapy.

Certainty is the element in the mind/body response that we need to utilize for maximum results in all forms of healing.

Before we continue, does the above data indicate that cancer is real and asthma is not? No. Asthma is very real. So is cancer. A person who loses a limb will not regenerate a new limb regardless of their power of belief and expectancy. There is no programming for limb regeneration in our body. It doesn't happen. There are some things that the human body can do and there are some things it cannot do. Our goal as hypnotherapists is to maximize the healing process for each client that we have. Everything our client experiences is very real if to no one else than the client. Note that in the asthma study 3 out of 10 people didn't benefit from the water in their inhaler.

They needed the medicine to affect physiological change in the lungs. So, let's continue with what those chances are in another critical area, that of pain control.

Pain analgesics have been tested time and again against a placebo (an inert pill) and it has been found that about 35% of all people utilizing a placebo for the reduction of pain experience about a 50% reduction in pain. We cannot know exactly why this third of the population responds so well to a placebo pill. We also don't know if the same group would respond better or worse to other pain reducing treatments.

What we do know is that on average, about 1/3 of people need nothing more than a placebo (including the appropriate mind/body response) to gain remarkable relief from pain.

Ernest Rossi (*Psychobiology of Mind Body Healing*, 1993, Norton Publishing) has catalogued a number of maladies that seem to at least in part improve with the administration of "placebo treatment," implicating at least three major body systems in the mind/body healing response. In simple terms: All of the following disorders, diseases and symptoms respond at least in part to placebo treatment indicating some degree of mindbody healing capability.

Category One:

The Autonomic Nervous System is Implicated

Hypertension
Stress
Cardiac Pain
Blood Cell Counts
Headaches
Pupilary Dilation

Category Two: The Endocrine System is Implicated

Adrenal Gland Secretion
Diabetes
Ulcers
Gastric Secretion and Motility
Colitis
Oral Contraceptives
Menstrual Pain
Thyrotoxicosis

Category Three: The Immune System is Implicated

The Common Cold
Fever
Vaccines
Asthma
Multiple Sclerosis
Rheumatoid Arthritis
Warts

Dr. Frederick Evans, a clinical psychologist has discovered that about 55% of the effectiveness of numerous drugs is actually wrapped up in the placebo response itself. He says in his contribution to a recent book studying that matter (Placebo: Theory, Research and Mechanism, 1985, Guliford) that ..."in other words, the effectiveness of a placebo compared to standard doses of different analgesic drugs under double blind circumstances seems to be relatively constant. This is indeed rather remarkable and unique characteristic for any therapeutic agent. The effectiveness of the placebo is proportional to the apparent effectiveness of the active analgesic agent."

"It is worth noting that this 56% effectiveness ration is not limited to comparing placebo with analgesic drugs. It is found in double blind studies of non-pharmacological insomnia treatment techniques (58%) and psychotropic drugs for the treatment of depression such as tricyclics (59%) and lithium (62%). Thus it appears that placebo is about 55-60% as effective as active medications, irrespective of the potency of these active medications."

In the next section you will learn how the placebo effect directly influences healing and how it is very different from a modality of healing including hypnosis, hypnotherapy, or any other form of therapy. The mindbody connection is powerful. While hypnotic suggestion is not a placebo and healing doesn't take place with hypnosis because of the placebo response, this information does have powerful impact on our work as you will see in the next part of the book.

Expectation that Changes Outcomes

The placebo effect is the expectation of improvement actually changing outcome. The placebo effect is the therapeutic effect of hope aroused by partaking in a specific therapy, process or treatment.

Hope has been defined in psychological literature as the perceived possibility of achieving a goal. (Stotland 1969) The placebo effect is measurable by comparing bogus therapy with actual therapy, bogus drugs (inert pills) compared to real drugs.

The placebo response appears to be a self-reinforcing loop of improvement whereby the individual believes to experience some improvement, does experience some improvement, pays attention to it and therefore internally responds as if improvement is happening, once again expecting to find more improvement.

Someone who suffers from chronic fatigue who undergoes therapy that might reasonably be expected to help the person will have a built in placebo effect as the person watches an occasional improvement and then the body responds favorably to the improvement which could be both a combination of therapy and placebo effect.

The placebo effect, hopefully, is an important part of hypnotherapy, much like the response of various drugs by people is partially the placebo response. However, the placebo effect is not equal to hypnotherapy though it is sometimes the same as hypnosis. "Physicians have always known that their ability to inspire expectant trust in a patient partially determines the success of treatment." (Persuasion and Healing, Frank, 1993)

We see the doctor as a healer and therefore when he prescribes a medication or course of action we expect that course to work. As we improve the placebo response helps most people improve toward the goal whether a placebo is involved or not. Until the mid-twentieth century, most drugs prescribed by medical doctors were actually toxic and so the entire history of medicine until the last half century is really the study of the power of the placebo effect and response.

"Hypnotic procedures favorably affect those bodily systems that are most reactive to psychological inputs- notably, the cardiovascular, gastrointestinal, and respiratory systems and the skin (Crasilneck and Hall 1985).

The well-authenticated hypnotic cure of warts is particularly noteworthy because warts are caused by identifiable viruses. Apparently hypnotic suggestion can induce immunological changes in the skin that combat these viruses. More remarkable is the finding that this procedure can cause warts to disappear on one side of the body only (Sinclair-Gieben and Chalmers 1959)." (Persuasion and Healng, Frank, 1993)

Hypnosis is just as effective in removing warts as surgical procedures whether the person has experienced failure in previous treatments or not. Interestingly, you can paint inert dye on warts and tell people that the ingredients in the dye will make the warts go away and that works just as well as hypnosis and surgery also! In these three procedures is an apparently powerful placebo response at work.

The Nocebo Response

The placebo effect can also be seen in it's reciprocal "nocebo" responses. One kind of nocebo is seen in the patient (who dislikes   doctors and traditional helping professionals) who is prescribed medicine and actually has many side effects to the "medicine" when in fact the person is experiencing side effects to the traditional helper. Many people simply don't like medicine and do not trust the traditional doctor. There responses are in line with their expectations in many instances. Researchers have found that typical "side effects" to doctors and traditional professionals include nausea, diarrhea, and skin eruptions (Wolf and Pinsky 1954)

The   Nocebo   is   Not   to   be   Taken   Lightly!

In 1992, Dr. Clifford Meador of the Department of Medicine at Vanderbilt Medical School read   an article called Voodoo Death describing how it is possible for people to die a hex or voodoo like death. I will   explain   Meadord's   significance   to   this   in   a moment. The article was by a physiologist Walter Cannon. There are three components in such a hexing death.

1) The victim and all family and friends must believe that the ability and power of the hexer is genuine and will indeed cause death.
2) All previously known victims of the hexing must have died, unless the hex was removed.
3) Every person known to the victim, including family and friends, must behave toward him as if he will die. This involves leaving him alone and isolated, even by his closest relatives.
Cannon concluded that death will occur in a few days if these elements are in place.

Meador published this article and the case of an older white man who was dying from what he believed to be esophageal cancer. Meador was an internist and consulted on the case. The entire story is detailed in Larry Dossey's (MD) book, *Be Careful What You Pray For.* What I want to share with you was through this man's tragic first bout with his life ending, he asked Meador if he could just live until Christmas. It was summer and his condition was grim. The entire staff, friends and family did everything they could to help the man and he amazingly improved. Dramatically so. He was healthy and you wouldn't know he had cancer. In January he was re-admitted to the hospital and died within 24 hours. The cancer turned out to be one and only one nodule. It had not spread as had been suspected. A previous liver scan showing cancer was a false positive. The only thing that could be determined was that "...he died thinking he was dying of cancer, a belief shared by his wife, family, his surgeons and me, his internist."

This kind of nocebo response is very powerful indeed. Although you cannot tell someone with metastatic cancer that they can safely go on with their life and ignore treatment, never offer a negative review for a person's prognosis as a hypnotherapist. Why? Consider the following sampling of studies and papers.

Research in patients being treated for stomach cancer showed that 1/3 of patients who received placebos developed nausea, 1/5 developed vomiting and 1/3 lost hair. Certainly the cancer played a confounding role in nausea and vomiting but in hair loss? (Fielding 1983)

Cases have been reported where patients become addicted to placebos. One extreme in this research showed a patient who took 10,000 placebos in one year. (Rhein 1980)

In another study, two thirds of patients receiving a placebo developed evidence of streptomycin toxicity-streptomycin being the antibiotic they believed they were taking- including high and low frequency hearing loss, a known side effect of using aminoglycosides. (Wolf and Pinsky)

Finally, in the Framingham Heart Study, in which thousands of residents of Framingham, Massachusetts have been followed over decades, women aged 45-60 who believed they were likely to suffer a heart attack were 3.7 times more likely to die from coronary conditions than women who didn't consider themselves particularly coronary prone. (Voelker 1996)

Personality and The Placebo Response

What personality traits of people seem to be threaded to responding well to the placebo effect? Research shows that it is often individuals displaying anxiety, people who can be dependent on others for help, people who are emotionally reactive, people who are conventional, and people who can accept others in their lives. Some studies have shown that people who tend to be less responsive tend to be isolated and mistrustful. (Lasagna 1954)

Utilize the Mind/Body Response in Hypnotherapy

The placebo response is like a self fulfilling loop. The placebo response MUST be utilized effectively to improve the probability of improvement on the part of the client, regardless of the symptom.

1. A person expects a change of some kind or of some magnitude.
2. A person experiences some change of some kind or magnitude at some time.
3. A person believes they are improving thereby creating optimism.
4. The body responds biochemically to the optimism..
5. A sense of more improvement is experienced.
6. More improvement eventually is evidenced.
7. A person feels better.

There is a reasonable question that arises. How do you maximize the placebo response without blatantly lying to an individual? In other words if someone has stage IV cancer and are virtually certain to die in a very short period of time, how do we maximize the placebo response without building up false hope?

It is unethical to hold out hope for a person's life who is about die. It is unethical to tell a person that an arm can be re-grown where it has been cut off because arms do not regenerate. A person who was born without eyes will not see because of hypnotherapy. We must be ethical to be credible for the placebo effect to work.

You can act positive about someone's outlook or outcome but if THEY do not believe that you are credible and competent your "positive attitude" is meaningless. Therefore, we are looking for the point of "optimization."

> **Optimization is the point at which your credibility and skills meet the clients expectation and belief in the potential for improvement.**

If you make claims that are too outlandish, your credibility is reduced and your belief or expectation of the client healing or improvement is then virtually irrelevant in the clients improvement. On the other hand if you are credible and skilled and your client hears no positive potential they might still improve but the placebo impact is lost and that reduces their chances of improvement!

So, again, how do we maximize the placebo response for optimization in healing?

In most but not all cases our job as a hypnotherapist is to create a believable future where problems arise but where healing could be experienced if certain positive signs are experienced along the way.

Here is a sample of what I often share with my clients both in trance and out of trance. This is not a script that should be replicated for each client you see but is a guideline or sketch of how you want to frame reasonable and realistic futures that your client will likely experience so you can optimize the use of the placebo response.

"Your tinnitus is very loud and has been for some time. The good news is that over time most people's tinnitus can improve.

*"You will begin to notice periods of time
where you are briefly less aware of the
noise or maybe it will go un-noticed for
a period of minutes or even an hour
sometime soon.*

*"When you find yourself
saying, 'Is it still there?' , this will be a
defining moment. It is then that you know
that you are experiencing brief moments
of quieter experience and then you will know
that you can begin to experience, with more
regularity moments that are like those brief
interludes. Anything the brain experiences,
it can remember and virtually duplicate.*

*"If you experienced a few moments of
silence you can then later experience two
sets of moments back to back just like the
first set of moments." This doesn't mean
your tinnitus will vanish into thin air, because
it is in fact, at least partially a memory of a
sound you have heard.*

*"Always remember that bad days can follow
good days but that when you have a good
day you must highlight that day on your
calendar to remind you of what you just
experienced.*

*"It is possible to have a good day and
that means that it is possible to have two
good days back to back eventually.
"Then when you have had two days back
to back you can know that it is possible*

to have more days back to back.

*"Always remember that the brain, the
mind can remember wellness and quiet
as well as it can those times which
are not so good. The good days
eventually become our new baseline
from which we measure our progress
in the future."*

This is not only effective utilization of the potential placebo (the mind/body) response but it is excellent trance work as well. The unconscious mind can believe each idea because it is built on a simple presupposition, one on top of the other. The critical faculty of the mind is bypassed because it is believable and thereby you optimize the placebo response!

Understand that if the person does improve eventually it does NOT mean that it was because of the placebo response, but the placebo response MAY have helped the person improve, BECAUSE of your credibility and skill of framing suggestions. In addition, please always remember that you just read a two page sample guideline on how to utilize the placebo effect. One ten minute reading of a "script" will not change anyone's life. This line of thinking is a common theme that underlies each and every session of your work with your clients.

In drug trials, those who test the efficacy of a drug do so in comparison to the response to a placebo. These kind of trials typically take 4-16 weeks of using a drug or placebo before results are experienced. Allow yourself the same opportunity to maximize your work!

It is very common for a hypnotherapist who is new to the field to do a rapid change technique (of which we will discuss in depth later), have a client experience a remarkable metamorphosis in the first session, only to have the client return to his symptoms within hours, days or weeks, and the hypnotherapist never knew what happened. Why? Because the client believed that hypnosis doesn't work. He was better for awhile, but then "it came back."

The error is the belief on the part of the hypnotherapist that because the client leaves seemingly healthy that he remains healthy once back in the real world. This is normally not the case with rapid change technologies. Certain rapid change technologies like the procrastination cure I will discuss later, normally do take hold and stabilize within the person. Miracles also definitely occur as the title of my audio program "The Miracles of Hypnosis" implies but they wouldn't be called miracles if they happened with every client in every session. Usually it takes a great deal of work for miracles to happen!

Miracles tend to happen with greater regularity when the client has an almost spiritual faith and belief in the hypnotherapist's ability to create the desired outcome.

This only happens when the client perceives the hypnotherapist as credible, completely worthy of his trust and holds the belief that the therapist wants the healing or change to happen almost as much as the client. *The therapeutic alliance is the foundation for healing, for miracles and for long term change.*

The Elements of a Successful Therapeutic Alliance

1. The hypnotherapist cares deeply for the experience and welfare of her client.

2. The hypnotherapist learns everything possible about what the client is experiencing, both from the client and from other sources, including books, articles, interviews with others and the hypnotherapist's mentors.

3. The hypnotherapist is knowledgeable about all forms of treatment and therapy the client may consider for their problem, symptom, challenge or disease.

4. The hypnotherapist is thorough in both the pre-screening and the case analysis.

5. The client knows that the therapist cares and wants the very best for him.

6. The client wants to improve. They are there with you because they want to get better, not because someone sent them.

7. The client is willing to do what it takes to get well.

If the hypnotherapist can communicate with the client about his problem, then the two individuals will be using the same map and be on the same page. In other words, if the client is suffering from bulimia, the hypnotherapist must understand the experience of bulimia through interviews with others, their mentors, and read books and articles about bulimia to understand what the client is experiencing. If the client needs to educate the hypnotherapist because of the hypnotherapist's inexperience and ignorance the client will not likely get well.

The educated hypnotherapist not only understands hypnoanalytic techniques and strategies but they understand the problems, conditions and symptoms that the individual experiences. This demands the hypnotherapist to have a good working knowledge of pertinent medical and psychological literature. The hypnotherapist who is willing to learn about what his client really experiences will be destined to work with highly motivated clients for the rest of their career. The hypnotherapist who can truly align himself with the client in understanding the difficulties the client is facing will always be in demand from the public because of the empathy, breadth and depth of knowledge the hypnotherapist has.

The mind/body response is directly related to the therapeutic alliance because the respect, trust, certainty and expectation the client has in the hypnotherapist is in large part what will determine the success of the therapy. After this respect and trust has been endowed upon the hypnotherapist, then creating a believable future is important to the healing process.

The suggestions and future vision of the therapist in the scenario below are best used at the end of a session of hypnoanalysis. These themes were also utilized in the preceding example of a client suffering from tinnitus. Now we use the same techniques to optimize the mind/body response.

"...now we have learned a great deal today about how the experiences you had directly caused you to feel the pain you have long after the physical cause for the pain disappeared.

9 out of 10 people who experience back pain after the organic cause is gone have the experience because the stresses and emotions of their life have piled up and have been signaling us to take care of ourselves.

We're going to start doing that now.

It's time to start being as concerned about yourself as you have been all the other people in your life.

Now as each day goes forward you will find that you will experience moments of comfort and calm. Some moments will go quite awhile and others will be brief but you will have moments where the pain is almost completely gone.

Warning:
In the above example, the signal of pain is not something that can be diagnosed by the hypnotherapist. The diagnosis must be given by a medical doctor, probably with an x-ray and we cannot assume any pain is an emotional signal. We are not able to make that assumption! Therefore, we must rule out any organic cause of pain before we begin our work. At this point, we can utilize hypnoanalysis to find the time and emotional roots of the onset.

Hypnotherapy Handbook

8

Our Last Scheduled Session:
How People Get Better and Worse

Insight, in hypnoanalysis, is the recognition of how certain events or patterns created an illness, symptom or problem in the first place. Insight is very important in the healing process. Quite often a client will have an "AHA!" experience early in therapy. This often comes about when the person has regressed to the causal event after seeing several similar and later events first.

One cycle of chronic illness is this. The experience of pain or some other somatic brings about various "negative emotions" (like frustration and anger) which creates certain behaviors within the client that bring about certain responses from other people which often reinforce or diminish the somatics.

Somatics===> "negative emotions" ===>
Behaviors===>Others==>Responses===>Somatics

A woman hurts her back picking up her baby. (Pain, stretched muscle) The pain is a somatic symptom. It is very "real." The woman gets assistance from her husband for a few days and she is given a much deserved break. She begins to feel better and the husband eventually returns to his routine of work and entertainment. She begins to feel neglected, doing all the work again herself. At the same time she may accidentally strain a muscle or experience another "minor mishap." (This is not always the case, but is often enough to note it here.)

The part of her mind that felt deserving of the "break", that felt deserving of the husband's love, attention and assistance signals the woman through the same pain which brought such relief previously. Her pain again brings assistance from her husband and this time the pain is not the organically caused stretched muscle but a very vivid memory. Part of her brain is literally re-living the past experience and is doing so intentionally to bring her the attention and relief she deserves. The feelings of neglect or loneliness trigger the protective mechanism that so effectively helped the woman before. The husband again shows attention and eventually the symptom begins to reduce.

This pattern continues for months or years and doesn't cease because the couple never talks about the feelings they experience. In an ideal world, the woman would feel free to tell the husband about her feelings of neglect and loneliness but she doesn't in this world. Had the couple communicated their feelings and discussed how to handle duties such as taking care of the baby or spending time with each other the psychosomatic symptoms would in all likelihood have faded long ago.

Recognizing this pattern is the beginning of wellness for this woman. Her likelihood of getting better is very high indeed and we could reasonably expect significant symptom reduction with hypnoanalysis!

We probably have a sort of "story synthesizer" in the cerebral cortex (in the brain!) that tends to create a general context for our life. This concept may also have some significant right brain inter-relationship as the right brain tends to create a context for the details of life. This story synthesizer was originally postulated by Susan Vaughan in her excellent book, *The Talking Cure*, and is one good model for looking at our life experiences and healing. Vaughan rightly notes that our dreams tend to have common threads and themes that recur. This is because of the neurological wiring that currently is the status quo in the brain. The themes and threads are similar because the wiring is the same.

Neurons (brain cells) are linked together in a certain fashion. Each day those connections and brain cell links stay the same until *something* happens to change the patterns. Hypnotherapy then strengthens, weakens, or eventually breaks the patterns. It just takes time! When I speak of "re-wiring," or "installing" or "un-hooking experiences," this is what I am talking about. Over a period of days, weeks, and sometimes months, I have seen people's minds change the way they think about themselves and their experience. These changes often precede major reduction in the volume of tinnitus, the elimination of purging for the bulimic and emotional stability in most clients.

In regression therapy we go back in time to the memories that originally started experiences we now don't want anymore. By going back we see how the brain built the experiences we now have and we can figure out how to re-wire the brain by first recognizing the old patterns and then re-configuring them into something more productive.

When a client suffers from tinnitus, I will often use a metaphor in and out of trance to illustrate how the brain works. This metaphor assumes that client knows that here in the Twin Cities, the old major north-south highway in town is 35W. It's very congested and was unbearable until a few years ago when 35E was constructed to ease congestion and create another artery going north to south in the Twin Cities.

"Tinnitus is often much different from what we used to think it was. We used to think that all tinnitus was generated from the cochlea in the ear. We used to think that the inner ear sent all these noises into the ear. Then we found out we were not as smart as we thought we were. When the nerve was cut between the brain and the ear the brain still heard the noises and sometimes the noises got louder!

"It became obvious that there are highways in the brain like 35W. These highways are laid down and have lots of potholes...they are beat up, congested and old. There are also plenty of possible other highways that we haven't even laid down yet. We can lay down new highways anytime we want. We simply have to make something like highway 35E. 35E isn't congested, doesn't have potholes and traffic moves smoothly because not as many people use it.

"35E is the highway without tinnitus and 35W is the highway with tinnitus. We won't make your tinnitus disappear because your brain is like a highway system. The highways that have the tinnitus on it will always be there but they don't have to be driven all that often do they?

"So let's start forging new highways today by creating new memories instead of listening to the until now ever present memory of tinnitus. We don't expect the tinnitus to disappear and we realize that we are used to driving on 35W because we've been doing it for 30 years. But when we think about it we can start making new highways and eventually choose to drive all the time on highway 35E when it is completed and can handle the traffic!"

The metaphor gives the client reasonable, credible, tangible, real hope for the future and builds optimism and the possibility that they will experience quieter and better moments than they have been. The mind/body response has a real opportunity to engage and begin to heal the body, if possible.

Self Hypnosis
and
Guided Imagery for Healing

Self hypnosis is the experience of being able to dissociate yourself from one aspect or life experience into another, real or imagined life experience. Self hypnosis can take the form of auto-suggestion which is trance that is completely generated from within the client or it can be experienced by the use of a third party tool such as an audiocassette or a video cassette. At the end of several weeks of therapy and sometimes within the framework of therapy itself, teaching your client to use self hypnosis or giving your client cassettes that can help them while you are not there can be very constructive to her healing process. I like audiocassettes instead of having the client generate their own self hypnosis because tapes completely reliable. The cassette is designed by the therapist for the client and says all that needs to be said and in the same positive and affirming fashion each time the cassette is listened to. Auto-hypnosis (the ability of an individual to use self hypnosis without the aid of tapes) is a powerful tool as well but it takes discipline to utilize on a regular basis.

In this section, you will be given a number of templates for guided imagery (scripts that you can adapt to your client's specific needs) that you can model so that you can create audiocassette tapes for your clients. These templates and scripts were all designed by Holly Sumner, a respected and internationally known hypnotherapist. When you make an audiocassette for your client, personalize the cassette for your client. Simply reading the template given here will do only a limited amount of good for your client. If you can personalize the cassette to the client however, the added dimension of self hypnosis with audio cassettes can play a valuable role in the healing process.

Stress Reduction
Copyright 1999 Holly Sumner

*Find a comfortable spot to sit or lie down in and close
your eyes. Take a breath in, hold it for a moment, and
then just exhale fully. Throughout this exercise merely
breathe in and out regularly.*

*Now, simply imagine and remember what the sky looks
like on a nice sunny day. A nice sunny day when there
are puffy white clouds scattered here and there. The
kind of clouds that you used to love as a child because
you could imagine they were all kinds of things. Castles
and kittens and lions and magical things.*

*Remember how it felt to be laying there imagining all
the
wonderful things that you could see in those clouds.
How carefree you felt on days like that. How relaxed
and free. Perhaps you even feel like smiling. That's
right... just lying there using your imagination. There is
nowhere else you have to be... nothing else you have to
be doing but imagining that you are looking at puffy
white clouds in a blue, blue sky.*

*Perhaps you can even feel the sun on your face. Maybe
you can feel a light, gentle breeze as it blows softly over
your body. The temperature is just right... and you are
so very comfortable. Just lying here and watching the
puffy white clouds just float on by.*

*Allow yourself to watch each cloud... what do you see?
What does it look like? And with each cloud that you
watch... you recall those days when you were a child and
did this... just lying there watching the clouds float*

161

by. There is no where else you have to be... nowhere else you have to go... nothing to do but enjoy watching the clouds pass by.

Worry Reduction

Copyright 1999 by Holly Sumner

Worries...we all have them. They are part of life. It would be unrealistic to think we could simply "send them away", however, we so often give those things that worry us more power than they need. More power than they deserve. They can loom larger than life, magnified way out of proportion.

The script below can help defuse the amount of power given to worries:

Close your eyes, take a deep breath, and see, sense, and feel yourself standing in a large field. Perhaps it's a place you have been before. Perhaps not. It is somewhere you would like to visit.

The sky is a brilliant blue and there are a few puffy white clouds scattered here and there. A gentle breeze blows across your face and brings the scent of the flowers that grow in this field. It's a warm and pleasant day. Just the right temperature. Take a deep breath and notice the fragrance of your favorite flowers that gently waft their scent on the breeze.

And as you stand in this beautiful, pleasant field, know that it's a wonderful day. You have plenty of time to spend here... there's nowhere else you need to be. There is nothing else you need to be doing except enjoying being here... enjoying the sunshine... the breeze... the scent of the flowers... even the sounds of birds singing in the background. It's a perfect day and you are here in this field enjoying it.

Maybe you even feel like dancing... like spreading your arms wide and dancing. Dancing for the sheer joy of being in a beautiful place... with plenty of time to enjoy it... with nothing to disturb or hinder your joy and excitement.

And then perhaps a worry crosses your mind? And then perhaps even another one? Yet, as this happens you realize that you do not need to let worries hinder your joy... or get in your way... or keep you from enjoying this day... They do not need to keep you from enjoying life. You are in a place where you can simply release worries... and let them go.

Imagine gathering up all of your worries. That's right, simply being able to collect all those things that seem so bothersome... so troubling. Imagine you could hold any worry that you have right in your hands... hold them right in front of you. No matter how big any worry feels when it's in your mind... when you hold it in front of you... you notice how small it really is. It's easy to simply hold it in your hands.

Take a moment and collect any worries that come to your mind. It's as though you can pick them up and place them right in front of you. See, feel and sense yourself picking up any worries that have drifted into your mind and place them in front of you. That's right...

163

line them right up in front of you... one by one. See how small they look!

And now, as you look at the small little worries placed in front of you... you notice that there is a basket containing bright balloons and ribbons right next to them. There is also a helium machine. What fun it would be to place each and every worry that is lined up into a balloon!

Yes, you can do exactly that! See yourself taking a worry... placing it inside one of the balloons and filling it with helium and tying it with a ribbon. Notice how light your worry feels as it bobs gently in the breeze while you hold the ribbon. You can let go of the ribbon and watch as the balloon drifts off into the sky, taking your worry with it. Watch as it gently floats away...

You can take another worry, place it in a balloon, fill it with helium and tie it up with a ribbon. It too, feels light and airy and it's so easy to let go of it and watch it gently float off into the sky. How bright and beautiful the balloons look against the blue sky. How wonderful it feels to let your worries drift off...

You can take all the worries that you have lined up in front of you and place them each into their own balloon filled with helium. Just tie off each balloon with the ribbon and allow it to float off into the sky.

How pretty all those balloons look dotting the sky! Feel yourself smile as you realize just how easy it is to allow all your worries to drift off...

164

When we dwell on things, we often make things far worse than they really are. Sometimes we add drama and magnify our emotions. Circumstances as they really are, and how we perceive them rarely match. In truth, we often make fantasy out of reality.

Unfortunately, we often make those fantasies very negative. We see ourselves as foolish, clumsy, or complete failures. Instead of giving ourselves material for success and positive reinforcement, we pick on our faults.

Ever go to an adventure movie? In such movies there are heroes. The brave adventurer that saves the planet. Why are these kinds of movies so popular? Maybe it's because so many of us secretly wish WE were just like the hero...maybe even that we were the hero!

Hollywood has been smart enough to cash in on human nature. Why not use that nature for your own success?

Ego Strengthening
The Princess/Knight
Copyright 1999 Holly Sumner

Perhaps you have been feeling a little down lately? Feeling like you cannot do anything right? Other people always seem to do things right, don't they? Why can't you? Maybe you feel like a nobody. Like you are no one special?

Maybe it feels or has felt that no matter what you do you can't succeed? Perhaps you have felt like a failure.

And perhaps you are thinking these very same thoughts as you are sitting here right now? Maybe you do this often? Just sitting and thinking? And as you do you find that your thoughts drift off and that you are daydreaming. As you are daydreaming... just sitting there and thinking. And as you sit there and think... and just allow your thoughts to unfold... it's as though you are in a scene. Perhaps you can see yourself in the scene... or maybe it's as though you ARE in the scene...

Only this time, instead of dwelling on those same thoughts... your mind takes you upon a journey. That's right a journey... and you can see yourself as you go upon this journey. Soon you find yourself walking up a winding path. And as you continue along you find that mists are rising... it's as though everything around you has become very foggy.

Yet, you are not afraid at all. You have no fear, for you can see some light up ahead. You know the fog is only for just a short distance and that there is comforting light up ahead.

Soon, you see yourself stepping out of the mists and into a place absolutely bursting with sunshine. It is like no other place you have ever been before or have ever seen. True, you can recognize the plants, trees and flowers as kinds that you have seen before... but the land looks different.

And as you look around... you notice that off in the distance is a large building. You blink your eyes for that building is a ... castle! You know that you are not looking at a castle many hundreds of years later... but that you are looking at a castle as it WAS several hundreds of years ago. It's as though you are there during it's time.

Somehow you have been somehow mysteriously transported to another place and time. A magical time of Knights and Princesses. Oh what it must feel like to be a noble Knight or a beautiful, brave Princess? How wonderful that would be. After all, Knights and Princesses aren't nobodies! Knights and Princesses are not failures.

Wouldn't it be wonderful if you could meet such a person? Maybe a little of their ability for success and doing things right could rub off on you? Ah... but maybe
that is wishful thinking...

Soon you notice that people are coming out of the castle grounds toward you. They all look afraid. Many of them are running and looking confused. You wonder what is going on? What could be happening?

One of the people from the castle runs up to you and asks for help. You ask what is wrong. They tell you that there is a horrible dragon that has been terrorizing them. They are scared and there has been no one to protect them. They plead with you to help them.

But what can you do? After all, if you are a nobody... why would it be any different here? Yet... as you watch everyone running for their lives... you wonder what if you COULD do something?

Maybe you are still not sure that you can help these people, but you decide to walk closer to the castle to see what is actually happening. It is a long walk... and you are a bit apprehensive. But you continue to walk toward the castle.

And you keep walking and walking...coming closer to the castle. After a bit, you decide that you need a short rest. Just a few moments would be nice. It's been such a long walk... and after all, you aren't sure what you are walking into!

You come to a large, leafy tree and decide that this would be a wonderful place to stop for a moment. The tree with all of it's bright, green leaves creates a nice, shady spot. The perfect place in which to rest.

And as you walk up to the tree, you notice a noble white horse simply standing under the tree. What an incredibly beautiful steed. He is tall and majestic and looks just like the type of horse that a Knight or a Princess would have. He has a colorful blanket under his saddle, and there are ribbons flowing from his bridle. There is a long silver sword attached to the saddle in a leather holder. Exactly the type of horse you would see in a medieval storybook.

If you had a horse like that you think to yourself that maybe you could slay dragons! As you think that... it's almost like the horse can hear your thoughts and agrees... for he proudly shakes his head just as though he is saying, YES!

Perhaps you still feel a bit apprehensive, but you decide to go ahead and you climb up on the horse. Suddenly, you feel like you have never felt before. Here you are on a majestic horse... his mane and tail are flying as you gallop towards the castle. You are off to slay dragons!

You gallop toward the castle brandishing the sword. People are still running away from the castle but now you see the hope in their eyes. Someone... a proud Knight or a brave Princess has come to defeat the dragon!

You ride into the castle and then you see the dragon. He's like every dragon you've read about in fairytales. He's huge! And, yes, he is snorting fire. His eyes are gleaming red... and he's noticed you!

Your horse rears up... but not in fear... in challenge. This is the moment. You are facing a horrible dragon. Lives may depend upon you. Are you up to it? You've failed so many times before. Yet, even as you think this... you see yourself holding the sword and leaning forward in the saddle and yelling, "charge!"

You and the horse race toward the dragon. He lunges at you and you and the horse move out of the way. It's just like a movie where you and the horse are one. You and the horse instinctively know which way to move. The dragon continues to lunge at you... but he never manages to catch you.

You reach out with the sword and attack the dragon. You spear him with your sword... and he simply disappears! The dragon is gone! You are amazed until you realize that all anyone had to do in order to slay the dragon was try. No one had tried until you!

And now you can see all the people who live in the castle come streaming into the courtyard cheering! The dragon is gone... the dragon is defeated!
YOU have defeated dragons! You have done the impossible. And you realize that there have been many things you could have done... but you never even tried. Maybe it's because you thought you would fail? But look what happened when you DID try... you defeated a dragon! Imagine what life would be like if you weren't afraid to fail. If you had confidence in yourself. If you believed in yourself!

A Place of Healing
Copyright 1999 Holly Sumner

Imagine yourself standing at the foot of the most beautiful mountain you have ever seen. Notice that it rises... oh so majestically... flowing up from the green grassy ground at your feet... reaching toward the sky so far up that it seems that it touches the very heavens themselves. And as you look upward at the top of this majestic mountain, you notice that there are clouds that swirl gently around it's peak. These clouds are made of soothing, healing colors of violet, blue, gold, green and pink.

Suddenly you know that this is a special mountain, one that you have never seen the likes of before. And now, perhaps you even vaguely remember legends of such a "healing mountain". These legends are known to you from somewhere in the back of your mind... just like whispers that float upon the breeze... something that you know is there... but can't quite touch. But you know it's real.

Perhaps these whispers on the breeze sound like soft, sweet music... such as you have never heard before? A sweet and gentle melody that calls to you and stirs a wondrous chord within you... a chord of hope, peace and harmony. A joyous song. A song of healing.

There is also a subtle fragrance in the air... one of freshness... on of renewal... Smell just how sweet and pure it is... A smell so soft and gentle that you could almost wrap it around yourself like a blanket to soothe you... to heal you.

And now you have come to realize that maybe not everyone can see this mountain? Maybe it's only there for those who need some healing in their life? Someone like you. Yes, someone just like you.

And as you stand there at the foot of this mountain you notice that there is a path winding it's way up toward the top. Wouldn't it be lovely to walk this path and reach the summit? To actually feel those cool clouds of healing colors swirl around you? You know that if you could just reach those clouds of colors, you could walk right through those mists and feel those healing colors flow right through your body... to touch you... helping to heal you. To renew you. Can't you feel the wonder of this mountain path?

But, perhaps from where you stand it looks too far... too hard to climb? Yet, as with any path you take in life no matter how far, how hard... it can be reached. Yes, it can be reached... simply by taking one step at a time.

Just by placing one foot in front of another. That's right. One step... and then another... and then another ... until you have accumulated many steps. It's simply a matter of taking it one step at a time... one day at a time. It all adds up. It doesn't matter how large or how small those steps are... they all add up. Your steps will be just perfect... just the perfect stride for you.

This path is just like that. You need only take one small step at a time. There is no need to rush... you have plenty of time. Each step that you take will bring you closer to those healing clouds of color. Each step will be the perfect size... covering just the right amount of ground and at just the perfect pace for you. You will get exactly where you need to go at just the right time.

And now, picture yourself walking right up to the beginning of that path... placing one foot in front of the other. That's right. Easily and effortlessly... one foot in front of the other. You are on the path to the healing colors. You just need to take one step at a time and move along this path. And as you do so, you may notice things as you stroll easily and effortlessly along the path. Perhaps there are flowers scattered here and there along the way. Take a moment to enjoy each and every flower... for you have plenty of time... nothing else you need to be doing... nothing else to do but enjoying the stroll up the mountain path towards the clouds of color. There is plenty of time to enjoy this stroll.

You may meet others on your way along this path... perhaps a guide who will go with you if you so choose. You need not be alone on this journey... this path. You can choose to have a healing guide to walk with you. Your healing guide knows the way... knows exactly which is the best path to take. Your healing guide can help you over any rough spots... perhaps a spot that is just a bit hilly or uneven. Your guide will take your hand and walk with you to show you the best and easiest way to go.

That's right... just picture yourself walking with your healing guide. Maybe you can see their face... maybe you can't. Either way... it's just perfect. Your guide is there to keep you safe and free from any harm. To show you the way and assist you whenever you need help. Feel how safe and confident you are walking with your healing guide.

Continue walking along the path up the mountain with your guide, enjoying the scenery. You can still see those glorious clouds of healing colors swirling around the top of the mountain. And as you walk along the path with your guide, you know that you will be able to reach the top. It may take some time... but that is just fine. You have plenty of time to stroll up the path at your own pace. Each step you take will bring you closer to those clouds of healing colors.

At times the path may seem a bit hard... a bit steep... but for every step of the way your guide is with you. It's as though you can watch yourself and your guide as you go along...

As you are walking you suddenly come to a spot where the path comes to a rocky incline. To continue any further you would have to climb upwards. Perhaps you are a little nervous – it doesn't look all that easy. You know the path continues onward after this point... but you can't quite see the path – it's above your head. Perhaps you feel a little frustrated?

Your guide looks at you and gently tells you to notice things about this incline. See how there are rocks that are perfect hand-holds and foot-holds? It may look difficult... but if you take it step-by-step... one little part at a time... it really is not that difficult at all. It just takes a bit of patience.

See yourself reach up and find a perfect hand-hold and feel when you boost yourself up. Your guide is standing by ready to assist you in any way you need. Just allow yourself to place your feet in just the perfect spot to help you move upwards... in just the right spot to grab the next hand-hold. And as you do so... you can feel yourself climb slowly upwards with your guide right alongside of you... helping you... protecting you.

And now – you've done it! You've managed to climb up the incline and can now continue along the path. As you look upwards you can still see the healing clouds of color but you notice that you are getting nearer and nearer to them. Each step you take – each little bit you climb is helping you get closer and closer to the top.

Feel yourself continuing on the path. For each obstacle you meet... you and your guide find a safe way around it. It may take a bit of time... but that is just fine. You have plenty of time. Notice how proud you feel – you are making a difficult journey. You are doing it! It's simply taking one step at a time.

You and your guide continue along the path. Your guide will help you over any rough spots as you go along. See *yourself walking up the mountain path towards the clouds of healing colors.*

Now you are almost at the top of the mountain. You can almost touch those swirling clouds of healing color. But... just as you are almost there – you notice that there is a crevice in the path. It's just wide enough so that you can't jump over it. You are so close to those clouds... but the crevice is just too wide...

As you stand there wondering how you are going to get to the other side of the crevice your guide turns and points to the side of the path. At first you cannot see what the guide is pointing at. All you see are a bunch of flowers and trees. Then you notice that there is a fallen log! What if you were to push the log across the crevice?

You walk over to the log... but it is very heavy. It's good that it is thick and sturdy but that makes it too hard for you to lift. Then you remember... you are not alone. Your guide is with you. What if the two of you tried to lift the log? You know it will work!

See yourself and your guide as you slowly move the log into place and push it so that it spans the crevice. See how it fits over the entire crevice just like a bridge. All you will have to do is walk over that log and you will get to the other side.

But perhaps you are a bit nervous? After all, even though the log is thick and sturdy... it's not all that wide... You know you have traveled a great distance and have overcome many obstacles to get this far. You know you can walk over this log to get to the other side

175

of the crevice if you put your mind to it. If you believe you can.

See yourself as you slowly walk... step-by-step over the log and see yourself as you safely step down onto the other side. Feel how proud you are! You've done it. You were able to find a way around a very difficult obstacle and now you are here at the top of the mountain!

See yourself walk into those beautiful healing clouds of color. They float gently over you just like a light breeze. Feel as those colors flow into your body... into every cell and tissue and organ within your body... infusing it with those healing colors. Feel the strength and vitality of those colors as they flow throughout your body.

Take time to savor this feeling... you have plenty of time to experience this feeling...

Grounding For Anxiety Sufferers: Pre-Induction

Copyright 1999 Holly Sumner

One effect of anxiety can be feeling disconnected or out-of-kilter with things and the world around you. Here is a good "grounding" pre-induction for any anxiety-reducing script:

Find a comfortable chair preferably with arms that you may rest your arms on. It also is best if your feet can comfortably touch the floor. Take your shoes off and sit in the chair keeping your back fairly straight and with both feet touching the floor.

Close your eyes and take a deep breath, hold it for a moment and then release it. During this exercise continue to breathe in and out gently. As you sit in the chair, notice how it feels to be sitting in the chair. Allow yourself to find the most comfortable position for you. Now, take your time notice one-by-one all the different areas of your body. Some you will be able to feel touching the chair.

Notice how the top of your head feels... maybe you can feel your scalp and how your hair touches the skin of your head. Just allow yourself to think of your head... there is nothing else that needs your attention... just how your head feels. And as you notice how your head feels... allow it to feel oh... so... calm and relaxed. You might even imagine warm, soothing, gentle sunlight softly flowing over your head. It's just the right temperature... warm and soothing. Continue to breathe in and out as you notice how relaxed your head feels. Even the thoughts in your head feel soothing and gentle.

And now, notice how your neck and shoulders feel. Perhaps you can feel how your neck and shoulders feel up against the chair... maybe not... but your neck and shoulders feel warm and relaxed. Feel how effortlessly your neck holds your head. Feel the sunlight flow down from your head... down through your neck and down your shoulders. Allow yourself to gently move your head, neck and shoulders if you wish. Feel how good it feels to gently move and stretch oh so gently. That's right... take a deep breath, hold it for a moment, and then let it go. There's nothing you need to do but notice how wonderful your head, neck and shoulders feel.

Now, notice how your back feels against the chair. Feel how supported it feels up against the chairback. Feel how solid the chair feels against your back giving it perfect and total support. Feel how easy it is to notice how the chair feels against your back from the very top of the chairback right on down to where it meets the small of your back. So very connected and supportive.

And now, notice how your arms and hands feel as they are supported by the arms of the chair. Feel how your arms curve to meet the chair. That's right... take a deep breath, hold it for a moment, and then let it gently out. Feel how your hands... your palms feel against the arms of the chair. Soothing and warm... connected and supported. Yes, that's right... you can move your hands to notice the texture of the chair... how it feels. It feels very pleasant to notice how your hands feel against the chair. Just allow your hands and arms to relax as the chair supports your hands and arms.

Now, notice how your hips and buttocks feel against the chair... how easy it is to just sit and be supported by the chair. As you sit there you can notice exactly how it feels to be sitting in the chair... supported...comfortable... relaxed. You can feel how the chair feels up against your body... even how your clothes feel against the chair and your body. That's right... you can even move and stretch a little... allowing yourself to feel comfortable in the chair.

Now, notice how your legs feel against the chair. Feel how they fit comfortably against the chair...how supported they feel. How comfortable they feel... relaxed and comfortable.

Now notice your feet. Feel the floor that they are resting on. You can even wiggle your toes and move your feet. It feels so good to be able to touch the ground... the floor... effortlessly and easily. Notice the texture of the floor. Is it smooth and cool... or is it warm and fuzzy? Is it made of wood or is there a rug or carpet? Whatever kind of surface your feet are resting on, notice how that feels as you wiggle your toes and rub the bottoms of your feet against it. Take a deep breath, hold it for a moment, and then gently let it out.

(Now begin your experience for your client's anxiety reduction.)

The Lake of Anxiety...
The Lake of Peace
Copyright 1999 Holly Sumner

Maybe you've known for some time that you've had fears or anxieties. Perhaps you finally know that it's time to face and conquer them? But maybe you have been a little fearful of taking that path...for it's a path that you have to walk alone?

Perhaps all your friends... your family... your guides... all wish you well and want to help you conquer these fears and anxieties. But you know ultimately it is you who must face these fears... these anxieties within you?

And now it is time. Perhaps it will be difficult. Perhaps

it will be hard. But it is a path you know you want to take.
For by taking the path you pave the way to having a life free from anxieties that hold you back. Those that have kept you from living your life to the fullest?

And now see yourself standing in the middle of a circle of those who wish you well. Perhaps you know them. Perhaps you don't. Maybe your Guides are there. Maybe Guides that you haven't yet been in contact with? Perhaps there are friends there around you that you haven't seen in a long time. Maybe it's family you don't know well. Maybe one or two good friends are there. Whoever's in this circle around you... know that they all wish you well.

And as you stand there circled by those who wish you well...those who wish a full, happy life for you... see them present you with a walking stick. Notice how the stick is decorated. Maybe there are special things on the stick...perhaps a feather from a type of bird you admire. Maybe there is a crystal at the top of the handle? Maybe there are beautiful and intricate designs carved into the wood.

Notice how special this walking stick is. All of the people in the circle of caring are presenting you with this walking stick to help you walk on the path to freedom from fears and anxieties. Maybe they can't walk with you on the path... but they can lend their love and support by giving you this walking stick to ease your way. So even though you may have to walk this path alone... you aren't really alone.

One of the elders in the circle tells you, "if ever you feel really fearful... or afraid... simply take a deep breath... and then let it slowly out. Then just allow yourself to think about things... an answer will come to you."
And now... see yourself as you set off upon the path.
See yourself walking along a path that goes off into the distance... yes, it is a very long path. But you are prepared and you know it is time for you to face your fears and anxieties. The path leads to the place where you can face and remove any of those fears and anxieties... you know the path eventually leads to The Lake of Anxieties.

At the moment, perhaps the path is a bit winding and maybe you can't totally see exactly where you are going. But you know where it leads and you can do this... it's just a matter of taking it one small step at a time. And you have the walking stick to help you along the way.

See yourself as you continue walking along the path. After awhile you come to a fork. Which way should you go? Maybe for a moment you are scared. What if you take the wrong fork? What if you get lost?

Then you remember what the elder told you. So you take a deep breath... hold it for a moment and then slowly let it out. This calms you down a little... enough so you notice that there is a small sign beside one of the paths. It says, "this way to the lake". Wow, before you had been so afraid and so upset you didn't even notice the sign! But by simply taking a moment to allow yourself to calm down... there it was. It was there all the time!

And now you see yourself setting off along this path. Feel how more confident you are feeling in your abilities

to make the right decision with each step you take?
Perhaps you still are a little afraid or anxious... after all
you know you are going to a place that is called The
Lake of Anxieties. But, look how well you are doing so
far! You are facing the obstacles and you are finding
how to get past them... how to get around them... how to
move past those obstacles.

And now you continue along the path and see that a
giant tree has fallen right in the middle of the path. It
mustbe hundreds of feet in girth! It is so high that you
can'tsee over it! In fact, it looks so big... so long... that
it might take days... maybe weeks to walk around it.
And it looks way too high for you to climb over. Still, you
remember what the elder told you. So, you take a deep
breath, hold it for a moment and then allow yourself to
become calm and clear. And when you have become
calm and clear you notice that from a branch of another
tree is hanging a strong, thick vine. You realize that you
could use it like a rope to help you climb over the tree!
You can just pull yourself up and over the tree. And so
you do... and you easily and effortlessly climb over the
tree.

Each time you come to an obstacle... simply take a deep
breath, hold it for a moment... and then allow yourself to
calm down. In that way you can face each and every
obstacle in a clear manner. Sometimes it will be quite
easy to find the way around an obstacle. Sometimes it
will be more difficult. But you can do it!

See yourself continuing to walk down the path with your
walking step. See yourself come to obstacles and see
yourself finding a way over, around, or through them.
With each obstacle you face... feel yourself becoming

more confident. Perhaps you still are a bit anxious or afraid after all this path IS leading to a place called The Lake of Anxieties. But you are successfully walking this path! You are doing it very well!

Finally, off in the distance you see a gleaming lake - it's as though there is light sparkling off the lake. You know this is The Lake of Anxieties. From this distance it doesn't look too bad. Why is it called the Lake of Anxieties? You stop and wonder. What if you can't handle it? What if you get there and you won't know what to do?

Then you remember what the elder told you. So you take a deep breath... hold it for a moment and then slowly let it out. This calms you down a little... enough so you feel confident in your abilities to continue. You know you will face whatever the Lake of Anxieties can throw your way. And that you will be able to do it to the best of your ability. Who could ask for more?

So, you continue down along the path with each step taking you closer and closer to the lake. And as you come close enough to see the lake you understand why it was gleaming from a distance. You see why the light was sparkling off it's surface. For the lake is bubbling... bubbling very rapidly just like it was boiling.

Perhaps you are afraid? Perhaps you are anxious. After all the lake is churning and bubbling and you can hear those bubbles loud and clear. And as you look closer at those bubbles... you can see each of those bubbles contains some things. You can see pictures and scenes of things you have been anxious about. It's like all your *fears and anxieties are bubbling away right in the lake before you.*

You may be very, very fearful at this moment... but... then you remember what the elder told you. So you take a deep breath... hold it for a moment and then slowly let it out. This calms you down a little... enough so you feel confident in your abilities to find a way around those bubbles. You know you can find a way to maybe break those bubbles? That's right... if you could break those bubbles... they'd no longer be able to contain or hold any of those anxieties! You'd be able to release them and let them go.

But how to do so? What if the water is bubbling because it is hot? How could you reach those bubbles... and how could you break them?

Then you recall your walking stick. The bottom of the stick has a point on it that helped you walk along the path. What if you took the stick and reached out and broke a bubble?

See yourself reaching out and poking a bubble with the walking stick. Pop! See the bubble pop and the anxiety that it contained just drift off. See yourself reaching out and popping another bubble. And another...and another... and another until you have popped ALL the bubbles in the lake.

And now look as the entire surface of the lake has become clear and smooth as silk. And now that the bubbles are no longer there it is quieter. Quiet enough to hear the birds singing... perhaps the sound of insects... the sound of the breeze in the trees.

What a wonderful feeling! And you did it... you freed the lake from being a bubbling, churning mass and have allowed it to be what it now is... a beautiful, calm lake.

Meet Your Inner Listener

Copyright 1999 Holly Sumner

Sometimes when we are feeling alone, anxious, or depressed it is amplified by the fact that we may feel we have no one who will listen to us with unconditional love and without passing judgment.

What if there were someone like that? Someone who would listen to you and not make fun of you? Not pass judgment, or allowed you to get whining out of your system?

This may be a difficult task in the external world. Even if you do find someone who is willing to listen to you there are circumstances that you can run into. What if they are having their own problems? Can you trust them?

Well, you do have the perfect person to listen to you right in your own inner world! Your "inner listener" is right there day or night. Sound like pure fantasy? Well, perhaps it is... perhaps it isn't. How many times have you "talked" out a problem just by having a mental dialog with yourself?

This technique takes that principle one step further by giving you an interactive experience with your Inner Listener - that part of you that is always willing to listen. That part of you that always has time for you, that cares for you and that you can trust.

185

*Find a comfortable spot to sit or lie in. Close
your eyes and take a full, deep but gentle breath.
Hold it for a count of four and then exhale to a
count of five. Take another breath and really feel
the air fill your lungs. Hold this breath for a moment
and then allow yourself to exhale gently. Know that with
each breath you take you will feel more and more
relaxed.*

*Imagine yourself at a mountain retreat. You are partially
up one of the mountains. The air is fresh, crisp, and
clean. The sky is a beautiful and clear blue. The other
mountains that you can see from here rise up into the
sky, dotting the horizon. Perhaps their peaks are
covered with snow. The sun is shining and warm upon
your face.*

*You are at a spot where there is a clearing. There are
rocky outcrops here and there with taller grasses
growing. Perhaps there are a few mountain flowers
growing and waving gently in the breeze.*

*Over at the side of the clearing you see a path that leads
gently up the mountain. It is as though there are rock
steps carved into the mountain. They are just the
right height to easily step up... just the right space
apart. You know that you can climb each and every step
easily and effortlessly.*

*Now, take another deep, slow breath and see yourself
climb each of those stairs from one to ten. Place your
foot upon each of the steps... one at a time. You will be
able to climb each individual step easily and effortlessly.
One. And as you see yourself taking that step, mentally*

say the number one to yourself. See and feel yourself taking that step... climbing up the mountain path.

Now, take another step. Place your foot upon the next step. Two. You will be able to climb this step easily and effortlessly. And as you see yourself taking that step, mentally say the number two to yourself. See and feel yourself taking that step... climbing further up the mountain path.

Now, take another step. Place your foot upon the next step. Three. You will be able to climb this step easily and effortlessly. And as you see yourself taking that step, mentally say the number three to yourself. See and feel yourself taking that step... climbing further up the mountain path.

Now, take another step. Place your foot upon the next step. Four. You will be able to climb this step easily and effortlessly. And as you see yourself taking that step, mentally say the number four to yourself. See and feel yourself taking that step... climbing further up the mountain path.

Now, take another step. Place your foot upon the next step. Five. You will be able to climb this step easily and effortlessly. And as you see yourself taking that step, mentally say the number five to yourself. See and feel yourself taking that step... climbing further up the mountain path.

Now, take another step. Place your foot upon the next step. Six. You will be able to climb this step easily and effortlessly. And as you see yourself taking that step, mentally say the number six to yourself. See and feel yourself taking that step... climbing further up the mountain path.

Now, take another step. Place your foot upon the next step. Seven. You will be able to climb this step easily and effortlessly. And as you see yourself taking that step, mentally say the number seven to yourself. See and feel yourself taking that step... climbing further up the mountain path.

Now, take another step. Place your foot upon the next step. Eight. You will be able to climb this step easily and effortlessly. And as you see yourself taking that step, mentally say the number eight to yourself. See and feel yourself taking that step... climbing further up the mountain path.

Now, take another step. Place your foot upon the next step. Nine. You will be able to climb this step easily and effortlessly. And as you see yourself taking that step, mentally say the number nine to yourself. See and feel yourself taking that step... climbing further up the mountain path.

Now, take another step. Place your foot upon the next step. Ten. You will be able to climb this step easily and effortlessly. And as you see yourself taking that step, mentally say the number ten to yourself. See and feel yourself taking that step... climbing further up the mountain path.

And as you see yourself reach the end of the steps... you have reached another clearing and you are feeling relaxed. So very, very relaxed. Allow this feeling to spread over your entire body, from the top of your head to the tips of your toes. *Take a few moments to enjoy this sensation...the sensation of being totally relaxed. Just focus on how very good you feel.*

And now that you are here at this clearing, you see that there is a spot that is just perfect to sit down upon. It's a smooth, flat rock set in the middle of the clearing. The views from this rock seat are wonderful! You can see the rest of the mountains off in the distance... you can see the green valleys below. It's very quiet and peaceful here at this place.

Take time for yourself here at this place. Take the time to notice your surroundings. Take time to notice how serene and happy this place allows you to feel. There is nowhere else you need to be right now... nothing else you need to be doing. Just taking some time for yourself and allowing yourself to feel happy. Safe. Secure and peaceful.

That's right... take all the time you want and need to soak up this wonderful feeling. Isn't it wonderful to feel so free? So happy? So content?

And as you enjoy this feeling and look around at the scenery and the views you notice that you can see the path you just came up. And as you look at that path you notice a figure slowly coming up the path. As you watch this figure climbing the path you notice that he or she has almost a glow about them. As though their entire being is emitting a very soft golden glow.

The figure grows closer and you are curious and excited to meet this person. You just know that this person is someone you want to meet... it's almost as though you can intuitively sense this person's inner being.

And now the figure has reached the top step and gently walks towards you. They stop just a short distance from you and ask your permission to sit down with you. See, feel, sense, and hear yourself allowing this person to sit down next to you.

Perhaps there are questions you would like to ask this person? You may ask them anything you wish. Perhaps you would like to ask them who they are? As you do so, this person tells you that they are your Inner Listener. They tell you that they are here in your life whenever you want or need them to listen to all you have to say. Hear them tell you that they will always have plenty of time to listen to you. They will never be too busy for you... it is their pleasure to talk with you.

Perhaps you still have questions? Is this really your Inner Listener? Is this someone you can trust? Go ahead and take some time and ask questions. This is YOUR Inner Listener and therefore they will always answer truthfully any questions you wish to ask. Perhaps you want to make sure that they are your true Inner Listener? Go ahead and ask them and allow some time to hear their answer. You have every right to ask any questions that you wish.

Perhaps you want to ask them their name? What you should call them? Go ahead and ask them and allow some time to hear the answer. That's right.
See, hear, sense and feel yourself talking with your Inner Listener. Take all the time you want. Your Inner Listener will always be there for you anytime you need

*or want them. They will always listen and hear you.
Perhaps at times they will talk to you and ask questions.
But, those questions will never be judgmental. It's
because they want to know more... to understand what
you are thinking... to understand what you are feeling.
To give you unconditional listening and an objective
discussion.*

*Your Inner Listener will never tell you what to do... but
they will always listen to the ideas you have and help
YOU decide what to do. They are the end you can
bend... your sounding board... a person to talk to who
will listen to you with their undivided attention.*

*You can talk to your Inner Listener about anything... you
can tell them anything. You know that your Inner
Listener talks to you alone... so anything you tell them
or discuss with them is solely between the two of you.*

*Perhaps you are just feeling down... or a little
depressed. Your Inner Listener is there to spend time
with you listening to your feelings. Sometimes just
having
someone to listen to you and care about you can help
you move on and not dwell on problems. It's true that
your Inner Listener cannot make decisions for you
or that they will never tell you what to do... but they can
and will listen to you so YOU can decide what you should
do.*

*Maybe sometimes you don't need to DO anything.
Maybe sometimes you just need someone to lend an
ear? Your Inner Listener is happy to listen to you and
wants*

to listen to your thoughts, ideas, and opinions. Maybe your Inner Listener will ask questions about what you are saying... so that they understand... and you understand and know exactly what and how YOU feel.

That's right. Now... just take some time to get to know your Inner Listener. Each time that you meet your Inner Listener... and as you spend some time with your Inner Listener you will be able to develop an easy communication style with them.

And each time you do so, it will become easier and easier to allow yourself to contact that part of yourself that is your Inner Listener.

Healing Touch... By an Angel
Copyright 1999 Holly Sumner

Touch is sadly lacking in today's society. It may be because we fear inappropriate touch or the consequences of touching someone and having them perceive it as inappropriate.

Touch, in the proper way and manner can be very healing both physically and emotionally. Many healing modalities such as massage or Reiki have gained popularity in recent years. But what if you can't find someone near you that practices any of these modalities? Or what if you can't afford a session?

The most powerful healing being there could possibly be in the Universe, in my opinion, would be an Angel. What if you could imagine a healing session with an Angel? The power of the mind is very powerful!

I like to imagine that my healing Angel is giving me a Reiki session. (a hands-on healing modality)

You have entered a pleasant and comfortable room in which there is a massage table in the center of the room. The light in the room is dimmed but not dark. There is soothing music playing softly in the background. Perhaps there is a light fragrance in the air... something that smells wonderful to you. Something that brings up pleasant memories.

Now imagine yourself lying fully dressed on the massage table. You are completely comfortable. If you wish, you can imagine that a pillow is placed under your knees to give a bit of support for your back.

And as you lie there upon the table, into the room walks the most beautiful Angel! Perhaps you stare in awe at the Angel for the first few minutes. Imagine having an angel giving you a healing treatment? How wonderful and awe inspiring. You must be a very special person!

After a short while though, you feel yourself feeling comfortable in the Angel's presence. Perhaps it's because the Angel exudes a calming influence. Perhaps it's because you know you deserve to have a healing treatment from an angel. Perhaps it's because it just feels right.

The Angel touches your shoulder and smiles at you and you know you can relax and just enjoy your healing treatment. The Angel moves to the top of the table and places it's hands on the crown of your head. As the Angel does so... you can feel the light weight of the Angel's hands. Notice how warm the Angel's hands feel placed on your head. Notice how very soothing that feels. The Angel may keep it's hands there for quite some time. Perhaps it's for five minutes. Perhaps it's for ten minutes. Perhaps even longer. Feel how relaxing and wonderful it feels to have the Angel's hands upon the crown of your head.

And now the Angel moves it's hands and places them over your forehead. As the Angel does so... you can feel the light weight of the Angel's hands. Notice how warm the Angel's hands feel placed on your forehead. Notice how very soothing that feels. The Angel may keep it's hands there for quite some time. Perhaps it's for five minutes. Perhaps it's for ten minutes. Perhaps even longer. Feel how relaxing and wonderful it feels to have the Angel's hands upon your forehead.

And now the Angel moves it's hands and places them very lightly cupped over your eyes. As the Angel does so... you can feel the light weight of the Angel's hands. Notice how warm the Angel's hands feel placed over your eyes. Notice how very soothing that feels. The Angel may keep it's hands there for quite some time. Perhaps it's for five minutes. Perhaps it's for ten minutes. Perhaps even longer. Feel how relaxing and wonderful it feels to have the Angel's hands placed over your eyes.

And now the Angel moves it's hands and places them over your ears. As the Angel does so... you can feel the light weight of the Angel's hands. Notice how warm the Angel's hands feel placed over your ears. Notice how very soothing that feels. The Angel may keep it's hands there for quite some time. Perhaps it's for five minutes. Perhaps it's for ten minutes. Perhaps even longer. Feel how relaxing and wonderful it feels to have the Angel's hands over your ears.

And now the Angel moves it's hands and places them over your jaw area. As the Angel does so... you can feel the light weight of the Angel's hands. Notice how warm the Angel's hands feel placed over your jaws. Notice how very soothing that feels. The Angel may keep it's hands there for quite some time. Perhaps it's for five minutes. Perhaps it's for ten minutes. Perhaps even longer. Feel how relaxing and wonderful it feels to have the Angel's hands over your jaws.

And now the Angel moves it's hands and places them over the area of your throat very gently. The Angel may not be quite touching your throat area... it may be that the Angel is holding it's hands over the area of your throat if that is more comfortable for you. As the Angel does so... you can feel the gentle warmth flow from the Angel's hands even if the Angel is not touching you. Notice how very soothing that feels. The Angel may keep it's hands in this area for quite some time. Perhaps it's for five minutes. Perhaps it's for ten minutes. Perhaps even longer. Feel how relaxing and wonderful it feels to have the Angel's hands placed near the area of your throat.

And now the Angel moves it's hands and places them over your upper chest area...where your heart is. As the Angel does so... you can feel the light weight of the Angel's hands. Notice how warm the Angel's hands feel placed over your heart. Notice how very soothing that feels. The Angel may keep it's hands there for quite some time. Perhaps it's for five minutes. Perhaps it's for ten minutes. Perhaps even longer. Feel how relaxing and wonderful it feels to have the Angel's hands over your heart.

And now the Angel moves it's hands and places them over your stomach and abdomen area. As the Angel does so... you can feel the light weight of the Angel's hands. Notice how warm the Angel's hands feel placed over your stomach. Notice how very soothing that feels. The Angel may keep it's hands there for quite some time. Perhaps it's for five minutes. Perhaps it's for ten minutes. Perhaps even longer. Feel how relaxing and wonderful it feels to have the Angel's hands over your stomach.

And now the Angel moves it's hands and places them over the tops of your upper legs. As the Angel does so... you can feel the light weight of the Angel's hands. Notice how warm the Angel's hands feel placed over your legs. Notice how very soothing that feels. The Angel may keep it's hands there for quite some time. Perhaps it's for five minutes. Perhaps it's for ten minutes. Perhaps even longer. Feel how relaxing and wonderful it feels to have the Angel's hands over your the upper part of your legs.

And now the Angel moves it's hands and places them over your knees. As the Angel does so... you can feel the light weight of the Angel's hands. Notice how warm the Angel's hands feel placed over your knees. Notice how very soothing that feels. The Angel may keep it's hands there for quite some time. Perhaps it's for five minutes. Perhaps it's for ten minutes. Perhaps even longer. Feel how relaxing and wonderful it feels to have the Angel's hands over your knees.

And now the Angel moves it's hands and places them over the top of your lower legs. As the Angel does so... you can feel the light weight of the Angel's hands. Notice how warm the Angel's hands feel placed over your legs. Notice how very soothing that feels. The Angel may for five minutes. Perhaps it's for ten minutes. Perhaps even longer. Feel how relaxing and wonderful it feels to have the Angel's hands over your the lower part of your legs.

And now the Angel moves it's hands and places them over your ankles. As the Angel does so... you can feel the light weight of the Angel's hands. Notice how warm the Angel's hands feel placed over your ankles. Notice how very soothing that feels. The Angel may keep it's hands there for quite some time. Perhaps it's for five minutes. Perhaps it's for ten minutes. Perhaps even longer. Feel how relaxing and wonderful it feels to have the Angel's hands over by your ankles.

And now the Angel moves it's hands and places them over the bottoms of your feet. As the Angel does so... you can feel the light weight of the Angel's hands. Notice how warm the Angel's hands feel placed over the bottom of your feet. Notice how very soothing that feels. The Angel may keep it's hands there for quite some time. Perhaps it's for five minutes. Perhaps it's for ten minutes. Perhaps even longer. Feel how relaxing and wonderful it feels to have the Angel's hands over your the bottom of your feet.

Now the Angel has you turn over and you lie on your stomach. And now the Angel moves it's hands and places

them over the heels of your feet. As the Angel does so...
you can feel the light weight of the Angel's hands.
Notice how warm the Angel's hands feel placed over
your heels. Notice how very soothing that feels. The
Angel may keep it's hands there for quite some time.
Perhaps it's for five minutes. Perhaps it's for ten minutes.
Perhaps even longer. Feel how relaxing and wonderful
it feels to have the Angel's hands over your heels.

And now the Angel moves it's hands and places them
over the back of your lower legs. As the Angel does so...
you can feel the light weight of the Angel's hands.
Notice how warm the Angel's hands feel placed over
your legs. Notice how very soothing that feels. The
Angel may
keep it's hands there for quite some time. Perhaps it's
for five minutes. Perhaps it's for ten minutes. Perhaps
even longer. Feel how relaxing and wonderful it feels to
have the Angel's hands over your the back of your legs.

And now the Angel moves it's hands and places them
over the back of your knees. As the Angel does so... you
can feel the light weight of the Angel's hands. Notice
how warm the Angel's hands feel placed over the back
of your knees. Notice how very soothing that feels. The
Angel may keep it's hands there for quite some time.
Perhaps it's for five minutes. Perhaps it's for ten minutes.
Perhaps even longer. Feel how relaxing and wonderful
it feels to have the Angel's hands over the back of your
knees.

And now the Angel moves it's hands and places them
over your lower back and hip area. As the Angel does
so... you can feel the light weight of the Angel's hands.
Notice how warm the Angel's hands feel placed over

your lower back and hip area. Notice how very soothing that feels. The Angel may keep it's hands there for quite some time. Perhaps it's for five minutes. Perhaps it's for ten minutes. Perhaps even longer. Feel how relaxing and wonderful it feels to have the Angel's hands over your lower back and hip area.

And now the Angel moves it's hands and places them over the small of your back. As the Angel does so... you can feel the light weight of the Angel's hands. Notice how warm the Angel's hands feel placed over the small of your back. Notice how very soothing that feels. The Angel may keep it's hands there for quite some time. Perhaps it's for five minutes. Perhaps it's for ten minutes. Perhaps even longer. Feel how relaxing and wonderful it feels to have the Angel's hands over the small of your back.

And now the Angel moves it's hands and places them over the upper part of your back. As the Angel does so... you can feel the light weight of the Angel's hands. Notice how warm the Angel's hands feel placed over the upper part of your back. Notice how very soothing that feels. The Angel may keep it's hands there for quite some time. Perhaps it's for five minutes. Perhaps it's for ten minutes. Perhaps even longer. Feel how relaxing and wonderful it feels to have the Angel's hands over the upper part of your back.

And now the Angel moves it's hands and places them over the back of your neck. As the Angel does so... you can feel the light weight of the Angel's hands. Notice how warm the Angel's hands feel placed over the back of your neck. Notice how very soothing that feels. The Angel may keep it's hands there for quite some time.

Perhaps it's for five minutes. Perhaps it's for ten minutes. Perhaps even longer. Feel how relaxing and wonderful it feels to have the Angel's hands over the back of your neck.

And now the Angel moves it's hands and places them over the back of your head. As the Angel does so... you can feel the light weight of the Angel's hands. Notice how warm the Angel's hands feel placed over the back of your head. Notice how very soothing that feels. The Angel may keep it's hands there for quite some time. Perhaps it's for five minutes. Perhaps it's for ten minutes. Perhaps even longer. Feel how relaxing and wonderful it feels to have the Angel's hands over the back of your head.

And now the Angel returns to the top of your head. As the Angel does so... you can feel the light weight of the Angel's hands. Notice how warm the Angel's hands feel placed on your head. Notice how very soothing that feels. The Angel may keep it's hands there for quite some time. Perhaps it's for five minutes. Perhaps it's for ten minutes. Perhaps even longer. Feel how relaxing and wonderful it feels to have the Angel's hands upon the crown of your head.

The Angel now touches your shoulder gently and leaves the room. And now take a deep breath and notice how wonderful you feel.

Filtering Away Pain
Copyright 1999 Holly Sumner

Imagine a filter... maybe it looks like a transparent coffee filter... maybe it looks like a silken light... however your filter looks for you... it's just perfect.

Now imagine stepping onto that filter. See how it circles the place where you are standing. Now watch as it slowly moves up your body... filtering out any pain. It slowly moves up your body and simply filters out and removes any pain in your body.

See as it rises over your feet. Feel how gently it is removing any pain from that area of your body. See as it rises over your ankles. Feel how gently it is removing any pain from that area of your body. See as it rises over your shins and calves. Feel how gently it is removing any pain from that area of your body. See as it rises over your knees. Notice how it slowly moves up your body... over your knees and simply filters out and removes any pain in your body.

See as it rises over your thighs. Feel how gently it is removing any pain from that area of your body. See as it rises over your hips... slowly moving over your hips gently removing any pain or discomfort in your hips. See the filter as it gently moves up your body. See as it rises over your abdomen and stomach area. Feel how gently it is removing any pain from that area of your body.

See as it rises up past your lower back...up along your chest as it rises up the trunk of your body. Feel how it

201

gently removes any pain or discomfort from the trunk of your body.

See and feel as the filter gently moves up along your shoulder and upper back area. Feel how it filters out any pain or discomfort in this area of your body. Notice how it slowly moves and filters out any pain in your body.

See and feel as the filter now gently moves down and up again along your arms and hands. Feel how the filter is removing any pain or discomfort in your hands or arms. Feel as the filter continues to move up and over your neck area. Feel as the filter gently removes any pain or discomfort in this area of your body.

Feel and see the filter as it now gently moves up and over your head and pulls out any remaining pain or discomfort in your body.

And now imagine that a soothing golden light flows over your body soaking into every pore and cell bringing with it a healing and regenerating energy.

Wash Away Pain and Discomfort
Copyright 1999 Holly Sumner

Whenever I am in pain I find that warm baths often give noticeable relief. Baths are also relaxing which can help to alleviate pain as stress can amplify any discomfort we feel.

Use any deepening method you prefer and then use the below script:

Imagine standing in front of a gleaming building. See how it sparkles in the sunshine. And as you stand in front of this building, it feels as though the building has it's own presence... it's own feeling. It is a feeling of quietness and peace. It is like there is a serene hush around the entire building and the grounds upon which it
sits.

Even the birds sing quietly and reverently. The breeze which blows gently upon your face as you stand looking at the building seems to make no noise or sound whatsoever.

Now, allow yourself to walk closer to the building and see, feel, and sense yourself walking into this building. You come into a large lobby. The colors on the walls are all soothing colors... and there are even murals painted on the surfaces of the walls. Allow yourself to enjoy the murals... the different scenes depicted... angels... fairies... all done in soft, soothing colors.

Notice how fresh the air in the building smells... so fresh and clean. In fact, everywhere you look or walk is incredibly clean and fresh. Immaculate. Peaceful.

As you continue to look around you notice a hallway that leads off into another area of the building. At the entrance is a woman... a woman unlike anyone you have seen before. There is an almost other-worldly glow about her. There is a pleasant smile upon her face and she is happy to see you here in this place. She doesn't speak just merely smiles at you and gracefully moves her arm pointing the way down the hall.

Off in the distance you can hear sweet melodic music. It wafts towards you and feels oh, so inviting... so very inviting. Peaceful. Serene. Pleasant, safe and inviting.

You find yourself walking down the hall feeling safe but excited at the same time. Where will the hall lead? You know it must be someplace good... for you can feel the specialness of this place. It feels almost sacred. You feel very honored to be walking down the hall and excited about what you will discover at the end of the hall.

And as you continue walking along the hall, listening to the sweet melodic music you see the end of the hall. There is a golden light that you can see... as though the hall opens right up into a golden heaven.

See, feel and sense yourself stepping into this golden room. Feel the golden light upon your face... feel the incredible energy that this room exudes... powerful...yet gentle at the same time.

And now you notice that in the room is a large tub... clean and sparkling. It is filled with the most clear and sparkling water you have ever seen. There are screens around the tub to ensure your privacy. The same woman you saw at the beginning of the hall to this room gracefully points at you and then the tub. She smiles at you and then quietly leaves the room. You are alone in this wonderful place and you feel amazed that all of this is just for you!

On the side of the tub there are bottles of all kinds of what appears to be bath oils. There are fluffy towels and candles and beautiful soaps. Everything you could possibly want for a luxurious bath is right here waiting for you.

See, sense and feel yourself preparing to get into the tub. You feel safe and secure. Everything you could possibly want to have a relaxing bath is right here for you. Maybe you see yourself lighting some scented candles. Maybe you see yourself selecting some bath oils or salts.

The water looks very inviting...and you allow yourself to step into the tub and immerse yourself. The water temperature is just right... it feels silky smooth... warm and comforting. It feels better than any bath water you have ever experienced.

And as you immerse yourself into the water you notice something... You notice that any aches... any pains... and discomforts you had before simply are being washed away. As the water flows and moves around you... caressing you... it's as though the water washes away any aches... any pains... any discomforts.

You can move easily and effortlessly. Feel as you move your hands, arms and legs in the bath water. Feel how good it feels to have the water soothe away any discomfort you might have had.

And now that you have no discomfort - you are free to notice other sensations instead. The feel of the warm soothing water over your skin. The feel of the scented air over your skin. How it feels to effortlessly move your *body... stretching and sensuously moving just like a cat. Maybe you've not been able to move like this for a very long time. But you can move like this now... and it feels wonderful.*

Take your time and enjoy this special bath. The candles are casting a soothing light... the music is soothing your mind... and the water is soothing your body and soul. The water will stay just the right temperature no matter how long you allow yourself to enjoy this bath.

Allow yourself to feel every muscle and inch of skin on your body. Notice how wonderful every part of your body feels. Take your time and allow yourself to be immersed in this soothing bath. Feel how it cleans any discomfort away... and how it brings a feeling of soothing and gentle sensations... wonderful sensations over your entire body.

And when you are done for now - allow yourself to use the fluffy towels... notice how soft they are. Notice how wonderful you feel.

And when you are dressed, feeling wonderful and relaxed and free from any discomfort the woman returns. She smiles at you and tells you in a soft ethereal voice... "this is your place... just for you... and you may return here anytime you wish... anytime you need... simply by thinking yourself here. You can bath in these healing waters anytime you need or wish. You may simply bathe away any pain or discomfort."

The woman then smiles at you and seems to float up the hall....

9

Hypnosis in the Relief of Pain

We are fortunate indeed to have such a powerful tool at our beck and call to help people experience relief from pain. Various forms of hypnosis can have differing effects on the different kinds of pain.

Pain certainly is the mindbody's way of getting our attention to do something to help ourselves. Headache pain might be a warning of a TMJ that needs correction or that the eyes are straining to much at work every day. (Headache pain can have many causes, including those that are rare but deadly. This fact helps the hypnotherapist always remember that they are a complementary therapist and not a medical doctor.)

Back pain can be dull and achy, or sharp like a knife being thrust in and out of the back. Back pain can be so severe that turning to the left or right can be impossible. Like headaches, back pain can have many origins and we must have those in the medical profession do a complete diagnostic check for causes before we go to work.

Pains that people experience inside, around the organs of our body, are particularly upsetting as one is never quite sure what pains in the cervical area, the kidney area, the abdomen, the appendix region, the heart and lungs and so on might be caused by. Worse, the duration of pain in these areas is often ongoing and can bring on a host of anxiety induced disorders.

In short, pain is caused by many different things and is experienced in different ways by each of us. We all have a different "threshold" or "tolerance" for pain. The exact same degree of pain in one person may be experienced as five or ten times worse in another person.

Pain is experienced in the brain and becomes a full fledged memory, sometimes a memory that "loops" for long periods of time, maybe even years or decades. Neurons (brain cells) release neurotransmitters from the axon (sending arm) of one cell to the dendrite (receiving arm) of another cell. Neurotransmitters are like taxi cabs that carry information from cell to cell. The more taxi cabs there are bringing information from cell to cell the more information is sped through the brain in any one instant. In the case of pain, information sent from cell to cell can be overwhelming to the brain.

Meanwhile the brain also has an emotional response to the pain. Both the pain and the emotional response to the pain are stored as memory. The brain is forever aware at the unconscious level of what caused the pain, the pain itself and the emotional response to the pain, *and* the circuitry used to create, experience and remember the pain!

Pain is complex and it's perceived intensity is different from ethnic group to ethnic group and person to person. Dr. Maryann Bates has discovered that Hispanic patients report the highest intensity of pain and that Polish and French Canadians on average experience the lowest levels of pain. The way we are taught to deal with pain obviously plays a role in our experience of it.

There are also cultural difficulties in coping with pain as it relates to our belief about disability. When people believe that the experience of chronic pain is equivalent to disability the individual tends to not want to work at their job. Making matters worse is the fact that charlatans hawking a pain free life in our culture has placed an unrealistic expectation on those who suffer from chronic pain. These people partake in pain relief remedies and treatments only to find that they do not fully recover from the pain. Then it becomes "obvious" that they must be disabled as they have failed to get well. Inappropriate and unrealistic expectations can be very harmful indeed.

In this vein we look at one of many "pain syndromes" known as fibromyalgia. Fibromyalgia is a syndrome of numerous pains experienced in body tissues throughout the body. Fibromyalgia is not a disease but is identified as a collection of symptoms. Fibromyalgia affects 3-10% of entire populations in our world's advanced societies.

Fibromyalgia can include headache pain, numbness and tingling in the hands and feet, pain of the chest, lower back or jaw pain, insomnia, mental fuzziness...all of which are also symptoms associated with other syndromes and ailments including lupus, rheumatoid arthritis, depression, migraines and irritable bowel syndrome among others.

So what is fibromyalgia? Is it a physical or mental disorder? My belief is that it is not relevant which, if either, it is. The pain experienced with fibromyalgia may be initiated in the tissues in the body or it may be initiated in the brain itself. One doesn't know which is which. There is no tissue damage that would cause the pain experienced with fibromyalgia so it is possible that at least a significant portion of the pain experienced with firbromyalgia is generated from the brain itself. This can be good news for treatment, but is rarely well received by the sufferer of fibromyalgia.

Dr. I. John Russell at the University of Texas, San Antonio has found abnormally high amounts of a neurotransmitter called Substance P, which is found only in spinal fluid. This neurotransmitter apparently causes neurons to send pain messages to the brain even when their is no source of the pain! Meanwhile three other neurotransmitters tend to be abnormally low in fibromyalgia sufferers. They are serotonin, dopamine and norepinephrine. Serotonin helps regulate substance P and tends to also play a role in depression when Serotonin levels are low.

For some reason women tend to produce less serotonin than men and it is no coincidence that 80-90% of fibromyalgia sufferers are women and over 2/3 of depressed individuals are women. Fibromyalgia is just one of numerous pain syndromes. Help is available and hypnotherapy can play a complementary role to that of taking anti-depressants, added magnesium and increased physical activity, all of which seem to help the symptoms in many individuals.

Regardless of what pain syndrome is being experienced (chronic back pain to fibromyalgia to headaches), using various forms of hypnotherapy, therapists can help the client reduce both pain and suffering in most cases. Remember that pain and suffering are not the same experiences. Pain is a physical sensation and suffering is the result of emotional interpretations of the sensations. At intense levels of pain, almost all people will suffer greatly, but at lower levels of intensity pain is experienced very differently from person to person.

There are three goals when working with people who suffer from pain.

1) Reduce the pain immediately.
2) Reduce the pain over the long term.
3) Reduce the suffering from the pain.

Trance in and of itself is enough to reduce pain simply by definition. Trance that begins with relaxation typically reduces pain as muscle tightness tends to increase pain wherever it is being experienced in the body. Relaxation also tends to bring on deeper breathing which may oxygenate the body tissues, again reducing pain. The next step in facilitating trance is often that of placing awareness and attention on some idea, thought, or location, much like watching a movie that you are engrossed in. With conscious attention units being utilized with the focal point of attention there is little "space" for pain to be experienced.

Next we often ask and test the client to see if the "critical faculty" has been bypassed. In other words, are suggestions being critically considered or accepted without judgment? If they are being accepted free or relatively free of consideration, then the client has allowed himself to dissociate from the present external experience. Suggestions are now accepted and believed. In many clients you finally experience an automatic response to body experience change suggestions. For example, suggestions for a hand to increase in temperature are not only accepted but realized as a bodily fact. This typical progression of trance induction alone is often enough to begin the reduction of pain in and of itself. Once trance has been induced we know there are several approaches that can be effective in helping the client.

Reminder: A hypnotherapist will only work with a client for pain control after a complete diagnostic exam has been performed by a medical doctor. Covering or cloaking pain symptoms can be deadly.

A) Hypnoanalysis

The first approach at gaining long term pain reduction is that of traditional hypnoanalysis (regression and ego state therapy). It's very important to find out what is causing the pain. People often suffer from everything from chronic back pain to the pains of fibromyalgia for reasons that have nothing to do with typical causes of short term pain. Utilize the CARPeTS model approach that has been described in detail in this book.

Using regression you will probably uncover some common themes in your clients who suffer from pain.

1) Don't be surprised if you find repressed rage in your client.. Hostility and anger

seem to go hand in hand with a large percentage of cases of pain, including everything from rheumatoid arthritis to fibromyalgia.

2) Don't be surprised if you find specific and generalized experiences of ongoing guilt with your client. The criticism of the self could come from within the self or from others, but it is held and maintained by the beliefs and values the person lives by and the connection, if there, should be enlightening to the client.

3) Don't be surprised if you find tendencies of **perfectionism** in your client's personality. Perfectionism is not a characteristic found in the "normal population" so this common thread seems to have- a legitimate correlation to the experience of pain. I particularly look for traits in people that reveal extreme neatness, self criticism, a low sense of self esteem and a drive to be someone or accomplish something that is really founded and driven by an inner sense of inadequacy. Using hypnoanalysis we want to bring the connections between the perfectionism and pain to the conscious mind of the client if indeed they do exist.

4) Don't be surprised if you find the "need to be good" within your client. People in pain often are people who are very religious or people pleasers. If the link between the "need to be good" and pain is indeed there we will need to bring it to the attention of the client in trance so she can integrate that insight back into her life. Religious beliefs are often difficult to work around because they are so rigidly adhered to.

B) Misdirection of Attention

An excellent tool for pain reduction both in session and for the client to use on her own is that of misdirection of attention. Someone who has significant pain might be urged to focus all of their conscious attention onto some other task or project. This is not to be confused with the "just ignore it" advice so often given. Attention and pain are directly related to each other. Change the focus of attention and you change the conscious experience. When attention is completely flowing in another experience then pain is not experienced. When attention is largely placed on a pain free event, pain is reduced.

As a hypnotherapist you can offer posthypnotic suggestions to pay closer attention to some activity or experience each time the client consciously begins to experience their pain in consciousness. The client must allow experiencing pain to not be a failure but a reminder to focus their attention elsewhere.

C) Guided Imagery

Use a well crafted script that will take the client on a long journey where they are seen walking, running, or participating in a variety of physical experiences that you know that they have enjoyed in the past. Not all of these experiences have to directly effect the part of the body that is now in pain but at least some of the experiences should. This accomplishes several things in the brain.

First, the experiences prove to be somewhat misdirecting and therefore the pain is felt irregularly to begin with. Secondly, the experiences allow the brain to experience other sensations than pain so that at least some re-programming can take place in the brain where pain was once felt. Finally, the brain will be confused at times when images of relaxation, calm, peace, etc. are given thus creating more mental diffusion while in trance. This at least temporarily reduces pain.

D) Dissociation

Dissociation is a wonderful tool for dealing with pain, at least in the near term. Dissociation, in this case, is a blend of all these techniques that create a different experience in the mind than that which is being experienced in physical reality.

Return the client to an earlier time in life where there was no pain and have the client experience this time period, preferably verbally to you, reassociating to the past experience as fully as possible. By finding a time which is positive and happy the client may experience less pain for two reasons. First it is possible his body will experience more good hormones like serotonin which tends to correlate with less pain and secondly it provides a new set of experiences for the brain to focus on, those that are happy..

E) Manipulate the duration and intensity of pain.

You can for example create a mental image that the brain has a fuse box with switches. There are two switches for each part of the body from head to foot. By flipping one switch you reduce almost half of the pain. Flipping the second switch reduces almost all of the pain. Have the client practice in his mind with flipping one switch and do not have the client flip the second switch until he shows success of some kind with the first switch.

F) Change the meaning of the pain.

As discussed in A, you have the ego state responsible for exacerbating the pain, while in trance, explain to you the purpose for the pain. Then negotiate an agreement with the ego state to reduce the pain with the promise of some other behavior that will help meet it's need.

G) Post Hypnotic Suggestions

Post hypnotic suggestions can be given to activate the mindbody healing response. "As each day goes by you will find yourself experiencing discomfort. What is interesting is that as each day goes by you will find yourself, calm, relaxed and free from discomfort for longer periods of time as each day goes on. You will also find that you will experience days where your discomfort will be aggravated and it hasn't been like that in a long time. Each time you experience this you can know that shortly the discomfort will diminish and you will begin to feel better...happier...and more comfortable shortly thereafter."

Post hypnotic suggestions that are believable to the unconscious mind seem to be listened to and obeyed with more regularity than those that are obviously false statements.

10

Emergency Hypnosis: 'How To Successfully P.A.N.I.C. (TM) In Any Emergency Situation.'

Copyright 1999 by C. Devin Hastings

The use of hypnosis in emergency or crisis control situations is a little utilized application of hypnosis. After reading the following case histories, you will receive clear and detailed instructions on how to successfully use hypnosis in almost any emergency situation. Some applications include the following:

- Reduction or Elimination of Pain
- Prevention of Shock
- Control of Bleeding
- Lessening the Severity of Burns
- Accelerated Healing
- Increasing a person's chance of Survival in Trauma.

The material is presented in such a manner that even if you are a new practitioner you will still be able to confidently apply this information. You will read some amazing examples of how others have used hypnosis to create astonishing results despite

217

horrifying injuries. Please understand that this chapter and the applications of hypnosis contained here are in no way to be construed as medical advice. Furthermore, the information presented in this chapter is not meant to be used as an adjunct to medical care and not to be used as an alternative to any advice given by a physician or other qualified medical professional.

Suggestion Changes A Life

The six year old boy and his baby sitter were standing by the side of a busy road in New Rochelle, New York. They were waiting until the traffic cleared so that he could cross the road and go home. When the time was right, his baby sitter told him to go and so he ran for the other side of the road to where he lived. His mother had gotten home from work earlier and was taking a short nap before having to deal with the responsibilities of being a single mom with two children in New York.

As the young boy began to sprint across the street he saw out of the corner of his left eye a hand reaching out for him. It caught his attention and because of that he did not see the car that was heading straight for him on his right side.

He was told later that the car never stopped. It struck him and threw him high into the air. Witnesses said he spun around 3 times before landing on the road and rolled into the arms of an elderly woman. Years later, he still remembers seeing himself as he rolled down the street.

After being hit by the car, the next thing he remembered was being in an ambulance and someone saying to another person that because the boy was young and had not stiffened with fear, his injuries were minimal and that he would be just fine. He remembered the phrase: "loose as a rag doll". Then, everything was just bits and pieces as he faded in and out of consciousness.

Now, many years later, I (Devin Hastings) remembered the power of those words and I thought to myself that the childhood adage: "Sticks and stones may break my bones, but words can never hurt me!" is incorrect. Indeed, quite the opposite is true. Not only can words create deep damage but they can also help to powerfully heal broken bones and other injuries.

My First Experience with Suggestion in a Crisis

All of these memories and thoughts flashed through my mind as I looked down at a wounded man bleeding on my porch. It was four in the morning and someone dressed in army fatigues had literally dropped an injured person off at my house and left without a word. The rescuer had banged on the door and yelled to call an ambulance and once he knew that someone was awake, he left. When I cautiously opened the front door, all I saw was his back as he hopped into what appeared to be white Subaru station wagon. To say that this all was a bit unnerving would be an understatement. After all, how often is one woken from a sound sleep to discover a person bleeding all over their porch?

Stepping onto the porch, I looked down at my new guest and saw that blood was pouring from his head and was covering his face which was looking ghostly pale blue-white in the porch light. The laceration on his head appeared quite deep but that effect was due mostly to the swelling of the injured area. Apparently what happened is that this guy had fallen asleep at the wheel and had driven off the road into a tree. This was my guess because I didn't smell any alcohol.

My step-brother Mike was with me and so while he was calling 911 it occurred to me that this situation was not so different from one I had experienced many years ago. The circumstances were a bit different but one thing was the same: this man's unconscious mind was ready to uncritically accept any suggestion. I knew this because as a hypnotist I had learned that in trauma situations, victims spontaneously enter deep trance. I also knew that years ago some person's words had burned into my mind with the assurance that I would be okay. Therefore, I knew that I too could help this man.

When Mike returned from calling an ambulance and we made him as comfortable as possible I decided to use hypnosis to help him. The first thing I did was to reassure him that he would be just fine and that help was going to be there very quickly. I then told him that I was thoroughly trained in emergency response techniques and that I could do whatever was necessary for him to be just fine. Once he understood this I then made him aware that his injury was in fact minor and that the bleeding would soon stop. Right after this, I asked Mike if he had seen a TV special where a doctor had stated that head wounds bled a lot because it was Nature's method of cleaning a wound and that once the wound was cleansed, the bleeding just naturally stopped. While saying these things, Mike and I had been using cloths to staunch the blood flow. Approximately 90 seconds later the blood flow decreased and then quickly ceased. Observing this, I knew that the victim was still in deep trance and so I then told him that since the blood flow had stopped I could actually see that his wound was even less severe than it had initially seemed. I then gave him suggestions that he keep his eyes closed and think of a time when he felt perfectly relaxed and safe. When he indicated to me that he remembered such a time, I had him describe to me his feelings. While this was going on I continued to deliver suggestions designed for his benefit. I made sure that he would be able to report to doctors any sensations that would indicate other injury but that he could feel comfortable while doing so. It is possible to completely mask pain using hypnosis but in this case that could have prevented the attending medical personnel from detecting any other problems.

When the ambulance arrived, I instructed the victim that he was on his way to a hospital and that shortly after that he would be home sleeping safe in his bed. I then told him that he would continue to remain very relaxed and calm and would be able to easily answer any questions the doctors or nurses might ask.

The bleeding man was then removed from the porch and after talking things over with Mike, I returned to bed. As I fell asleep I wondered how things would have been different for me if no one had spoken encouraging and healing words that I could hear even if they weren't consciously intended for me.

How Emergency Hypnosis
Could Have Changed this Woman's Life

Years later, in 1991, I was at an international martial arts tournament watching one of my teammates

221

compete. Alison was very quick and powerful for her size and was beating her opponent without much trouble. Then, as Alison executed a perfect side kick her opponent dropped to the floor and performed a damaging foot sweep. The biggest problem was that it was poorly executed. The sweep landed high on her leg forcing her knee sideways.

As Alison's knee bore the brunt of the impact, her face contorted with pain and she crumpled to the mat clutching her knee in agony.

The referees immediately halted the match. Due to the angle of the leg, they could tell that this was a very serious injury. People seemed to swarm around her as our instructor and on site emergency personnel went to Alison's side. Within moments she was whisked out of the stadium on her way to a hospital. She required major surgery in order for her to be able to walk again. Alison was advised to avoid any form of martial arts for the rest of her life because of the strain that would be imposed on her knee joint and the possibility of an even more debilitating injury. I still wonder what difference it would have made had Alison had the benefit of emergency hypnosis.

I would like you to use Alisons' story as a valuable imagination exercise. What would you have done if you could have helped? How would you have applied your knowledge? What would you have said? As I have thought long on this particular situation I'll share with you some of my thoughts on what I would have done.

First of all, I changed the situation just a little bit. In my inner scenario, I was the first one on the scene and qualified medical help would take some time to arrive. Next, because I am CPR qualified and have studied Red Cross Basic Emergency Response techniques (*and I recommend that every person take something of this sort*), I can do some basic assessment work. In other words, I want to know if there is any other condition that supercedes the obvious injury. For example, what if a person has started to vomit from pain. You want to be sure that your victim will not choke to death while you are focusing on their knee. This means, do your ABCs.

Is the victim going into shock?
Can they breathe?
Are they coherent?
What medical condition do they suffer from?
Are they wearing an emergency I.D. bracelet or necklace?

This is all information that you can relay to the emergency personnel when they arrive

After being sure of the nature of the situation, I would then utilize the most powerful tool in the world, the victim's imagination. If, in your assessment, the wounded person should not be moved (*and in most cases this is true*) then help them to imagine in some way that they are most comfortable not moving. If you have heard a client tell you that they could not move while in your chair, then you know you can do this for someone lying down on a floor. How? Tell them. You would look them straight in the eye and tell them that after they close their eyes they will remain still for just a couple of minutes while you do an assessment. Remember that time distortion is a natural by-product of deep trance so as soon as those eyes close, get your client in a deep, healing trance. They will stay perfectly still until help arrives. You tell them that they must close their eyes because that way they can focus on the areas of their body that you ask questions about.

Now, let's assume that my injured teammate is on the mat and I have gotten her to close her eyes. You'll notice that there is a post hypnotic at work here because I told her that after she closes her eyes she will remain still for a few minutes. I would even get ratification of that hypnotic suggestion by asking her if she will do what I ask so that I can help her. Once she nods her head, I would reinforce the suggestion to remain still and then continue with my work.

"O.K. Alison, as you close your eyes you know you and I can both see that your leg or knee is injured. (*Interesting that at that actual point in time she really can't see it....*) So let's check out the rest of your body to see if there is anything else we need to know. How is your (*pick a healthy body part*)? All right then, your left arm feels just fine? Good. Right from the shoulder down to the fingertips?

At this point, unless contraindicated, I would then touch the fingertips and ask if there is sensation there. As the client answers yes, I would couple a suggestion of growing comfort with this:

"You can feel this touch at your fingertips? Good. Now, I want you to focus on your fingertips as you wiggle those fingers. Good, you are doing great! Now, I want you to allow that arm to remain nice and relaxed for me, ok? Just pretend that your muscles feel so loose and limp and relaxed. That's it! Just keep moving those fingers but let the other muscles relax beautifully and deeply....Now...keep the fingers moving as you relax more and tell me about the toes on (the uninjured leg....)".

(Are you noticing that what I am doing is a disguised progressive relaxation? As I do this, I am loading suggestions for health and healing all along the way.)

Now, one of the most powerful techniques for getting a person away from experiencing pain is to move them in one direction or another on their time line. Physical pain is only experienced in the present so you have a few options: move them forward or backward in time. I prefer to do both.

"Alison, didn't you tell me a while ago about some trip you took to the beach in Greece? Where? Oh, the sand was white? Is it true that when *you are lying on the sand, you can feel the warmth soaking up into your body like you are lying on a big, comfortable heating pad*?"

Now that I have my clients mind in the past and focusing on feelings of comfort, I'm going to have her move into the future and tell me about her next visit to the beach or whatever most effectively captures her attention:

"So Alison, pretend you're back in Greece. *You're lying on the sand feeling the warmth soaking into your body.* If you could go anywhere else in the world, where would you go?"

Now we use a nice technique called future pacing:

"So, once you are all healed, do you think you are going to make plans to go there? Sure... why not? Yeah, while you are healing you can make plans to get there and you can enjoy that as much as your trip to Greece."

Notice that there is some ambiguity here so that her mind can make the most appropriate and powerful connections. The point here is to create a pleasurable and powerful association in her mind. The future looks and feels good and she is connecting that with healing at a subconscious and conscious level. Once I have woven these themes into my client's mind, I then proceed to the next healing step. That is, to make sure that all other modalities applied will benefit her:

"All right Alison, as you can hear, help is arriving. I want you to notice that as they move you around and talk you'll notice that all sights, sounds and sensations that are part of what's happening can actually help you to relax more and more.........because you'll pretty much be concentrating on breathing nice and evenly while you wiggle those pretty fingers...wiggle those fingers.....and notice those good sensations.....once in a while ..... notice how good you feel with your eyes closed...you'll think to yourself that soon this will be over and you'll be home in bed.......such a nice comforting thought, isn't it? ....as you remember how all of this seemed to just pass in a comfortable..... haze............keeping your eyes closed unless the medical personnel ask you to open them........and you know they can only help you to feel better because they are so well trained and everything they do helps you to heal quickly Alison....that's true isn't it?"

The final step is to insure that she can respond appropriately to any questions or requests from doctors and nurses.

"Alison, one of the nice things about how....you are feeling so comfortable right now...is that you can stay beautifully and wonderfully relaxed even when anyone is talking to you or around you. In fact, you'll notice that it is a natural response of the mind and body that nothing will disturb your inner peace of mind. You can answer any questions, and if there is anything else in your body that needs medical attention, you can bring that to the doctor's attention without it disturbing because you are feeling peaceful and relaxed now .....aren't you Alison? Good. You really are doing great and sooner than you think........we'll be looking back on this...talking about how well you've come through all of this....won't we? Yeah, it's a story to tell isn't it?"

The Basics of PANIC

Every situation is unique and challenging. For just as many questions answered by the preceding situation there are just as many raised. For instance, what if a person is screaming in agony? What if there are multiple injuries? In a nutshell, do the best you can. There are questions and scenarios that are best explored during an actual training session and of course only real life experience will truly teach us completely. In the meantime, use your imagination to come up with your best possible response.

How do you do this? You apply your imagination to what you want, not what you don't want. So, this brings us to the nuts and bolts part of this chapter: What is the best way to get what you want in an emergency situation? You follow a fail-safe procedure that always creates effective results.

In NLP there is a technique called reframing. In other words it takes an existing reference and allows a person to use it differently. Briefly stated, what once was a bad thing, is now not as bad or maybe even a good thing. Applying this theory I therefore decided that the best thing to do in any emergency situation was to P.A.N.I.C.

There are 5 steps you need to know. As the acronym P.A.N.I.C. suggests, the first step starts with the letter P. P is for positive. Be positive in everything you say and do. Even if you have never been involved in an emergency situation before, I will tell you how to congruently act positive. In other words, I will show you how to believe in yourself and your ability to help in an emergency situation even though you may never have been in one before. However, it is important for you to have a framework in your mind upon which to build your imagination around. It's like putting walls on a house frame.

Your emergency response frame is:

Positive
Action
Notice
Imagination
Calm, Control & Credentials.

Follow these steps in order and you have a solid, never fail procedure that will help you in any high tension situation.

So how can you realistically act like you can help in a situation you've never been in before? The first and most important thing to realize is this: be positive about not being perfect. So many people do not attempt certain things because they are positive they are not going to be perfect at it the first time. So, reframe it! Celebrate the fact that you are perfectly human and that you will not do a perfect job. Once you realize this deep in your mind, you will then be free to do the best job you can. Once you are positive about not being absolutely perfect in the situation you *will* discover yourself not being nearly as bothered by scared, negative self-talk.

How can you counter some residual negative self-talk? Remind yourself that if you had trained for this kind of work and had been in hundreds of situations like the one you're in, then you could expect a more educated, professional response from yourself.

Now you might be thinking to yourself that this makes sense but what if you're still really nervous? How can you act positive in front of someone who is *really* depending on you? After all, they are looking right at you, aren't they? (*remember my mentioning mental pictures that immobilize?*) In the past, you might have pictured yourself as being the focus of this person's universe and you might even have imagined the disastrous results if you let them down or something like that.

Fire this image into your deep mind: Standing behind you in the eyes of the victim in a crisis is the entire, massive and overall enormously successful United States Medical System.

Now, you are an important part of the medical system that your victim depends upon but you are not all they are focusing on. People who are hurt *really* believe in our medical system. Especially when they are hurt. The good news is that you are just a small part of that system. As soon as you create the image in that person's mind that they are about to be saved by this massive system, your role becomes much less crucial and much easier.

You would have to practically go out of your way to make major errors because of the victim's deep belief in the power of our sophisticated emergency response system. So to feel and therefore act positive, all you have to do is picture yourself as an important but small part of a huge, and I mean huge medical team. By the way, this again is an NLP technique. It is called changing submodalities. You are changing how you represent things in your mind and therefore you are changing the impact of those negative thoughts and images. You are eliminating self-doubt.

With this idea of transforming negative self-talk within your mind, I want you to also change your idea of the kind of impact your suggestions will have on an accident victim. **As a hypnotherapist you know that for a suggestion to work you must have 4 elements working in your favor.** *Trust, Desire, Belief and Concentration.* Of these 4 you have 3 instantly in a crisis situation.

Desire is the single most important key to change. You certainly have desire on the part of the victim. For instance, don't you suppose the man choking next to you in the restaurant desires to stop choking? Of course. Concentration? I don't know about you, but if I was choking and you asked me to pay attention to you so you could help, I believe that you would have my undivided attention.

So how do you get someone to believe in your abilities? You don't. Well, not really. Belief in the life- saving capability of our medical system is your saving grace. "Help is arriving any minute now and you're going to be just fine." Since the person you are helping truly desires to believe that they will be fine, then you utilize their desire and belief . Finally, before we move on to the next step, be positive that you are making some kind of a difference and be assured that you really do have the powerful (*albeit unwitting*) blessing of the entire United State Medical Establishment working on your side.

The second step is to Act, even if you're just clearing your throat (*could you possibly use that as a*

post-hypnotic suggestion to yourself to remain calm?)
while you're trying to think of something to say
besides "HELP! Someone's hurt!" Picture it this way:
to start a chain of events in action it only takes the first
domino to fall. Nature takes care of the rest. So, as the
saying goes, "fake it 'til you make it." It is a known
fact that if you act as though you can do something,
you will begin to believe it.

What is one thing you can do? Ask the person
what their name is. Then use it. "Stephanie, you're
going to be fine."

Act. Act as if the situation is not as bad as it may
be. Act as if you've seen compound fractures a
thousand times. Act alert but nonchalant. Your
beliefs and expectations will influence those beliefs
and expectations of the person you are helping.

So what if you are still doubting your ability to
help? Say the following words to yourself: "I am a
hypnotherapist and this is the kind of situation where
hypnosis can be used." Bear in mind that hypnosis is
the power of words. Just talk to the victim. As a
specially trained healer you know the deep value of
communication. Do *not* underestimate the difference
you can make in someone's life just by talking to them.

Step 3. N is for Notice. Notice what is going on.
There are a few important things to really pay
attention to . A very important thing to notice is what
you can and can not do. For instance, notice if the car
is likely to explode or if the house is going to burn
down, etc.. The reason is that by noticing these things
you will know if you have to move the accident victim.
As previously mentioned, never move someone unless
you have no choice.

Another important thing to notice is how the
victim is responding to your efforts. If what you are

doing is not having *any* kind of positive effect, change what you are doing.

What else can you notice? Look for something that the victim can focus on. If they are in the home, look around for an object or photos that they can talk about. Your purpose here is to distract and ultimately tie up the conscious mind. This is so you can more easily access their subconscious and begin to deliver healing suggestions.

Speaking of that, what can you notice to help deepen and compound suggestions? If it's a car accident, look for something that can be used like the passing of other vehicles or the flashing of ambulance lights. They tend to be hypnotic anyway. The point is to look for something rhythmic. If their breathing is fairly normal, use that. Use the sound of a ticking clock. Listen for music. A rotating overhead fan. Be creative. Be imaginative.

Finally, have your client notice what you tell them to notice: "Notice as I place this cool washcloth on your head how good it feels.... As *you notice that...* you may notice that *you are beginning to relax* just a little bit *more* or perhaps you are noticing that you can allow those forehead *muscles* to *relax more.....*"

Notice all the embedded commands and syntactic ambiguities. Notice how easily this produces trance.

Step 4: Imagination. The most important thing is to imagine yourself making a positive difference in someone's life. One way or another you are using your imagination, so be sure to use it in your favor.

What else should you imagine? Imagine yourself using only words and phrases that are appropriate. *Avoid* words and phrases that can paint damaging pictures. Here are some things you and others around an accident victim should *never* utter: Paralyzed, scarred for life, disfigured, coma, "I don't know if they'll live, "look at all that blood", "I've never seen anything this bad!" I'm sure you get the idea. It's things like this that get the victims imagination working overtime in the wrong direction.

This brings us to our next point in step four: now that we know how to avoid creating damaging images, what can be done to create helpful, healing images? Well, in NLP there is a thing called Pacing and Leading. This is where you step into a person's model of the world (pacing) and you guide them to a better place (leading). This is very similar to the 3 F's. Feel, Felt and Found. "I know how you feel. I have felt the same. I have found that if....." Of course, if you're a man dealing with a pregnant woman, do not try this. On a more serious note, how would a man help a woman about to give birth say, in a car or a bus? You would use a technique of reiteration. You repeat back to a person almost verbatim what they tell you about their situation. "Let me see if I understand you...." or "So what you're telling me is...." or "you said you are experiencing discomfort in your (arm, leg, etc...)

Note: avoid using the word pain. It is a word that actually creates harmful images and feelings.

Your goal is to establish influential communication. Another method to accomplish this is by using Truisms. This alternative method of pacing by actually leading is a classic technique that allows suggestions to zip in virtually undetected. Here's an example:

"You have been sick before?"
"Yes."
"You have recovered every time from sickness?"
(obviously) "Yes."

"You've heard of people being hurt before?"
"Sure."
"So you know that people have been in far worse situations and have come out just fine, right?"
"Sure."
"So you know there is an excellent chance that *you are going to be just fine, right?*"
"Yes."

By the way, never miss a chance to embed a command. You'd be amazed at how powerful they really are. Remember to nod your head in the affirmative as you send in those healing suggestions.

The main point here is this: You are using *your* imagination to powerfully influence the other person's imagination. This is where your training as a hypnotist is most effective.

Finally, imagine yourself using self-hypnosis to prepare for success in any emergency situation.

So here we are at step 5. C is for calm, control and credentials. If nothing else sinks in remember this: Breathe. You'd be amazed at how much calmer you can feel when you breathe. Take a BIG deep breath as soon as those butterflies start flexing their wings in your stomach. That will calm them. If necessary, take a few deep breaths.

Remaining calm is a truly powerful tool. Think of the phrase 'actions speak louder than words.' A calm person is wonderfully reassuring. Additionally, acting calm communicates an impression of competence. You may not have a clue what you're doing but if you're calm about it, the other person will benefit greatly and think you're just great.

Your air of confidence will positively influence the accident victim as well as others around you. This brings us to the issue of control. Someone has to take charge. This is essential. How do you do this? Once people see that you are calm you merely tell them that you are trained for this kind of situation and would they mind helping you? By the way, those are the only credentials you need to deliver

Anyway, remember it is imperative to get gawkers out of the way. Have them form a perimeter some distance around and away from the victim. Give them a mission. Tell them that what they are doing is extremely important because they are protecting the hurt person. You could even drop hints that they could be the first ones to talk to the press. Maybe they'll even be on TV if the news people see them first? Have them find things like blankets, water, pillows, police, phones, Band-Aids, first-aid kits, etc... Doing this not only gets them out of the way but also away from the hurt person. It is amazing how a little dignity can go a long way.

Also, you want people far away because it will be more difficult for an injured person to hear and utilize negative remarks made by gawkers. Remember this: you are isolating the victim so you can deliver pure, positive and powerful suggestions without interference. Do it calmly and with control and you will make an incredible difference in someone's life.

Now you know the 5 steps on how to successfully P.A.N.I.C. in any emergency situation.

Hypnosis is a wonderful tool that truly can change lives. The evidence is before us in black and white. As a hypnotist you are a healer and should an emergency situation ever arise, you now have the information to create a positive change in someone's life.

Walk with the Angels.

11

Impotence: The Hidden Pain
Hypnosis Can Help

Copyright 1999 C. Devin Hastings

Impotence is a subject that is difficult for many to deal with because it is an uncomfortable subject. However, it is an area where you as a hypnotist can truly make a difference in a person's life. So as you read this chapter bear in mind that there are two benefits you will derive: First you will learn how to expand your healing skills to profoundly help people. Secondly, you are going to find out how to significantly increase your income.

Let's focus on enhancing your healing skills for a moment. People who come to see you for impotence are in pain. When you help a person or a couple to restore fundamental intimacy to their relationship you have powerfully helped to change their lives for the better.

As a healer you help to alleviate pain. Therefore, you need to understand how an impotence sufferer is in pain and how you can help. I will explain this to you. Additionally you will learn about the different types of impotence. This serves two

237

purposes. The first is you will have credibility in the eyes of your client. They will believe that you know what you're talking about. Secondly, if you convey an understanding of a person's problem and tell them you know how to fix it, they will tend to believe you.

In order for you to be able to communicate these things to your client you must know how to establish, from the beginning, clear and professional communications. How to do this will be clearly explained later in this chapter. Part of being a consummate professional is being aware of certain things that you must do and certain things you must never do. Forewarned is indeed forearmed. Interpersed in this chapter you will also learn of a few, shall we say, interesting case studies. Experience is a great teacher.

Finally, you can expect to know how to easily establish rapport and legitimacy with medical professionals in your area. As a bonus I have included a few crucial points that will help you to secure clients and many referrals.

Keep this in mind: you are helping people in a powerful manner that actually has been documented to have lasting effects. You are saving these people money because their other choice is to keep paying for drugs. That means paying financially and physically. (*By the way, feel free to use the preceding line of reasoning when presenting your services to a prospective client.*) For this you deserve to be well-compensated.

Now, what did a very popular anti-impotence drug promise to do? It promised to successfully change millions of people's lives in a cost-effective and safe manner. Millions and millions of dollars have been spent on this product because of the amount of pain that would be eliminated and the amount of pleasure experienced. Did it work? For some. Here's the catch: what if the drug does not address the cause of the impotence? It won't work. Let's look at the facts: In the first 3 months of its release, Viagra sales exceeded $410 million . By the end of the following quarter, its sales had fallen to $141 million.

What do these statistics mean to you as a hypnotist? They tell you loud and clear that you have a lot of potential clients out there with a demonstrated history of spending their money on a solution to their problems. All of these men suffer from a hidden pain called impotence and they want an answer. Just think, they were willing to try a drug that for some had very serious health consequences. Read between the lines here: They are willing to try just about anything. This is good news! Here's another exciting thing to think about: what if you could attract some of the market that is already using Viagra? In other words, those men will still continue to use the drug but what if you can somehow use your skills to help them? A point to give very serious consideration.

Now, with these thoughts in mind of how many people there are that you can help and you know that they are looking for an answer, what do you do? Well, first of all you learn how to help them and then you let them know about your skills. The remainder of this chapter will be dedicated to giving you the information necessary to effectively help men suffering from impotence. You can even help those people suffering from impotence due to vascular injury or disease. Also, as I mentioned, I will share with you some sure-fire techniques on how to build your client base.

Please understand this caveat very carefully: You must always have a doctors approval before working with anybody in any manner what so ever that is medically related. *This includes making sure your client has had a proper medical examination.* Furthermore, you should never engage in a practice or give advice that in any way contradicts advice or instructions given by a duly licensed medical professional. Finally, the information given in this chapter is not meant to be taken as medical advice. The information provided is to be utilized within your professional capacity as a hypnotist only. You are not practicing allopathic medicine. You are practicing hypnosis.

All right then. Let's move on to the business of how you can help someone suffering from impotence. First of all let's define our focus. This article is dealing with impotence as it afflicts males. Due to a variety of reasons not the least of which being today's law-suit happy society, I do not work with women when it comes to sexual issues. Obviously, the context changes a bit if you the reader, are a woman. All the techniques used are non-gender specific. The only thing that changes is the reference material.

Speaking of techniques, I do want to mention that some of the methods I will be referring to are advanced in nature. Since this chapter is focusing exclusively on the hypnotic treatment of impotence it is assumed that the reader is either familiar with the techniques mentioned or can learn them. If you want to learn more about these advanced techniques I suggest you consult the following three sources: *The Miracles of Hypnosis* by Kevin Hogan. It is a phenomenal 12-tape guide to creating powerful hypnotic change. Another excellent source for highly

effective   hypnotherapeutic   techniques   is
Hypnoanalytic Techniques by John G. Watkins.   The
third source I recommend is *Heart of the Mind* by Steve
and Connirae Andreas. This is an NLP text.

Before we move on to the actual hypnosis
applications I want to cover something else that is very
interesting.   A short while ago I mentioned that it
appeared that Viagra had not addressed the cause of
some men's impotence. So guess what? According to
an article in the Florida Orlando Sentinel dated on May
23rd, 1999 there is a new drug for impotence! The
article goes on to talk about how this new drug called
Uprima , generically called apomorphine, targets the
brain instead of the peripheral nervous system.
Specifically this drug will help send electrical
impulses from the hypothalamus in the brain down
through the spinal cord to increase blood flow to the
penis. Do you remember that I mentioned you could
tap the existing Viagra market?   Here's how: tell
people that are already using Viagra that they can try
you're all natural method of hypnotic visualization
before trying *another* drug that *may* also have serious
side effects. In other words, state that it is possible to
create a similar beneficial effect as apomorphine but
without the serious cost financially and physically.
People have a history of doubling up on drugs if they
think they will obtain an increased benefit.   That is
terrific leverage for you. If someone thinks that your
skills can enhance the effect of a drug they are taking
and they want it bad enough, you have a ready made
client.

Also, for those potential clients that tried and
gave up on Viagra, suggest that you have an
alternative that can possibly create a beneficial
response similar to that of apomorphine. I suggest you

use the generic name because that helps you to avoid any name infringement.

Before I provide powerful evidence that supports the idea that a similar effect to that ascribed to apomorphine can be obtained using hypnosis, I would like you to consider this: think of the visualization already associated to the drug. 'Electrical impulses (travelling) from the hypothalamus in the brain down through the spinal cord to increase blood flow to the penis.' As a hypnotist you know that the most powerful sex organ is the mind. Imagine if you had millions of dollars to promote hypnosis as an answer to impotence. What would be a better publicly- acceptable visual than the one described? Aren't you glad Takeda Chemical Industries Ltd. of Japan and Abbot Laboratories Inc. are doing your advertising? As Kevin Hogan states: "Never pay for your advertising when someone else will."

Now I said that I would provide the proof that you can use to show to a potential client. Please remember that according to a published description of the effects of apomorphine, what happens is that signals are sent from the brain to the genitals generating a response. Look at the reality of the statement. An incredible generalization has been used to help create in a person's mind a specific effect. Milton Erickson would be proud. This also leaves you a lot of room to show how you can help.

Here's what you do: First quote a success statistic such as.... "Crasilneck (1977, 1979b) reported another follow-up study of 100 cases; 87 reported freedom from the problem (impotence) 1 year after the termination of treatment." *Clinical Hypnosis: Principles and Applications (P.385) by Harold B. Crasilneck, Ph.D and James A. Hall, M.D.*

You can add the following: "Damacer, Shor, and Orne (1963) observed that physiological changes occurred consistently in hypnotically requested emotions". *Clinical Hypnosis: Principles and Applications (P.21) by Harold B. Crasilneck, Ph.D and James A. Hall, M.D.*

Then, you quote medically verified evidence that hypnosis can help a person to alter blood flow (*think of the implied image here*): "Some dentists and oral surgeons have found that under hypnosis a bleeding tooth socket can be caused to bleed more or less profusely by the appropriate suggestions."*Clinical Hypnosis: Principles and Applications by Harold B. Crasilneck, Ph.D and James A. Hall, M.D.*

You can also tell your client the following: "Erection and ejaculaton can even occur in a paraplegic with complete transection of the spinal cord." *Clinical Hypnosis: Principles and Applications (P.175) by Harold B. Crasilneck, Ph.D and James A. Hall, M.D.*

You then sum all of this up by asking your client if they now see how *hypnosis can create effects extremely similar to that of drugs...minus the side effects.*

Finally, ask your client if whatever drug they are taking can help them to emotionally get over the feeling of discouragement that they have felt as a result of their sexual dysfunction. At this point you must be very aware of unconscious signals provided by the client. If the eyes become watery or misty or if you notice flushing of the face or ears or even slight tremors in the lips or chin, you have hit an emotional hot button. Some men will of course state that if their equipment begins to work again then there are no problems. These are the guys who really need your services. Be aware that there will be an occasional client who truly can move past their difficulty but they are rare. As always, agree with your clients because you know that in trance you can learn the real deal from their subconscious.

So now you have some interesting information on the advertising angle and you have a good idea of how to present compelling facts to persuade someone that you can help them.

The next thing to do is to get about the business of letting your client know exactly how you can help them. Remember the old sales technique of telling your client what your going to do; tell them your doing it and then let them know you have done it. This fits in neatly with Gerald Keins' maxim for suggestion effectiveness: compound, compound, and compound those suggestions even more.

Now let's talk about emotional impact. When someone calls you or walks into your office, what are they feeling? Well, you can definitely expect a great deal of embarrassment. From my experience I estimate that 1 in 15 people are able to express themselves with any kind of ease. Remember the expression, "Big boys don't cry." For many men, they have ignored a deep physical and emotional need. This only makes the situation worse. When a man walks into your office for impotence bear in mind that he is suffering emotionally as well as physically. Ask yourself how you like to feel rejected. Then realize that these people are experiencing rejection from their own body and perhaps from a mate as well. Frustration, isolation and loneliness are key emotions that you will see quite often. By the way, I have found it quite useful to use them as affect bridges to get to the heart of the matter.

Consider this next rather graphic point carefully and you will really begin to understand your client: How would you feel if you had to inject your genitals with a needle in order to have sex? What kind of self-esteem would you have?

What kind of self-esteem would you have especially if you had been to see other professionals who could not help you? Add to that a profound ignorance on the part of most men who suffer from this affliction. They just don't understand what is happening and therefore *they really feel out of control of an essential part of their identity.*

Let me share with you what this means. Very simply it means that you have a powerful and simple way to establish rapport with your client. Show them that you have a deep understanding of their situation and that very quickly they will also have an understanding of what is happening with them. You will then see the hope that they feel at being able to understand and therefore *control* what is going on. Think of your client being in a car without a steering wheel. Then, due to your skills they suddenly have the ability to steer the vehicle. Now, I wouldn't want you to possibly use this as some sort of metaphor or anything of the sort.......steering wheels being rather firm and all that. So now that your client feels that they can again get behind the wheel of their mental/physical vehicle, what do they need to know in order to do this? First, they need to know what type of impotence they have. So you explain that there are four kinds:

(1) Physical
(2) Psychological

(3) Mixed

(4) Unknown.

As far as I have been able to determine, unknown causes fit into the psychological category and mixed causes is self-explanatory.

What are the major causes of physical impotence? First, there are diseases of the blood vessels such arteriosclerosis, hypertension and high cholesterol. Part of this category includes venous leakage. This occurs when the penile veins are unable to close off properly during an erection. However, this is something that a doctors examination should have discovered.

The second leading cause of impotence is diabetes. This disease can damage both blood vessels (*in it's advanced stages*) and nerves. When nerves are affected, the brain cannot properly transmit the sexual stimuli that create an erection.

Also note that even during the early stages of diabetes extremely high blood sugar levels can cause a significant decrease in arousal and response.

Finally, another cause of physical impotence is, of course, actual bodily injury involving the spine and/or genitals.

At this point you may be wondering just how many things do you need to find out about your client. I have good news for you. At the end of this chapter you will be provided with a check-list of questions and a sample script from a case study.

So what is another common physical cause of impotence? Prescription drugs. There are roughly some 200 different drugs that can cause impotence. Pay attention to this concept: As people age they tend to use more and more medication. So when you have a client who may be advanced in years do not automatically attribute a lack of sexual response to their age. Look at their past and present drug history. And let them know this! Many people have been hypnotized into believing that when they get older they just start to fall apart. This simply is not true. There are many people in their 70's, 80's and even older who enjoy active sex lives.

While we're on the subject of drugs it is important to realize that substance abuse is another cause of impotence. And speaking of substance abuse, there is also this to consider: In a report in a 1994 American Journal of Epidemiology it was reported that men with diets high in caffeine, nicotine, sugar and alcohol experience a comparable amount of erectile dysfunction as do men who use recreational drugs.

Now let's move on to the psychological causes of impotence. By the way, this is where a properly conducted intake can greatly improve your chances of success. Here's one reason why: You install powerful hope into your client. One way to do this is to help your client gain a better perspective on his situation. You do this by asking for a percentage of *successful* attempts at intercourse or whatever is his exact presenting problem. By focusing on successful attempts you are already beginning the reframing process.

Of course, if the answer is zero or darn near it, then you know you first have to do some ego-building before attempting other hypnotic change.

While eliciting information from your client another very important thing to obtain from them is what they consider to be a mental representation of their problem. If you do this skillfully enough you will have a powerful metaphor as presented by their subconscious.   Many times I have found this metaphor-elicitation technique to ultimately provide critical information.   Something that I have found fascinating is how this metaphor will change according to context.   For instance, one man I assisted had a metaphor of a tired horse in a pen when he talked about his feelings of impotence *as they related to his wife*.   He loved her dearly but could only sustain an erection when he engaged in masturbation by himself. Here's the other metaphor he presented when he could maintain an erection: The pen was gone and the horse had a special place that it went to run in.   Even though this at first appeared like a superficial case it was hardly that.   A great deal of abreactive therapy actually occurred before I could do direct suggestion work to change his physiology.

   With the idea in mind that the subconscious will always leave clues to the cause, most of those clues fit into the following psychological causes:

   Stress--the bad kind.   Such as divorce stress.   I had a client whose ex-wife delivered powerful impotency suggestions.   She did this while they were in bed. That is definitely below-the-belt hypnosis.   A fair bit of regressive hypnoanalysis was required to discover this because he had buried this information with good memories of her.

   Financial stress will cause a man to see himself as less than a man and this inner image, of course, can wreak havoc.   Knowing this, you must remain alert to subtle signals from the client or spouse (if she is present) for what I call the echo-effect.   This is evidenced by the wife echoing her husbands feelings. I know this because I have had many wives tell me that their passion fades when their husbands are not doing well financially.

The stress of guilt is another very common cause. Let me caution the female reading this: Do not jump to this soap opera explanation of a man's impotence. It does occur but not as often as the media and other purveyors of guilt would have you think. And remember, as a healer you do not judge. If your personal feelings get in the way of your helping someone, refer them out to another professional.

Another psychological cause of impotence is depression. The causes for depression are manifold. An example of this is a very poignant case history of a client who had become impotent after he and his wife started trying to have another baby. The heart-breaking part of this story is that the couple had lost a child 5 years previously and the man was so hurt by the experience that, in his words: "....it hurts so much to think of the possibility of losing another one that *I can not conceive of another child.*" Indeed, he could not. How was this man's situation finally resolved? First and foremost a great deal of grief counseling was necessary. Though this father had gone to a counselor who had eventually pronounced him 'cured' all he had done was learned what was expected of him in terms of how men deal with this kind of thing. Obviously he was not cured if the thought of having another child frightened him to his core. After grief-counseling which included death-bed therapy, the father was then guided in such a manner so that he could allow time to heal his wounds. I utilized many NLP and hypnosis techniques in order to help accomplish in a period of 1 1/2 months what could have taken years. I also utilized death-resolution methods that are extremely healing but must be approached with an open mind. To get an idea of these , please refer to the excellent 2 volume set, *Regression Therapy, A Handbook for Professionals* by Winafred Blake Lucas, Ph.D.

To sum up so far, the major psychological causes of impotence are stress and/or depression. And remember, when dealing with your client it is imperative that no matter what the cause of the impotence, you must be clear and professional in your communications. One of the things that gets in the way of this is nervousness on the part of the hypnotist. A good way to deal with this is through post-hypnotic suggestions to yourself to maintain a calm and detached yet empathetic state toward this issue. Another thing that helps a hypnotist to feel calm and professional is to be thoroughly familiar with this topic. Additionally, it helps to remember that what you are primarily dealing with is an emotional situation. When a person focuses on the physical aspect of the problem it can cause feelings of discomfort. Therefore, it is important to remind yourself that focusing on the emotional aspect of this work will tend to draw a healers heart more into the process.

To be perfectly blunt with those of you who are feeling queasy remember, you are helping to heal a heart, not a penis. You can do this by perhaps thinking of the situation as a kind of phobia or anxiety problem.

Help the man understand that the odds are in his favor of improvement but do *not* bore him with numbers. Make numbers their friend. For example, did you know that an estimated 20 million men suffer from impotence? If you are clever, you will then do a powerful reframe with your client by making him one in 20 million rather than one alone in his world. Make sure he pictures this because this causes a re-perception of his situation.   Be sure to remind him that there is strength in numbers and that when enough people want something, they get it.

So what do you do if your client states that their doctor said their condition is permanent, incurable or progressively worsening but they're trying you as a last resort?   You use one of the most subtle and powerful tools in any hypno-salesmen's tool-kit: the yes set. But you are even more sneaky than the guy who sold you the underwater basket weaving set. You do it unconsciously.   Let me tell you the plan: your plan is to get your client to unequivocally question the predictive suggestions given to him. Before launching this stealth attack against limiting beliefs, do be sure that your client has a leg to stand on, so to speak. Make sure your client has the all the proper pieces in place so to speak. *(I had a man one time who was quite physically challenged with missing parts and he thought I could perform a major miracle in the form of a regrowth of certain parts.)*

Once you are certain you have a chance of success, here is how you proceed: First, you ask your client if they think that any sane doctor would state that "If excessive smoking actually plays a role in the production of lung cancer, it seems to be a minor one." *(Dr. W.C. Heuper of the National Cancer Institute as quoted in the New York Times, April 14, 1954)* When they say, "No, of course no sane doctor would say that!", you then ask, Then if a doctor did say that, perhaps it means that some doctors don't always make accurate predictions, right?   Once you get their agreement you then pounce (gently) on them with the good doctor's name and the institute he worked for. Then you set them up for the next brick to be taken out of the wall of iatrogenically induced limiting beliefs.

You do this by asking the following question: "What if a doctor actually stated that "For the majority of people, smoking has a beneficial effect." *(Los Angeles Surgeon, quoted in Newsweek, November 18, 1963.)* what would you think? If they need even more proof of how many experts are wrong, they can read the 392 page book, <u>The Experts Speak</u> by Christopher Cerf and Victor Navasky, Pantheon books, New York. This book features most noted experts being wrong about almost every major event, discovery, and human endeavor of the past seven thousand years.

Moving on from there, you are now ready to collapse the wall of limiting beliefs that they have anchored to these incredible authority figures. Here's how to bring down the Berlin Wall of Idiocy: You do it by analogy. By metaphor. By telling a story with these basic ingredients: If one car mechanic tells you that your car is broken beyond repair and impossible to fix and yet another mechanic states your car can be fixed and has in fact repaired cars with problems just like yours, which do you believe? Which mechanic would you spend your money on? You can deepen the power of this metaphor by having the client use their own car and a mechanic they dislike and one they trust. (Emotion sells!) When you get your answer, then you whip out even more statistics about how hypnosis has constantly proven traditional predictions wrong. You do this while reminding them of their trusted mechanic.....while they are looking right at you....

Then you clinch the sale with the final yes: Which mechanic would you rather spend your money on? *(A rhetorical question because you already have the answer!! Yes!!!)*

Your client has now been sold on the idea that they can gain control of their situation because you, as a competent information source, have shown them a path around their discouraging beliefs. Furthermore, you have given evidence that you are their trusted mechanic who can fix the problem.

Now what? Well, before proceeding on with the heart of the cure, you must know what you can and must not do. First of all, always listen for clues. Do this from the moment they walk in. Also, do be sure that your client is reasonably mentally stable. Your intuition will help you a great deal if you listen. One time I had a man go off into a world of non-sequiturs and bizarre body movements when he supposedly got into trance. To defuse this situation, I set off my burglar alarm. It was amazing how fast he came back to this world.

To sum up, be thorough and attentive. Be professional. Be aware of your limits *and potential.* The hope you project can be a balm to your client's soul. So healing and soothing.

Now let's move on to a few don'ts: Don't make false promises. Do not work with anyone who has any kind of medical condition be it emotional or physical, without a proper referral. Do not be afraid to ask for a referral.

Another thing to avoid: *never, ever, prescribe* anything. Even if it's aspirin or vitamins. To do so is a grievous mistake that crosses a clearly defined legal boundary. What I do is refer to published, verifiable research and I always say that whatever you do, it must be with your doctor's consent.

Following this line of safe reasoning, it is imperative that you *never diagnose.* If someone you talk to describes symptoms that scream at you with an obvious diagnosis, don't be tempted to diagnose unless you are a medical doctor.

All Right! You've got a good marketing concept, a good understanding of your client's point of view, some good tips and techniques to use to persuade your client, some good statistics to quote, some interesting case histories to learn from, some very clearly dropped hints for hypnotherapeutic success and of course the warning buoys. Things to avoid so you don't become bait for a lawyer.

How do you put all of this together? With a good protocol outline. Your client walks into your office and here's what you do:

I. Establish Rapport by empathizing with client. Do this by establishing clear and professional communications with a good understanding of their situation.

II. Case Analysis. Ask questions to elicit pertinent information. Determine if you can help and if you can, demonstrate to the client how you can. Do waking suggestions.

Give Hope. Break down the walls of limiting beliefs. Remember! If you are uncomfortable with the person in your office, move them on.

III. Hypnoanalysis: Do the tough work. More often than not, hypno-investigations will reveal a cause. Use whatever you can to ameliorate the cause.

Be prepared to cry. Crying clears the soul. Is it possible that tears we shed actually reflect those that need to be shed by our client?

Additionally, remember the power of hypnosis has been shown to create powerful effects so keep the door to your subconscious open. Be Creative!!

IV. Closure: Healing The Wound by moving your client into the future using future-pacing hypnotic metaphor, imagery and suggestion.

To sum up, become an ally with your client and then help them to find the cause of their problem. Often, this will bring insight which, in some cases, can effect a cure by itself without conscious intervention.

Now, before I close this chapter, I would like to share with you a questionnaire, a script and information that- talks about standard impotence treatments

Impotence Questionnaire

Remember, the purpose of these questions is manifold. First, you are gathering information to determine if this person is genuine. Second, you're determining if you can be of assistance. Be realistic. That will earn you respect. Third, you are creating rapport. Fourth, you are installing a sense of hope in your client. Fifth, you are beginning the hypnotic change process while gathering important information.

1)   How do you know you are experiencing impotence?   (*This is not a silly question. Many men have thought that not responding once, or twice or even a few times equals impotence.*)

2)   Have you seen a Medical Doctor.?   What has the Dr. said to you?   (*This sets you up to ask for the referral which you must have before proceeding with any hypnotherapy.*)

3)   What medications and/or treatment are you using?

(This gives you the opportunity to establish in your client's mind that you know what you are talking about. Hence, rapport. Also, this is when you can begin to give them an optimistic view of their situation. You accomplish this by letting them know that they can have control over their condition and they don't need to feel helpless by depending on doctors.)

4)   Have you been checked for diabetes? Is there a history of diabetes in your family? *(Remember, up to 60% of all diabetics suffer from impotence and there are roughly 8 million undiagnosed diabetics out there. Also, at this point in your mind you should be noticing physical factors that predispose a person to impotence. Obesity in particular because of all the typical concurrent problems such as high blood pressure, Type II diabetes, high cholesterol and so on.)*

5)   What other problems *(notice how open ended this is....)* have you experienced in the past? *(Think about it....if you do this well, you are setting up your client to regress for you right there. Once they are in trance, it will be easier to enlist their subconscious mind to help you find the answer. Plus you are getting information that may prove to be crucial!)*

6)   Have you had any stressful events occur within the last 3 years? 5 yrs? 10 yrs? *(Again, going for some kind of regression....you'd be amazed how many times I have had clients regress to cause without the benefit of any so-called induction! Look for anger! Remember, once they are really thinking about a past event, they are in a some kind of trance and go straight to the cause.)*

Key Point: At this stage, you should be very alert to those small tell-tale signs of significant information. Expect their subconscious to give you the information you need to help them change!

7)   Can you think of any relationship issues you have had in the past? Has this ever happened before? *(With the medical questions you are ferreting out any physical causes......with the relationship questions you are looking for possible emotional causes...of all kinds including self-inflicted punishment.   Notice that this question follows the others that are normally less threatening to answer.)*

8)   What does it mean to you that you are experiencing this difficulty?   *(Listen carefully....any family identification?)*

9)   What will it mean for you once you come through this experience? *(go ahead, laugh.....but it works! Plus, you have a good idea of how to set up their future. Better still, the subconscious will reveal where they really want to be.   This is to be viewed relative to sexual preference as well as other issues.   One other point, if they don't project themselves successfully overcoming this problem, find out why!)*

Script For Impotence Stress

Please note: this script is to follow after you have done your induction and deepening, etc...
All right John,   as you hear the sound of my voice allow yourself to begin to drift even deeper into a state

of wonderful, relaxing trance.....allowing all stress, tension and anxiety to flow from your body as you focus on the sound of my voice and all other sounds and sensations fading away becoming unimportant....as you once again.... begin to fully enjoy this state of healing mind John, I want you to think about your breathing.....

notice how even and relaxed your breath goes in and out, naturally in and out enjoying the natural rhythm your body has built into it...And as you relax more and more into a deep sleep allow your mind to focus on your body's natural ability to heal itself....thinking how when we nick our fingers the mind and body naturally, easily join forces to heal deeply inside John........

So, since your body does indeed have a deep wisdom to heal deeply inside John....then, how many different ways can it help you to go deep inside naturally, easily w/ pleasure feeling firm.... in your resolve to...now enjoy sex John....Remembering it is your right to now enjoy sex John....Finding it easy to....

Reject negative thoughts...Finding it easy to....

Reject negative thoughts....Finding it easy to....

Finding it easy to....Remember a time when you had a wonderful powerful, passionate love with your wife on your 2nd honeymoon...(your current partner, former lover, whatever. You should have a least one time to prompt client with.....get it from the intake...feed it back to him...in detail....try it, it works!)

(Remember to anchor a positive response with a post-hypnotic!)

Now John, as you find yourself more and more remembering these past wonderful times you are discovering you are forgetting the negative memories.....

the negative memories naturally fading away as you remember more and more positive ones...As you think more and more of the past, wonderful sex you have had with your wife you are feeling yourself.....looking forward to a future of deep, rewarding pleasure with your wife.....

You are feeling yourself with pleasure ... looking forward to a future of deep, pleasure with your wife.....Feeling your body surge with pleasure as the blood in your body naturally goes to where it belongs...

Allowing your mind and body to function naturally, easily, automatically sending blood to exactly where it belongs.....

Now....as you go deeper John....

Allowing yourself to experience a sense, a feeling, a certainty that your health is improving...

Feeling deep inside with pleasure as your body begins to function normally with health, for the rest of your life.....

(Emerge Your Client at this point.)

Standard Impotence Treatments

Obviously we must be familiar with any specialty area with which we are working with our clients. What follows are the current and standard treatments for sufferers of impotence. Whether you are working with people who suffer from impotence, pain relief or tinnitus, you should always be completely versed in standard and current treatments of whatever issue is presented to you or you should probably refer your client with someone that has a greater breadth and depth of knowledge in a particular area.

One method is vacuum devices. Now don't go out and tell your clients to grab the Hoover and expect miracles!

There is a device called the ErecAid System. Essentially, it creates a vacuum around the penis and this causes blood to flow into it.

Then, a tension ring that was slipped around the device is moved onto the base of the penis. This effectively traps the blood in the penis for as long as 30 minutes.

Depending on whose literature you read, this is a good thing or a bad thing. According to one manufacturer:

"With some men, minor side effects can occur, such as petechiae and ecchymosis. Petechiae (little red spots) are caused by placing the penis under negative pressure too rapidly. The penis may need to be reconditioned slowly after a prolonged period of inactivity. Eccymosis is a bruise caused by the penis being held under vacuum too long. Neither condition is painful nor serious....."

By the way, this device is NOT recommended for men who have sickle cell anemia, leukemia or blood clotting problems.

Remember, it is not your job to recommend any of these treatments to your clients.

Just be aware of what they are.

Viagra aka Sildenafil:

How does it work? Simply stated, it is an erection enhancer.

It does not cause erections but rather, it helps men to attain one when sexually stimulated. It does this by regulating vasodilation in the penis.

It is know as a phosphodiesterase 5 inhibitor. (aka PDE5).

PDE5 is an enzyme found mainly in the penis. This enzyme is antagonistic to cyclic GMP, which is the chemical responsible for increased blood flow and hence for erections.

Last I read, Viagra is around $10 a pill.

And last but not least...

Penile Injections and Implants

Let's face facts: neither of these is a great alternative. Implants require surgery and are now regarded as a last resort because they are the most invasive. Can you imagine how terrified a person must be to choose surgery over hypnosis?

The chemicals injected have a few different actions.

There are currently 3 different chemicals used. The first is Papaverine. It is an alkaloid derived from opium and essentially acts as a smooth muscle relaxant in the corpus cavernosa. This allows for increased blood flow.

The second chemical used for injections is Prostaglandin E1. Besides acting as a smooth muscle relaxant its action is similar to Viagra's in that it encourages an increase in cyclic GMP.

Finally, there is Phentolamine which is an alpha blocker. What this means for you and me is that it blocks the hypertensive effects of epinepherine and norepinephrine.

Do those words *(epinepherine and norepinephrine)* make you think of any over-the-counter drugs that Americans consume by pound? For colds, hayfever, etc...

Did you know that epinepherine is also known as adrenaline? When do we produce adrenaline? When we are stressed.

Do you know what adrenaline does? It causes increased blood pressure among many other powerful effects. Norepinepherine also increases blood pressure.

Now, think about what most impotence treatments attempt to do.....reduce hypertension. So, just reducing a person's stress can go a long way towards helping them....Right? By the way, those 3 chemicals are many times mixed in one package for a man to inject into the base of his penis.

Side effects of these injections can include burning and sometimes fibrosis of the penis.

Alternative Impotence Treatments....

You may be familiar with Yohimbe. It is shown to increase libido and shorten the latency period between ejaculations. The New England Journal of Medicine in 1981 also reported that yohimbe enhances the erectile function in patients with diabetic neuropathy.

In the August, 1987 issue of Lancet, a double blind placebo study was conducted which found that men suffering from any form of impotence showed a 62% improvement with yohimbe.

Again, let me stress that this is something your client's doctor should prescribe and oversee. So what are some everyday supplements that help? Nutrients such as vitamins C, E, zinc and essential fatty acids play an important role in a man's normal sexual function. All of these are needed to form both sperm and seminal fluid and are found in especially high levels in the prostate gland. Raw pumpkin seeds are one good source of zinc and essential oils.

One study indicates that 60 mg per day of ginkgo extract increased penile arterial flow in a group of patients who did not respond to papaverine injections.

Half of those participants regained potency within six months.

This brings me to an important point: If your client is looking for instant solutions tell him shots are about the quickest.

Otherwise, give him post hypnotic suggestions for patience.

Other herbs noted for their effects are ginseng and saw palmetto. Ginseng comes in many varieties but the ones you want to be aware of are: Siberian and Korean or the Chinese Red or White. There are other varieties like Panax Quinquefolius which is grown here in the states and very calming.

Saw Palmetto is noted primarily for its ability to maintain the prostate gland's proper hormone balance which is especially beneficial for older men.

Additionally, an optimally functioning prostate gland is needed for the biochemical and mechanical aspects of erectile function.

Remember, always refer to published studies and findings rather than prescribing. Just knowing about these alternatives will make you more competent because many of your clients know a little bit about them but they can always use more information to feel more in control.

12

Past Life Regression Therapy

Past Life Regression Therapy (PLRT) is a systematic, therapeutic model used in hypnosis to uncover suppressed, repressed and sublimated information which may be responsible for somatic phenomena, negative or harmful behavioral patterns, or life choices which are no longer serving the clients' best interests. It is at once an art, a skill and a science.

Once this information is retrieved through careful and meticulous regression techniques, it becomes the thoughtful task of the therapist to sensitively assist the client to understand this material as a reflection of their current life pattern. It is often difficult for the client to embrace the esoteric meaning of the regression, for the information and emotions can be painful or uncomfortable to confront. Remember, these memories or stories contain insights too powerful to be immediately incorporated. It takes a skilled therapist to reframe and interpret the information for the client. Sometimes that which is most clear and straightforward to the therapist is completely rejected by the client. The client has spent many years or many lifetimes keeping this significant information just out of reach of their conscious mind.

Past Life Regression Therapy is *not* a religion and not even a philosophical perspective. Many of my clients do not embrace reincarnation as part of their primary belief system. However, for some 3/4 of the earth's population, it is integrated into their religious ideology. For the rest it is an easy task, not even much of a challenge, to explain PLRT as a metaphoric tool created by the subconscious to elucidate issues which are either too painful or too distressing for the client to directly embrace. I have come to recognize three primary types of regressions.

First, and most common, is the historic regression. The client can identify the time and place in history, however loosely. They are rarely kings and queens, or power mongers. The average person has average past lives. This is not a value judgment. Royalty has the same lessons to learn - they just get to learn them in the public eye.

Archetypal (well known, heroic or dramatic characters in history and mythology) regressions are the most difficult to deal with and require a gentle hand and lots of reframing. In these regressions clients recall themselves to be Christ or his disciples, King Arthur or Morgaine, Napoleon or Peter the Great. You see the pattern. It is possible, of course that Napoleon is indeed seated in your office doing a past life regression. It is, however, rather unlikely. The information retrieved from these regressions must be reframed. They are valuable and important regressions and it is important for you, the therapist, to see the thread of emotion which drew your client to this archetypal realm. The work is valid, the emotions are real, but the package must be honorably released or we have, in effect, created a new dysfunctional ego state. This is the area where I have done the most patch-up work from other regressionists who do not recognize the appearance of archetype material.

The metaphoric regression is the third and most useful interpretation to use when working with clients who do not embrace reincarnation as a belief system. You may be using more conservative methods when it becomes clear to you that the most effective and efficient approach to a client's therapeutic process is PLRT. If your client is uncomfortable with the notion of past lives it is easy to explain PLRT as a metaphoric tool: "Your subconscious mind will generate pictures and emotions which will be profoundly relevant to you. The story you entertain in your mind will hold significant information, which will aid you in interpreting that which is presently occurring in your life." This explanation opens the PLRT door to many who would otherwise have rejected it based on their religious doctrine.

On initial interview, many clients will present survival mechanisms, behaviors based on religious doctrine or coping behaviors no longer required in the present circumstances or present lifetime. These behaviors persist as integral parts of the clients's personality until, using PLRT, they are able to isolate these behavior patterns and uncover their origins. Once the client has observed these dysfunctional patterns from the vantage-point of PLRT, they are often eager to release the pattern in their present-day lives.

There are, of course, many ways to accomplish similar outcomes, however PLRT has many unique advantages. The first and probably the most important is that the charged emotions and traumatizing events are far enough removed from their everyday life to make the retrieval process relatively easy. Secondly, the majority of clients have no idea how powerful this work can be. The result of their under-estimation is that there is little resistance. Clients can't hide from that which is unknown.

It is important to note that one could make several fine correlations between present time regression therapy such as the somatic bridge used in ego state therapy and dissociative conditions and PLRT. However I feel it is of utmost importance to keep these two types of regression in separate categories. It is the differences between the two which define them. It is definitely possible to use ego state therapy in subsequent sessions, but it would be wise to view these two approaches as separate, equally valuable tools in the therapeutic paradigm.

What brings a PLRT client to your door?

Many people seeking a PLRT are unaware of the driving force behind their curiosity. Their lives *seem* to be fine. Often they exhibit no outward signs of distress, depression or illness. They come seeking answers through what promises to be a fascinating journey to past lives. Here are some of the more conscious reasons clients will seek out a PLRT.
- Connections with people they are considering relationships with.
"I looked in his eyes and I melted. We must have been lovers in a past life"
- Connections with friends or lovers that have recently ended.

"If I can prove we were lovers in the past, perhaps I can persuade him/her to come back. I just know we're soul mates and are meant to be together"

- Information concerning family members; especially recently departed ones.

"I just want to know if we were together in a past life. It would be great if I never have to incarnate with that nasty uncle again." Or "I know my mother and I have been in opposite roles. I would love to remember what she was like as my daughter because I often feel like her parent now."

- A reassurance that they have had more adventurous lives.

"Was I ever *not* bored? Was there ever a time when I was free to make my own decisions?"

- Gender-based questions.

"I was never a man/woman! Was I?"

- Reasons to remain in or begin relationships with uncertain futures.

"It feels as if we have done this all before. Can you help me find out if it worked out well last time?"

- Curiosity about historic times and foreign places

"I have always been interested in... the French Revolution, the Dark Ages or Japanese cuisine." "I know I don't have a drop of Egyptian blood in me, but boy when I see pictures of the Pyramids, my heart just skips a beat."

- A desire to share their interesting New Age PLRT experience with family, friends or fellow workers.

"Wait 'til you hear what I did this weekend. You'll never believe who I was in a past life."

This is some of what I know can change for them during the next two hours regardless of their declared reason for coming.

- They might permanently and positively alter their view of life, death and the dying experience.
- They might view and comprehend painful life patterns and have the courage to discontinue them.
- They might heal or better understand the mind/body/soul connection.
- They might understand a complex human relationship, and understand that which had eluded them until now. When they have the opportunity to view it from a more distant or opposite perspective they can release their bias and accept others in a non-judgmental way.
- v They might gain insight into the opposite sex, which could help heal significant relationships in their lives.
- v They might be *so* moved by profound insights and revelations concerning regrets and poor choices they experienced in a past life, that they may change the entire direction of the current lives.

If they knew all that, I wonder if they would come so readily for their first PLRT.

A Word or Two about Karma

It is difficult to do PLRT work without a sense of what karma is and how it operates.

The Sanskrit and original definition of Karma is action. Over the past seven millennia, it has come to mean action and their consequences. The karma (cause and effect) is dependent on your own moral code of ethics. This code tends not to be malleable. Our sense of right and wrong is embodied as young children and rarely shifts without the influence of a dominant and pervasive force. A karmic act or action is committed for the attainment of something, which gratifies a personal desire. Karma neither punishes nor rewards; it is simply a universal law, which guides unerringly. This force guides us towards experiences which teach our soul the highest lessons of the universe.

One of those lessons is to harm none. If a mother steals a loaf of bread for her starving children during a war, she may not be held karmically responsible for that action. She may have been performing the highest form of sacrifice to feed her children and keep them alive. In this case there may not be a set of circumstances in her life then or in later lives which balance that action.

However, the same action, stealing bread, done by a mischievous adolescent, looking to see what he can get away with or done from a misguided sense of entitlement (the world owes me) will no doubt bring balancing action his way. That balancing action is rarely an eye for an eye, but it will, under closer scrutiny, be a perfect lesson for the offending action.

For example, this same offending adolescent as a more mature man may become a parole officer for juvenile boys and find that his teenage boys who steal or break the law are bucking the same system he bucked years earlier. If he remembers his youth he will understand both sides of the issue. This example is still a bit simplistic but it makes its point.

A Word about Good Karma

The very nature of karma is that it binds energy to it. If the action is good then it frees you from repeating the lesson. Freedom is an expansive experience, whereas karma is a contracting one. It pulls you back down into human experience until you understand and make the correct choices based on your own personal code of ethics.

A Word about Resolving Karma

The more often an issue is presented the greater the likelihood of one to reach resolution. The first lifetime an issue appears one may have only a 10% chance of resolution. The 8th time a person is romancing an issue, they may have an 80% chance to resolve it. This is mainly due to the fact that each time the issue is presented it is larger and more apparent until it becomes the soul's sole purpose to resolve it during that lifetime.

For example, a drug addict who has lost his youth and much of his future to drugs, struggles to kick the habit. He comes close to losing his life several times from drug-related causes, knife wounds, overdoses and infections. Several years later he completes a rehabilitation program and stays clean and sober. He still feels victimized by a culture which failed him, and left him to die on the streets of New York. He arrives at my door wishing to do a past life regression because someone spoke about it on the Oprah Winfrey show.

It was not a surprise to discover that this is one of many lifetimes dominated by substance abuse in some manner. However, what he uncovered was several past lives as a poppy grower, opium smuggler and den owner, and a rum runner and slave dealer. The balance is seemingly harsh but evident. Each lifetime the level of involvement increased and each lifetime had presented an opportunity to change professions. Each time he justified his actions because the money was very good. He knew each lifetime, that people were dying because of something he was involved in, but turned a blind eye. Only when he was on the opposite side of the equation could he understand the power of his past choices.

A Word about Personal Evolution

It seems that as we spiral up the evolutionary ladder, we find that we have all participated in behaviors, which we would now judge to be reprehensible. The fact is, we learn by doing and we have learned that some behaviors make us feel better than others. Over many lifetimes we make choices to participate in healthier and more productive behaviors. Your regression work will reveal lifetimes filled with poor choices and unkind actions. Your clients will recognize it now as negative behavior patterns because they have grown and are now ready to progress beyond them. That is what is evolution is all about.

I feel it is necessary for the accomplished therapist to cultivate a path to true compassion. If there is any trace of blame, judgment, shaming, or rejection in the tone of voice or timbre of the questions, the client will shut down and, I hope, go home. I sometimes see myself as a go-between or advocate for the client. They have been wrestling with some of these issues for decades. Now they reveal them and secretly pray that we will embrace them and support them in their painful and difficult struggle to reconcile past mistakes and poor choices. Many have made a difficult decision as in *Sophie's Choice* or the *Joy Luck Club*.

In times of great duress, we don't always make choices we're proud of, but we still need to know others will love and accept us. Some of my sessions are more like confessionals than therapy. Part of the power of PLRT is the flexible ability to move along the time line and clear away burdens of the soul which have stalked people for lifetimes.

Reinforce the notion of regression as metaphor whenever needed. The reminder will help relax your clients by distancing them from the sting of raw emotion. Let them know through past examples that you have seen and heard it all.

A Word about Depth Testing and Inductions

It is a commonly held belief in our profession that regression cannot be done and *trusted* if stage four (somnambulism) is not achieved. There are also some who believe that everyone can be a stage four given the proper induction. It is rare for these two thoughts to be held by the same person. So, if you believe that reliable regression can not be done unless somnambulism is achieved, then please depth test your client. However, if you believe that given the proper induction everyone can achieve stage four, then please, choose the proper induction.

Progressive relaxation for PLRT usually creates far too much tension in the client and they drift away ignoring your words. The progressive relaxation induction is often done more for the therapist than for the client. It helps the therapist gear up and settle-in for the session. If you insist on using progressive relaxation, then follow it with another induction such as the Dave Elman induction.

Entering Hypnosis with Your Client

It is fairly predictable and indeed helpful if you allow yourself to move into hypnosis with your client. I do it all the time, which is why I take verbatim notes. If I didn't write I would move right into the regression with my client and would be no help at all, just bouncing around in hypno-space without an anchor. Writing also helps to slow down the questioning process.

Your clients are actively experiencing emotions and absorbing tremendous amounts of information, which they are struggling to put into words. It takes far longer than we would expect for answers to formulate into full thoughts and sentences. Handwriting (please, no laptop computers - even if it is faster for you) will give your clients ample time to relate their internal experiences for you to record.

I watch my clients lips carefully before speaking my next question since many times their lips are struggling to form words. By paying careful attention I can give them the time they need to fully express themselves without firing out my next question and squelching their not yet expressed impressions.

Approaches to Regression

There are several approaches to regression. The first one I strongly recommend as an all-purpose approach. It is perfect for clients who are coming for their first regression, as well as more experienced clients.

- 1) You can ask their higher self or higher power to guide them to a lifetime, which is having the strongest Karmic influence over them right now. (The lifetime that mirrors most fully the life issues that you are involved with right now.)
- 2) You can use somatic/affect bridge approach. Emotional issues will anchor one back to another point in history when these same behaviors were operative.
- 3) You can use the time-line approach to place one in a specific time in history.
- 4) You can ask for the *origin* of the issue, similar but different from an affect bridge.
- 5) You can access information through the mother-line. This is similar to time-line work, but instead moves back through the mother's bloodline seeking out behaviors which have been passed down through multiple generations within one family.

PLRT Orientation Session

Below is a sample intake conversation to orient the therapist to PLRT.

Welcome. Why have you come to see me today?
"A friend sent me. I read a book or article about it. It was on Oprah last week."

What do you hope to discover?

What do you hope to experience?

This is usually a throwaway question. Rarely do clients state the true purpose of their regression. Their soul usually has a totally different agenda. People often want to find their present spouse, lover, relative, or boss in a past life. Some are looking for hidden justification for difficulties. A son may feel his father is too controlling and state of their relationship: "I think he was my slave owner in a past life because he treats me like he owns me now." More likely the shoe was on the other foot in the past, and this lifetime the son is discovering that ownership of any living thing is harmful.
Has anyone you know experienced PLRT?

"Yes a co-worker, my daughter etc."

If so, what was their experience like?

It is quite important to find out what type of experience it was. They may have some conflicting ideas about what is about to happen. Many clients think you're going to read their aura or look deeply into their eyes and tell them all about the many past lives they've experienced. It is important to know what they expect so you can correctly inform them.

What is going on in your life just now?

Key question. Get them talking about the now. Get real interested because you are about to hear the real reason they came.

What would you like to change?

This is often the set up for the regression. They don't know that. But you will more than likely see the thread that runs through the answer to this question and the regression symbolism and lessons learned.

Before the induction, tell the client the regression doesn't actually begin until they walk through a door of their choosing and hear you ask the question,

"Look down at you feet, are they larger or smaller than you know you feet to be right now?"

Beginning the Regression

Begin your regression by handing your client a few tissues saying, "you never know, you might need these". If they don't, fine. But if they do, it interrupts the flow to scramble to find a tissue and hand it to them. It moves them too much into present time and away from what needs to be cleared. It also makes them keenly aware of you as someone outside the experience.

After the induction of choice is skillfully employed, ask them to create a safe and protected space somewhere out in nature. Ask them where they are and prompt them to experience the scene with all their senses. Ask them to look around and notice an elevator, it may be directly behind them. Ask them to describe it to you "**in as much detail as possible.**" Their description will be your first opportunity to observe the client in hypnosis responding to your suggestions. Often the tone of the regression is already present. You will hear if there is creative detail or flat, monosyllabic responses.

If they don't answer within a reasonable amount of time, ask another question to prompt them. If still nothing, ask them to pretend, create or imagine if you have to an elevator. Encouraging them to pretend at this point is safe and nonpolluting. Prompt for more details, "is there a control panel to call the elevator? What does it look like?" Ask them to call the elevator to them and to describe the inside of the elevator "*in as much detail as you can*". Ask about the control panel inside. How many floors does this elevator go to? Whatever the answer respond by saying Good. Please, sound supportive. They are like children taking their first baby steps and they need feedback that what they are experiencing is what is expected of them.

"I'd like you to push the button for the highest floor this elevator will go to and let me know when the elevator has come to a gentle halt. When it does, and the elevator doors open, you will be standing in front of two white French double doors? I'd like you to describe in detail the French doors as you see them. What kind of hardware is on these doors?" The answer that is given most universally is two brass or

279

golden handles, which are S, shaped and mounted horizontally. They have to be pushed down like a lever. If your client reports seeing something different than handles, you might want to deepen them, or make a note that they are not completely able to see what is indeed present. They are creating something other than the place you are taking them to. This room is a real place. It does exit in the collective unconscious of our culture. If they have not found it, it may be due to fear, disbelief or they're rebelling against your authority. Most people are not accustomed to surrendering their control and venturing in to unknown territory. As they walk into the large round room, relax them with positive and supportive imagery. Ask them to call their guides, power animals or other divine figures at this time to guide them.

Let them know as they are opening the French door, that the room they are walking into is round and all the walls are covered with doors, dozens and dozens and dozens of doors. Each one leads to a past life. Assure them right away that the double doors they entered are unique. They are never locked and they will be able to find them and open them whenever they are ready to leave.

Ask them to walk to the center to the room, and take a few minutes to orient themselves. Look around and focus on as many details as you can. As they look around in silence, you can explain to them the possibilities are of what they're seeing. Explain that:

"Only 20 per cent of us really see. The rest of us intuit, sense, hear or have a knowing experience much like our dream states. Some people see all the doors in the room. Some see only one. If you see only one, it is because in the process of speaking about the regression process earlier, your subconscious mind already

*selected the lifetime you need to explore at this time. Some see all the doors as the same. Some see them as all architecturally different. It matters not how you see them. There is rarely any correspondence between the outward appearance and the lifetime revealed inside. So, take a few minutes and look around. When you feel drawn to a door, either because of how it feels or because of how it looks, let me know by describing it to me **in as much detail as possible.**"*

Once they have described the door, let them know that this door will remain open for the remainder of the session.

Now, please walk across the threshold and look down at your feet and let me know if they are larger or smaller than you know their feet to be now? (The regression officially begins now.)

Are they covered or bare?

Clean or dirty?

Are the coverings new or well worn?

Comfortable or not?

Good. Now follow with your eyes, from your feet to the top of your head and describe what you see?

Prompt them by asking if there if anything they are wearing on the rest of their body.

Tell me about your hair? What color is it and how do you wear it?

Are you wearing any jewelry?

How did you come by this piece?

Is it significant in any way?

What meaning does it hold for you, personal or spiritual?

Are there any markings on the physical body? (Tattoo, ritual scaring, wounded or missing body parts) It is not necessary to ask about tattooing etc., but be prepared for answers which reflect these options.

What color and texture is your skin?

What age are you or how old are you? Look at the back of your hands. It is easy to judge your age by the texture of your skin.

Ask if they are male or female; even if you think the clothing style gives it away, you never know.
Once this information has been gathered it is time to place the person in their surrounding.

Shift their focus to location

Are you indoors or out of doors?

Is this place familiar?

See what they say and take it from there. If they are in their house you can ask them to go to their room or their section of the house or to describe what is most precious to them in the house.

Emotion

Information is stored on the astral (a point within the human collective consciousness where all information of emotional content is stored) , in the akashic record (a repository or library for everything that has ever occurred anywhere) or buried in the subconscious by the sheer intensity of emotion. A person performing a daily mindless task like brushing their teeth will probably not recall it in a regression unless they were traumatized by something while tending to this mundane task.

I move people from strong emotion to strong emotion throughout the regression. Once I have the basic information, (who, what, when, where) I move through the years and have them experience the most profound moments of their life (the why).

I'd like you now to move to a strong emotion. First you will feel it in your body, then the scene will open up and you will be able to tell me what you are experiencing and why. Good, Now move to the next strong emotion and again let me know what you are experiencing. Take your time.

If your client has an unusually strong abreaction to an event, please stay with them in that emotion. They are releasing hundreds of years of suppressed emotion. Give them all the emotional space they need to express it. They may moan and groan holding their bodies as they rock back and forth. They may sob loudly for some time, coughing and creating much mucus. Let them be. Do not touch them, hold them or try to soothe them with calming words. Do not placate them (there, there it will be all right) It may seem like hours to you but in real time only a few minutes will have passed. Keep your eyes on them and bathe them in your grace, in a wash of compassion. Stay relaxed and know this is an incredible event you are privileged to witness. They are the bravest they have ever been right now before you. Honor them in that place. It takes much more strength to cry than to suppress emotion. Once they have exhausted themselves or the emotion, praise them and help them to refocus on the rest of the work at hand. Continue with the regression. The worst is over and you can pretty safely tell them so. Your words directly after the abreaction should be supportive, positive and loving.

If for some reason they cannot seem to connect to their emotions or they see only still photographs (usually caused by fear) I bring them to where all regressions eventually end up, to the last day they are alive in that cycle.

Karmic Viewpoint

It is important to note that towards the last day of all of our many lives, profound moments or crystallized realizations often visit us. Many of us who have attended to loved ones who are in the process of passing over will note a change of attitude, as they review their life and assess it from a dramatically different perspective from how they lived it. This new found perspective I call the karmic viewpoint. From here they can glean the lessons and come to terms with the demons they have been battling against throughout their life.

Last Day of Cycle Questions

What regrets do you have? Set up for next life.

What would you do differently knowing what you know now?

What was your proudest moment?

What was your darkest moment?

They say there is a lesson presented during each lifetime, what lesson was presented to you this life?

Did you learn it?

Were there any other lessons presented?

Did you learn those?

Was there a skill or vocation you mastered in that lifetime which would serve you now? If so, know that should you wish to study that skill now, you would acquire that skill with great ease... For deep in your subconscious mind the information is still present and retrievable.

Last Breath

Now I'd like you take your last breath, That's it, just exhale and feel yourself float up toward the ceiling. Good, now look down at your body and tell me what your thoughts and feelings are concerning the shell which housed your soul for all those years.

Good, now float further away, between the worlds.

We will now call in universal healers including religious icons and spiritual guides. Let me know when you see, sense, feel, hear or know that these guides are with you. Good, allow them to remove any scar tissue, physical or emotional, heal any wounds, remove negative mental messages, release any negative interference and smooth and soothe your energy field or aura. Just relax and let them do their work. Let me know when they are finished. Feel free to narrate if you choose to, I would love to share in your experience.

I ask them to narrate this part of the work even though it is often a trans-language phenomena. On occasion a client becomes psychically paralyzed or unable to accept the healing because of current shame or guilt oriented issues. I can coach them through the healing experience and sometimes we can even remove the blocks to deeper healing at the same time.

PLRT can stand-alone, be used as a fact-finding mission, or can incorporate other healing modalities and create a complete healing experience. I have seen incredible shifts of behavior and perspective just by using universal healers to end a negative pattern, or heal a wound.

You can ask the person to go to the bardos the place between lifetimes where you will discuss with your guides what lessons you will attempt to resolve in the next life cycle. Ask them to see themselves with the guide who is helping them plan that life. Ask them to remember what it was they had chosen to learn this time. Ask what lesson they had come to teach the significant others in their lives. Ask if they had learned it. Ask them to remember any karmic agreements they signed like a vow of poverty or if they had agreed to live that life to learn about a particular issue. All this questioning is helping to remove the blame and negative charge associated with the issues they were struggling with in that life time.

The End

Good, how do you feel? Are you ready to return to the large round room with all the doors? Good, let's go and remember you will have total recall of everything you experienced. I know there was much you experienced that you did not vocalize, but even these thoughts and feelings will be readily accessible when you return to full waking consciousness.

Count the client back up as you would any client experiencing a hypnosis session. Give them plenty of time to return. You may wish to offer them a cup of tea as you work together to interpret and assimilate the retrieved material.

13

Documented Case Studies
in
Past Life Regression Therapy

While transcribing my regression notes and poring over more than 15 volumes of carefully recorded data, it became evident that this important point had to be made: regressions are sensational, exciting, amazing, enlightening and life changing only to the person who is actually doing the regression.

As I began to read through hundreds of lifetimes, it was clear that unless you were that person, looking for that singular piece of information which would shed light on a shadowy and painful area of your life, the information is rather, well, flat.

What *is* always a wonderment and a trans-personal experience is that the needed information makes its way to the correct person at the correct time, presented in a manner which open the hearts and minds of those involved in the process.

It is impossible, and I won't attempt here, to describe the impact on the *therapist*, of watching a 6"2" 200+ pound, bearded man undergo and describe the emotional impressions of feeling a fetus living inside his pregnant body during a regression where "he" was a woman. How much more impossible to capture in words the impact of the experience on the *client*?

Yes, at times truth *is* stranger than fiction and on occasion I have felt that Hollywood should enlist a good regressor to assist in the movie making business. In the end though, the audience most fascinated with the retrieved information is composed of those making the deeply personal connections to their present life.

The magic of PLRT happens not so much during the regression, but during the therapy. I usually serve my clients a cup of herbal ttea after the session. It eases the transition back to the present time. It also allows me about 15 or 20 minutes while the tea is cooling to assist them in the therapeutic process of assimilation. It is during these few minutes that we work together to decipher the hidden meaning of their regression and why indeed that particular life was revealed at this particular time. There are many times when the light bulb does not come on until after they are reminded of what they spoke about before the regression. Often just by asking them to remember the pre-talk a shocked "Aha!" look passes over their faces. Those are joyful moments. Once the connections are made, magic happens. They begin to see correlations between the two lives and view them as mirrors for each other. Suddenly a simple story becomes a valuable teaching aid or powerful therapeutic tool. They look at their regrets from their regression and see this life as a natural extension of their previous choices.

The strong emotions they experienced during the regression serve as guiding lights as they re-chart the course of their future.

For Past Life Regression to become an accepted form of therapy it must be clear that it is not a miracle cure. Yes, there are times when spontaneous healings occur, but those healings are mostly observed as shifts in perspective, release of prejudice, forgiveness, understanding, etc. They are seen as miracles because the client did not spend five years on an analyst's couch. The insights were reached in just one or two sessions. Most importantly, the integration of the insights occurs during the "T" in PLRT. The trained therapist, bringing years of experience and wisdom to her sessions, will quickly discover that PLRT will have long-lasting positive results if the therapy after the regression is thorough and compassionate.

Read through the following case histories using this PLR Therapy to discover what you might expect during your sessions and possible results after your sessions are over.

Therapist note: It is important to note that information retrieved under hypnosis can seem fragmented and incomplete. At times there can be 30 seconds to a minute between comments as they go out to recover details and impressions. I will prompt my clients many times during a session. For instance, they may simply say 'Kitchen' in a dreamy far away voice. I can hear the amount of work it is taking them just to produce that single word. I will gently say 'tell me more'. They may say 'sunny'. I may again softly prompt, 'tell me more'. This may go on until I hear no new content or receive no further reply. As you read client transcripts, remember they are very far away and speaking is a tremendous effort. It would be irresponsible of me to report these experiences by filling in or rounding out their sentences or thoughts. Until they are fully out of trance and speaking in full sentences, I cannot know for sure what the connecting emotions are for them. Reporting on their experience at the moment it is happening can be very distracting for them. It may prevent their total immersion in a moment or in a lifetime. Clients have been known to answer in a very annoyed voice.

November 25, 1996 Mandy

Mandy came to do PLRT. Her major complaint concerned her mother, who has been unfair in allocation of affection, finances and time, between Mandy and her many siblings. She is feeling hurt, angry and unsupported.

Induction

Return to the lifetime that is having its strongest karmic influence on you at this time. As you step over the threshold please look at your feet and tell me everything you can.

"Gold sandals ...new ... smaller (than my own now) ... female ...white dress ... gold sash ... beaded headdress ... arm band ...skin soft and scented ... Headdress is ornamental* ...

How old are you?

Age 19 ...

Tell me about your hair?

Hair black and straight ...shoulder length."

Look around you and tell me what you see.

"Stone walls ... Counselor chair ... I belong here ... Comfortable...Bedroom ... Pretty room ... Couch ... Chamber ... Hairbrushes ... Bottles of oils."

Move ahead to a strong emotion and tell me what you are feeling and what is causing those emotions.

"Coronation ... Feeling happy ... I'm 19 ... He is my lover ... Proud and happy ... Lots of people ... Banners ...Food ... Dancers ... Treated well ... Head of the servants ... I am a servant! ... I obtain position through affair...Thermets his name. ... I am well liked. ... I'm very sweet. ...I have a very gentle nature. ... I'm not going to punish anyone. ... I'm good... Family not here ... Maybe they sold me. ... Not head of all servants ... Ladies in waiting ... I am their personal servant.
I am happy with myself...People think I have power because little white birds come to me. I'm blessed by the Gods.

I love this man. ... Maybe (present husband) ... Not sure ... He is good ... Just ... Kind and sweet. ... He adores me ... I'm very beautiful but not shallow. ... I go much deeper than that. ... Loves me for the person I am.
He has to marry...Can't marry me ... I'm not happy about it ... She is not a nice person ... Everybody knows about me...We become clandestine after marriage...She is nasty, selfish person ... wants to get rid of me but she can't because everybody loves me so ... protects me.

Please move ahead to the next strong emotion.

Twenty years old now... (She is speaking with much emotion now) She has me poisoned ... It doesn't kill me ... Puts me in a sort of a coma. So much hate ... I've never harmed her ... We began sleeping together when I was 16 years old ...

What lesson, would you say is being presented in this lifetime?

Watch out for nasty selfish people ... Three days ... He has me buried in a sarcophagus... Made especially for me... Jewels and very pretty. He puts me inside... Won't let them mummify me ... which seems odd ... I'm in *his* burial chamber. She is enjoying his grief. I'm sad for him... Not so much for myself... Little birds follow casket...

Move ahead to the next strong emotion.

I'M NOT DEAD! CAN'T GET OUT! I WAKE UP! CAN'T GET OUT!

He hates her ... Won't sleep with her ... Not effect she wanted. I take me two days to die... I don't hate her ...feel sorry for him ... His name... I keep calling... He only outlives me three years... Killed in battle ...We are together again... Love ... I love him so ... Trying to get back to him so he won't be killed anymore. When he is killed I am right there waiting for him. She is despised. ... Exiled by people ... Took on recklessness because I was dead."

Was there a lesson presented that was unlearned?

"I should have known she would hurt me... It was accepted back then... Don't understand why she would not back off... She never would have had his love anyway...

Do you know anyone from this past life in your current life?

She Is My Mother!

Where are you and what year do you feel this is?

Egypt year 12 (?) Comes to mind...

What are you feeling right now?

Heartbroken ... Betrayed ... I respond with distrust ... Deep down I don't trust people. ... Thought I did. ... Still loving and giving to people I am close to...

What regrets do you have from this lifetime?

No regrets ... I never would have given him up.
The regression ends here and we move into a healing session.

We did a Karmic release for issues around betrayal in general and her mother specifically.

Throughout Mandy's current marriage, her mother has often sided with her husband against her. She has considered leaving her husband on occasion but feels strongly that he would die if she did. Mandy had no real concerns about her emotions inside the sarcophagus or how she met her death. She makes some jokes about it and changes the subject. She is primarily focused on clearing away years of pain and abuse from her alcoholic mother and husband.

It is now ˙November 1998. Mandy had been working since November 1995 with me. In November 1996, she had worked with PLRT and retraced the above lifetime.

This next transcript occurred two years later. Mandy arrives wanting to work on her claustrophobia. After trance is established I suggest she fill herself with the feelings she associated with the word claustrophobia, an affect bridge. Her first words are

"Buried alive...Sarcophagus...Dark...I can't get out...Wrong man...He is very powerful...His wife did this to me. I am scared...It's dark...Difficult to breathe... Poisoned!

What lesson do you feel is being presented?

(Long pause, she is searching for the lesson, she knows there must be one or else why experience something so dreadful)

Stay away from married men ... But he was soul mate ... Self-control ... I was supposed to wait until next lifetime before we were to be together ... She was a bitch ... He was unhappy ... He is a Pharaoh (?) She tells him ... (his wife tells him that she poisoned his lover)...He wants to kill her ... He can't ... He becomes reckless in his life and in war ... In 30's still when he dies."

We call in the Lords of Karma, (universal healers) and ask them to remove all the scars from this lifetime.

When we first uncovered this lifetime in 1995, Mandy makes no mention of this phobia. She is primarily working on mother issues and feelings of betrayal from her family.

Lifetimes often have layers of information. In the first regression we asked to return to the lifetime which was having the strongest karmic influence on her at that time. Claustrophobia was not mentioned. In fact the first time Mandy mentioned her struggle with this phobia is when she decided to tackle it. Upon further questioning, she reports being plagued by this phobia for years. However, other issues demanded more immediate attention. She had, over many years, developed good coping skills to deal with it. Compared to the rest of her life, her claustrophobia was manageable. Mandy has not experienced this phobia since she completed this session.

Melody's Native American Regression

This morning Melody shows up looking poorly. She tell me as she is slowly making her way to the sofa that she is in serious pain and may consider having surgery on her neck again. She has had two in as many years. She has slept little during this week and with three kids to care for and drive to school, painkillers are not an option. She has tears in her eyes while she is speaking. Pain is very wearing. She states she is most upset because she looks forward to her sessions and is afraid she is in too much pain to relax and do our work. She is very angry with the doctors who butchered her these last two times. If they had done a good job she would be pain free. The doctors are surprised that she is in pain. They feel she should have made a complete recovery.

Induction

As you step over the threshold please look down at your feet and tell me everything you can about them.

Leather shoe...Moccasins...

Can you tell me about anything else on your body that you can see?

Leather buckskin clothing...Male...ornamental*

Are you wearing any jewelry, or do you have any physical markings?

Earring...ornamental necklace... shells

How old are you?

Age 25/26...Strong

Tell me about your hair.

Long Brown

Are you indoors or out of doors?

Outdoors...Clearing by a swamp...Sky over top of trees...Wilderness...I like it that way...I hate people... My brother...Darker hair...But same clothes...Older...He is my friend. Our parents died when we were small...Built *this* rather than live with others...We manage...We get along just fine...Hunt and trap...completely self-sufficient...Don't know if we go into town for coffee...Small but cozy...Animal skins cover bed...Family died of illness...Fever...Plates, cups...Tin cups...Brought them with us from old house...We don't have contact with civilization in any way...we were forced out ... Treated badly and left.

Please move ahead to a strong emotion now:

My brother is hurt. Tree fell on him...Leg is broken...bone sticking out of it. Really sick...Herbs ain't working...We wild-craft and make own medicines...

How old are you?

I'm now 32 years old... He's going to die...I see his eyes... they are green...Drag brother on a palette behind horse...2-3 days ride to civilization... He does not want me to take him...He wants to stay where he is... He is in agony...He must be dying...They are ridiculing us...Not a lot of sympathy...Or help...They are taking him away...Won't tell me where they are taking him...Want me to help in war effort...I won't do it...Tracking skills...Treating me like some kind of animal...They are taking him away...I'll never see him again...They just let him die...Didn't even try to help him...I brought pelts to trade for him to be helped.
I hate these people...I want to go home...They have beaten me...Put me in jail...a little box...They steal pelts...horse and let my brother die...**They hit me on the neck back here**...I die of a broken heart.

I was too stubborn to join them and then run away.

What lessons were presented in this lifetime?

Stubbornness is what killed me. I could have joined them and run off when the first opportunity arose. I shouldn't judge people now on how they treated me. I think badly of someone and think differently when they are nice. I have nothing but hatred and anger in my heart. Colonist...Revolution...Narrow minded assholes... Treated me like an animal... So much I could have taught them...Someone high up wanted to make us an example.

Let's move to your last breath in that lifetime?

Pity...Freedom... so glad to be free...Brother right there...Glad to be dead...I apologize to him...None of that matters here...So glad to see him and so relieved...They dragged me through the streets with hands tied in front of me.

Regrets:

I wish I had never gone...Could have given my brother a decent burial and gone on with my life. They just threw him in a hole in the ground. We speak language... trade food...Passing through.

Before returning we call in universal healers and all of Melody's guides. She died in great pain and with much anger in her heart. We ask them for a healing of her neck and to help resolve the anger she has toward herself for not listening to her brother when he asked not to go to the town, and towards the people in the town.

After the regression and healing are over Melody stands up smoothly and without assistance, gingerly moves her neck, shoulder and arm and finds there is no pain. She sits down in disbelief and pops right back up again because she can. She is laughing in shear amazement. We are both very pleased with the results of this regression.

When she returns two weeks later she is still pain free.

* Ornamental indicates they have no spiritual, sentimental or monetary value.

Monica the Gladiator

Monica had been doing PLRT for several months when she experienced this regression. Her pre-talk issue had to do with comparison. She was "discontent with her present life-except by comparison" She didn't wish to exchange lives with anyone, but bits and parts of other peoples lives were far better than her own. She had been aware of her comparing herself to other girls in grade school and it became a strongly charged emotion in high school. She admits to coasting on her good looks. "A girl can go far on a pretty smile." I had observed that Monica has never worn the same outfit or shoes to my office. She always dressed to accent her figure and complexion. Her taste was impeccable. At 33, she was content not to further her education, which would result in her remaining in the same position until retirement. In her field, it is usual to return to school for advanced degrees. She described this feeling of discontent and comparison as existing in her solar plexus and identifies it as a soul issue.

Induction (Sentences in Italics indicate my questions or prompts)

She begins with the description of the door to the past life. In this case there is some correlation between the door and the lifetime behind it.

Please describe the door in as much detail as you can.

"Cut into stone ... Narrow ... Dark iron bars ... Pegs ... Latched.

As you step over the threshold, please look down at your feet and tell me everything you can about your feet?

Dirty ... Men's feet ... Sandals ... Then strips of material ...Very worn ... Feet well formed and muscular legs ... Beautiful body ... Strong and young ... Hard ... Strong ... But gentle ... Skin ... Deep golden color ...

What else can you see?

My outfit ... Suede ... but cloth ... Dirty ... Ripped and wrapped ... Short over one shoulder ... Knife-type dagger ... Carrying tools and weapons on odd location (?)... Heavy headband ... Heavy ... Thick leather ... Metal ... I use it as a weapon...

Tell me about your hair?

Brown gold strands ... Long wavy.
Hard muscular ... Odd for this land ... Skin and eyes
unique for this land ... White teeth ...

How old are you?

...23 years old. Arabic or Araback ... I see Roman
numerals ... (can't focus in on them)

Are you inside or outside?

Outside ... Land ... see nothing but dry barren land ...
Bits of glass ... Wild life ... Creatures ... Receives no
water ... No rain ... Some trees in distance.

Please move to a strong emotion.

I'm alone and walking towards trees ... I make my
mark and leave ... I like the women ... I love the
women ... Fight the men ... Party ... Carouse ...
Conquer and move on ... They think I'm a God ...
Maybe I am ... I laugh at them ... They amuse me ... I
was just.

Please move to the next strong emotion:

Fear and Pain ... A little boy ... chained to a wall ...
With men who are also chained ... Prisoners ... Outfits
looks like ... Ministers (?)... Metal Helmet ... Made for
men of noble birth. He is very optimistic ... He is six ...
Thinks it's a game ... He's nice and friendly ... Playful
... Just there. Rome ... year 160 AD

Strong emotion (went back in time again, same lifetime)

Joy! Celebration ...My birth ... I'm a son ... in an ornate (crib) rounded like a boat ... Red and gold curtains ... Drinking and food ...

Moving ahead to another strong emotion please.

Celebration ... Women ... Very petite ... Juliet type gown ... Painted hats ... They are young and afraid.
I am a man. Older more mature ... Bought and bartered ... A deal ... Not love ... I'm floating above now. I'm a bubble of light ... Gold...A little man ... I can feel his perception. Condescending ... Amusement ... Celebration for me ... Not highly evolved essence of a man ... But highly evolved in the physical plane ... Superior strength and beauty.

Please move to the next strong emotion.

Sadness ... Nights ... Old man ... Hair is nothing what it used to be. Eyes still beautiful blue. Great sadness in his eyes. In a den of iniquity ... Black outfit ... Skin hanging from bones ... Flesh old and wrinkled ... He doesn't think much about past present or future. Everything he did was filled with confidence.
He laughs at himself ... He had so much ... Wasted it like a stallion conquering and impressing. He should have loved ... Treated women as objects – Mother (?)... He may have been bi-sexual ... But never loved. He did everything he could have done physically.
He did regain wealth and leadership ... Not same capacity as he was born into ... He was the best at the games ... Gladiator ... in his thirties ... His name is ...

(writers choice not to include it) ...won his freedom ... No regrets ... Just wishes he had done what a woman he met in a cave on a journey told him to do. She told him he was chosen ... He was to be a great warrior ... Fighting far ... Peaceful ... Prosperous ... Loved. Instead of accepting it as it was ... Instead of indulging in it ... He should have risen above it ... made it better ... His life was not meant to be with one ... but to transform many ... He did reach heights ... But not very transformative ...

What important lesson was presented?

Physical gifts were given to me ... I must not give myself over to them ... Should put my energy in spiritual growth ... Not supposed to ... Should put more energy into soul and spirituality and Leadership ... To bring the Divine essence to earth. That person was so incredibly beautiful ... He was gold ... A Divine God ... Physical God ... Everyone disappeared beside him ... It bothers me now ... When someone else comes into a room I want to be the center (She is now a gorgeous, stunning woman). Beauty is in essence spiritual...
That is beauty ... That is spirit ... Not important to be sexiest, most beautiful ... Develop ones essence ... That will shine forth.
Stop comparing! Beauty ... Beating yourself up ... Stop flagellating the self ... Material and physical aspects of self ... all else will fall away.

Let's move to your last breath in that lifetime.

He is Light
He is in a room ... Skies open up ... Light ... Pastels of the rainbow ... Angels coming for him ... Is his mother

... He knows ... He understands ... She comes to him ... She embraces him ... He cries happiness ... And Spirit and his spirit join ... Not become one ...Rise up into light...

He is young and beautiful again. He is a God once again.

Monica's regression is exciting for many reasons. First of all she has her epiphany during the regression. It appears that she was able to pull up from the life she was retracing and shift into the karmic perspective without breaking her tie to the more emotional aspects of that life. Her spontaneous commentary is incredibly revealing. Although the word is never used, Monica seems to be battling with vanity issues. Vanity is a taboo subject in our culture. Her higher self presents it beautifully for her to see by bringing her to a higher place of spiritual awakening. It is even highlighted by a note to her that what will follow will be important. Monica moves into this regression knowing that she is looking for a soul issue, but has no idea it will lead her there.

Another remarkable aspect of this regression was Monica's ability to retrieve a name, which she then researched. Monica discovered that that man did indeed exist. He is listed as one of the last great Gladiators in Roman history. It is stated that he had been trained from early on to fight and win. When he finally comes of age to be that which he was trained for, the arenas are almost empty and the excitement and glory are absent. His prize, fame, for striving so hard and so long evaporated. Had he been born several years earlier we all would have remembered his name. It was part of the vanity issue that Monica was working on even then. To be that good and not recognized, no longer a popular hero, was quite a blow to his/her ego. Monica has struggled with internal satisfaction vs. external adulation for many lifetimes.

Monica's current life experience has been a bittersweet struggle. At a time when achievement and the capacity to genuinely love is becoming a more important assessment of a woman's worth in our culture, she has been blessed with a beautiful countenance, not much professional drive, and much rage. Monica was able to easily make connections between the two lives. and has begun to pursue spiritual interests which are helping her to heal and to love herself more.

Marsha's Rages

A female Pediatric Nurse in her mid-twenties introduces into our first meeting that she is a husband beater. She has all the patience in the world for the sick children on her floor, but flies into blind rages with her husband and struggles for control with her colleagues. This beautiful petite woman is bright, articulate and soft-spoken. She arrives promptly and clearly states her belief that she had been molested as a child, and wants to discover the truth of the situation no matter what, or who, it reveals. She has no interest in addressing her rages at this time. She feels they may be related to being violated as a child. Here is what transpired during her first session.

After the induction I choose a bridge/somatic affect. I ask her to go to the source of the rage. (This session took place over 7 years ago. If it were occurring now, I would not ask her to return directly to an initial sensitizing event since it often produces abreactions which are too intense for a new team of client and therapist. Rapport needs to be established before such a journey should be embarked on.)

"This rage may or may not be from this lifetime."

I say it as a matter of course. She has already told me of her strong Christian religious background and education. I offer the comment because I feel I would be remiss if I omitted it. The client feels herself moving backward and to her surprise finds herself in her mother's womb as a fetus over-hearing a conversation between her parents. Her mother is crying and screaming that she will go insane if she has to carry another child. She is begging her husband for an abortion, which he coldly refuses her. He is quoting chapter and verse at her as sound reasons for maintaining the pregnancy and she is crumbling to the floor, beating her belly, sobbing hysterically. My client is the 6th of 8 children born to an Irish Catholic family. Her two older and nearest siblings are twin girls. There has not been a full year when her mother has not been pregnant since the conception of her first-born. I ask my client how this event is related to her rage. She says "Oh my God! This is not my rage, it is hers. I have been holding her rage all these years believing it was my own. I thought all of it was my fault."

I ask her what she would like to do about it. She said she wanted to separate herself from her mother's rage. I ask,

"Do you feel connected to any of the Archangels?"

" Yes, Michael."

" Please call in the Archangel Michael and ask him for his assistance in this matter." He appears in all his ruby red shining glory, flaming sword in hand. As she is describing him to me she stops and exclaims,

"Look I have a miniature sword just like his and I am waving it around the inside of the womb separating myself from my mother's rage and insanity. It is creating a wall of sacred flame as protection between the two of us."

"How do you feel now?"

"Calm, safe, protected, relaxed."

"What is happening now?"

"I am offering the sword back to Michael and he tells me to keep it and use it anytime I need to separate myself from my family's rage and insanity. He is almost laughing. He is fading away into a cloud of red smoke."

This was the end of our first session. I saw her two weeks later. She had not had a full-rage event since the previous session.

Could I have created this powerful visual for my client? Not during a first session. The imagery came from deep within her sub-conscious mind and brought with it healing on many levels. (Of course, it may also have been a very real astral healing.)

1) Religiously she got the desired support and commiseration from St. Michael. She had secretly feared an afterlife in hell for all the hurt she had caused others with her rage.

2) She has released the blame she had accepted in the womb.

3) She has returned the part of her mother's soul fragment that was given unconsciously to her as a fetus.

4) She has gained insight into her mother's life. She has in fact asked her mother if she had wanted an abortion when she was pregnant with her. Her mother denied it at first but soon opened up and told her the truth of her married life, which she had never shared with anyone before.

5) This helped heal the mother-daughter relationship as well.

I continued to see this client on and off for several years for various different issues. She and her husband are currently working on creating a family. This is something they had ruled out years ago because of Marsha's rages.

Max's Story

A Licensed Massage Therapist, who was also my client, referred this thirty-eight-year-old gentleman to me. Miranda had been seeing Max for close to seven years. Each week he appeared listing so far to the left side that he could brush his knees with the tips of his fingers. Miranda explained that she would work for most of the session just on his lower back to assist relaxing his muscle spasms which 'locked up his legs'. The spasms returned several days after each massage. He was rarely pain-free and experienced only a sense of lessened pain after the massage. The weekly process was often painful and loud as he vocally released energy while Miranda carefully and expertly helped release the spasms in his lower back and legs. Max would often say 'I can work through the pain, continue, or 'no pain, no gain'

The day of his regression Miranda drove Max to my office after his weekly massage. He requested that she remain. I was more than reluctant to comply, however Miranda was currently enrolled in my Hypnotherapy Certification Training Program, so I consented. Max's face softened and he relaxed into the recliner. He appeared open and ready to experience hypnosis. His mood was optimistic, and his humor was brilliant. I asked for his thoughts concerning his back pain and what he thought we might find as we moved backward through time, looking for contributing factors and perhaps the primary offense.

This is his story, but not his words as he is still Miranda's client.

Max is clear and stoic as he reports the details of this adolescent experience. It was apparent from the patter and rhythm of his words that he had dissociated from the events of that day.

Max was 16 years old, on a very successful high school football team. The coach was a 'no pain-no gain' type of person and had instilled that philosophy into his impressionable teenage boys. As the winning season continued to grow, life in the locker room became very important. The boys on the team had decided that the winning streak would be broken if they changed anything about the way they were currently performing. Someone suggested they not wash their team uniforms until the end of the season since *that* might change their run of good fortune. They all agreed. After all they *were* teenage boys. During that time Max developed a small pimple under the waistband of his unwashed athletic supporter. The pimple grew into a rather painful boil, which would have deterred most boys from playing, but 'no pain-no gain' was the banner under which this team played. So play Max did, until he was in such agony that Max finally asked his mother what to do. "Ask your father. How am I supposed to know such things?" He showed it to his father and received the name and address of a Doctor who would tend to the hot inflamed boil.

So this unattended 16-year-old boy, with an embarrassing boil on his lower back, went to the Doctor's office that afternoon. The doctor asked him to bend over and lower his pants (also embarrassing). He poked around a second or two and then asked, "Do you drink? You look like a beer drinking kind of guy, why don't you and some friends of yours go down to the bar, drink your fill and have your friends drop you by afterwards. I'll be waiting for you." So Max, a trusting soul, who we already know responds well to authority figures, returned that evening to the Doctor's office, very drunk. The Doctor instructed him to lie across the table and then swiftly lanced the boil without preparing Max in anyway for the shock or the inevitable pain. Max almost passed out from the intensity of the feeling. His friends dropped him home but Max told no one of what he felt was a shameful reaction to the pain, the embarrassing encounter or the deep sense of betrayal etched deeply into his soul that night. He is betrayed by his coach, who didn't rescue him, his father who didn't support or protect him and his Doctor who caused him great pain in a dishonoring way.

Fortunately, Max was a senior. He only had to finish out the year. His team continued to win and he did play, chanting no pain, no gain slogans to numb his mind and body. His coach, aware of Max's pain, was unwilling to lose a good player so ignores Max's limping and grimacing.

As years pass the pain in Max's lower back and legs prevented him from enjoying life to the fullest. Remember that Max is well programmed. He is stoic! He continued to do the same things everyone else is doing; he just suffered tremendously. At the time of our meeting, Max was a very successful entrepreneur. His business required him to drive a truck, with a clutch, many long hours a day. He was in intense pain most of the time. He somehow managed to participate in a rich family life as well. His wife was supportive and nurturing. Needless to say, Max is a remarkable man.

We begin our hypnosis session with a brief induction and some depth testing. Max is a willing and capable client. I check with Miranda that his pain is on the *left* side. Somehow my intuition says that with all the male betrayal, the pain would manifest on the right, or male side of the body. She reassures me it is on the left side. I deepen his trance. At this time, I am preparing to go back to the day at the doctor's office to discharge that horrendous event. I ask Max to focus on his back sometime before it was injured. He had just been massaged to release the muscle spasms before coming to my office, so I know he is resting comfortably. I see his face registering the request and he seems to disappear inside himself. Then his face grimaces in pain and he appears to be recoiling in response to what he is seeing in his memory. I ask him where he is and what is happening. In a voice louder and more emotional than I would have anticipated he is yelling "Stop Ma. Stop it!" I prompt again. Max begins to tell this story with full-blown emotion and great attention to detail as if this is the first time he is truly seeing this event.

Max is using his body to shield his younger sisters from getting a beating with the metal part of a canister vacuum cleaner hose. He has his back to his mother as he is yelling at her to stop. She is in a mad rage and continues to beat him across his lower back until she is exhausted. Max is 14 years old. He is the first born eldest boy in a culture which venerates his position.

He is old enough and strong enough to physically restrain his mother but feels that would be disrespectful. The feelings of betrayal, anger, love, loyalty and disbelief are all fighting for expression. His only solution is to make believe this isn't really happening and bury his strong feelings and memories. As I continue to question him it appears that this is just one of many painful episodes he experienced with his mother. I jot a quick note to Miranda asking if he has ever mentioned this during their sessions. She shakes her head no, as she watches the session unfold in pure amazement.

We continue to uncover and clear many events throughout the session. When we have accomplished all that I feel is reasonable in one (two-hour) session, I ask him if he would like to call in healers from the Light. He asks for some clarification and quickly makes the association to Martial Arts training in his youth and the ancient lineage of the ancestors called in before his class. He agrees. I ask him to ask the healers, the ancient ones to heal all the wounds he has remembered this day; to remove all the negative emotions stored in his lower back and leg muscles and to restore ease in his body. I then ask for the healers to remove any scar tissue which might reactivate the spasms. Max indicates when these requests have been fulfilled. I further request that they ease Max's thoughts toward his mother and father and assist him in finding forgiveness for the pain inflicted on him for all those years. Max weeps openly and releases much emotion during the healing. His shirt is soaked with sweat. Before returning to real time I guide Max to a healing place in nature where he can rest and allow the deep and profound healing to penetrate all the levels of his being.

When Max returns, he looks over at Miranda and points to me. "Now I see what you mean about her. I would never have expected anything like this." He is smiling. We speak about the session for about twenty minutes. He has a few questions about the ancient healers and wants to know if what he was seeing and feeling was real. I assure him, from my past experience, that it was.

Max now clearly remembers these early childhood experiences but states firmly he could not have recalled them before the session. He is anxious to return home to call his sisters and tell them what he experienced and to see what they remember.

He rises from the recliner, touches his back and smiles. He looks years younger and almost glows as one often does after a good cry. He walks across the room and gives me a big hug before he leaves.

I received a phone call from Max a week later booking another appointment. I am somewhat surprised. I receive another call from Miranda saying that his wife called her to thank her for bringing Max to my office. He is a changed man.

The day of our appointment the door opens and Max is standing there grinning ear to ear. "Oh by the way, I think I forgot to tell you when I called for the appointment, I have been pain free for two weeks!" He gives me a big hug and a sweet kiss on my cheek. He is joyfully beside himself.

During the two weeks he has become the emissary of his family, openly speaking to all his sisters about his memories and validating theirs. No one had ever spoken about their childhood before now. He is planning the first family reunion and is standing on a platform of remembering, sharing and forgiving.

I see Max two more times before I relocate to another state several hundred miles away. Miranda keeps me informed. His back pain has not returned and she now finally has the opportunity to work on his upper body.

14

Metaphor Use in Hypnotherapy
Copyright 1999 Mary Lee La Bay

A metaphor is the use of a symbolic image that is meant to have correlations to or be a substitution of something else. It is synonymous with a simile or an analogy. In hypnosis the use of metaphor is extremely powerful. The unconscious mind will sometimes more readily accept the message found in a metaphor than if it is given direct commands. When the conscious mind is listening to a story, the unconscious is searching for meaning and resolution. It allows the client to create their own change, learning without barriers.

A metaphor always includes imagery, but imagery does not always include a metaphor. In other words the metaphor will consist of a descriptive story while a guided imagery, in and of itself, may lack significant or relevant meaning to the client. If you, as the therapist, choose to create a metaphor for your client, be sure to collect detailed data on the client's background so that they will be able to easily relate to the metaphor. By understanding the client's goal, you can develop the action and resolution accordingly. It is most effective when the metaphor contains elements from the three main senses - visual, auditory, and kinesthetic.

During the induction it is recommended to use the imagery of going down a hall and choosing a door when the session is leading to a past life regression or a metaphor. Whereas an affect bridge is the preferred preamble to a memory from the past.

Metaphors of real life experience can be a useful tool for helping clients see their life experience in a slightly different light. You may be inspired to create metaphors or guide imagery for your clients. It's my experience however, that the client is often much more adept at creating their own metaphors. What the client produces is by far more elegant and intricately pertinent to their own inner sense of the issue. The following cases are interesting examples of several techniques combined within the client's own metaphorical imagery.

The Blossom

Patty had been in counseling for several years, yet still she sensed there was a block preventing a crucial step in her healing/growth that was refusing to reveal itself or be removed. She was referred to me by her psychoanalyst who felt that perhaps the roots of this problem would be uncovered by past life regression. During our intake interview, Patty described the problem as a "spiral of picking at myself." She was in crisis and conflict with her inner self.

As we entered into the session there was an expectation of discovering a past life. It is important to always stay neutral and non-intrusive in hypnotherapy as the subconscious mind is much more knowledgeable concerning what is there and what is needed than we could ever hope to be. As we move into the session, we will discover a most apt and elegant example of a client-created metaphor.

Once a deep trance was achieved, I guided her through the imagery of a hallway with doorways leading to the information that would be most helpful for her in the discovery and healing of the issues that had been discussed. Although I am presenting this session with mostly her side of the dialogue, in actuality I was asking many questions throughout. I will only present a few questions here that seem relevant to the coherency of the metaphor.

ML: Describe to me the door that you find yourself in front of.

P: It's arched, with vines. It's white, no pattern....wood.

ML: Are you ready to open the door and step through?

P: Yes.

ML: As you open the door and begin to step through what do you begin to notice around you?

P: Light. It's orange, yellow, warm. Almost a living room setting. The light comes from one lamp. The color is because of the lamp shade. The orange comes from that, not the bulb. There are clouds....fog....in the room. And trees, vine-like and craggy.

ML: And what else do you notice about this place?

P: It's quiet. 'No one has been there for a really long time. The light has kept it warm. It feels like there is life there. Feels like I've been here long ago. I was supposed to come back. I forgot something - maybe left it here so I would come back. I liked it there. Lots of books. I feel warm. The trees and fog make it cold. Like something is wrong. Something shouldn't be there. The fog is hiding something. The light from the lamp is false, so the trees are 'cragging' - bent like an old man. There is a beauty to them anyway - they survived. It's really the fog that scares me.

ML: How do you feel being here?

P: I feel bristles on my body. The hairs stand on end, my heart beats faster. It's not panic, but cold terror. Something is wrong. If I walked through it, the fog would freeze the sweat on my body. It's only near the books, and it curls around the lamp and at the base of the trees - at the end of the room. I have to get through it to get to the books. It's quiet.....there's a secret that hovers there. You know it, feel it and see it, but it's silent - so you don't know it's potential for harm. It has a life of its own. It's waiting for me to go to the books. I don't know if I'd make it to the books. Maybe if I reached it, it would cloud it so that I couldn't read it.

ML: Why would it be important to reach the books?

P: If I have the books I have knowledge.   It's something I need to know.   The knowledge from the book is warm - it's not frightening.

ML: What is the origin of the fog?

P: The fog comes from the other room. It's dark there. It comes from the mouth of something. Doesn't feel alive - more mechanical, with a life. Cold like steel but alive. It lives over there - waiting for me to come back. It wants me to fail. It wants me to try to get the book and fail.

ML: Why does it want that?

P: To show me I never could. It would gain control and power. It would be right. Everything I thought negative about myself is right. I'm incapable. It would win. It would triumph, I wouldn't exist so it wouldn't have to worry.

ML: What does it worry about?

P: I impose a threat to it's life. Anything of warmth ceases to exist in that sense. There would be no love. Doesn't want to feel love. It hurts. It doesn't see any redeeming qualities. Nothing good came out of love. It retreated to the dark side, put up a shield to say "this is who I am and what works. This is my truth". Then it would die, lonely. It doesn't care and it doesn't want to know that, but its true. It would shrivel and cease to exist. Nothing can grow in the cold environment. No nourishment.   It would rather have immediate domination and die than to let me win. It's history. It wasn't always that way.

ML: What was it like before?

P: When it was younger it had potential for the steel exterior, but I hadn't been introduced. It experienced love like a young bud on a tree, just opening. But it never opened. It didn't feel love. It gave love but when nothing returned and it felt unworthy, unattractive.... as if it had no qualities that mattered. It was told this. And it saw no matter how it tried - just opening one point of its bloom to show a little of who it was - it got torn out. The leaves....the petals.....it started to wilt and turn brown. No nourishment. It stopped trying. It was never cut from the branch. That would have been better. To have died quickly. But each part was ripped away slowly and painfully. Even
the most beautiful point, the best gift. It was never enough. It was thoughtlessly pulled out, sometimes purposely. Sometimes they just blew away unnoticed. All the other branches had beautiful blooms and were told that. They had potential for more. They never faded.

ML: Moving back to when it first emerged as a bud, before it had lost any petals, what do you notice about the blossom then?

P: It was perfect in every way. Perfect even while not being in full bloom. Just where it as, with potential. It needs to be loved - and told that no matter how it looks, or what it does, or doesn't do - it's beautiful because it is. It needs acceptance, support. Something or someone to believe in it just because it is. No other reason - not beauty or brains or faith.

ML: What could you do for that young bud right now to help to nourish it?

P: I could be there.   I'd tell it the difficulties it has gone through make it even more beautiful.   It knows truth and suffering.   It has a spirit that is very much loveable and I'm glad that it is who it is.

ML: How does that make it feel?

P: It feels hope.   I wouldn't say it trusts me.   But hope.   And maybe it lifts a veil to look and see whether what I said could be true.   It's cautious.

ML: When it lifts the veils to look, what does it notice?

P: It sees I'm still there.   It's curious, like a child testing its mom.   It builds on its sense of security.   It feels like what I said had some truth.

ML: What else would it like for you to do for it?

P: It wants me to let it go.   I've been hanging onto it.   That keeps it down.   It can't be free.

ML: What do you do?

P: I step away.

ML: What happens then?

P: It snaps up.   It's with all the other flowers.

ML: What is it doing?

P: He's thinking. Seeing what it's like to be with them. He's still looking at me even though from farther away.

ML: What is he doing now?

P: He won't bloom. He's not really liking being among the others. No substance. They are all about their bloom. Given what he's come through he knows more. He's deeper. He looks for me. To see if there is more I can tell him. Not necessarily about him, well, maybe a bit.

ML: And what do you tell him?

P: Love is everything. It doesn't matter if he's among them. I love him. And he can love them for where they are. Maybe he can share with them. That's love.

ML: How did he receive that message?

P: He didn't like it. He wants me to tell him more about him. How pretty he is.

ML: What do you tell him?

P: It's not about the external; the inner beauty will radiate.

ML: Why not let him hear compliments?

P: He'll get caught up in the beauty. He could lose his sense of self. If he did he would fade faster. He would be ashamed that he bought into it. He would be drawn to want it all until its all gone.

ML: Do you think that he could find a balance between the external and the internal beauty?

P: I don't know whether he could do it.

ML: What does he think about that?

P: He thinks he can. Since its been missing he's worried that he might forget.

ML: Feel how he feels now.

P: Strong, confident. He radiates love because he feels love for himself. He feels in his heart he's been out of touch.

ML: What else does he feel?

P: There's more to him than what you see. The ability to give and receive. There's a deep down, nagging voice.

ML: What is the voice saying?

P: "There's more. This is nothing."

ML: Now that he has this balance and accepts the exterior beauty, how has this made a difference?

P: It's made a difference because it's the way everyone looked at him. How he felt and others reacted.

ML: How does it feel now?

P: Feels good, because of the reactions.

ML: What does he notice as the benefits of his beauty?

P: He's noticed. There's more attention. He receives special favors.

ML: What benefits are received by the inner self by having the outer beauty?

P: It's easier to give. People are more open to communication with you. They'll allow you to approach. They're more open.

ML: How can the inner and outer beauty assist each other?

P: It's easier.

ML: What can be accomplished now that it is easier?

P: It wants to be known for its principles, struggles, knowledge,
experiences and how it manifests in knowledge. It doesn't want to be seen through the veil of beauty. He will blossom in a different way.

ML: How will he blossom differently?

P: There will be a warmth, a glow instead of just a physical bloom. It must be integrated. He can use the beauty to draw people in, to hear your truth. To see the real beauty. This would surprise people. They wouldn't expect more and that's exactly why you would do it that way. People shy away from the inner stuff. Once you have their attention, you can pull them in from the outer. It doesn't necessarily mean they're unaware. They haven't awakened to that in themselves. It can help them.

ML: How is the blossom feeling now?

P: Much clearer. Stronger. Like its OK to be both. Each has a purpose.

ML: How does it look now?

P: A little like both. It has petals. In the center, though, it has a glow inside. It's not in full bloom. It doesn't need to be.

ML: I would like for you to more completely integrate the two - the interior and the exterior beauty. If you were to hold the young bud that is aware of his perfection in one of your hands which one would it be?

P: My left hand.
ML: Do you see it there?

P: Yes.

ML: And now place the mature blossom, with its interior radiance, in your right hand. Do you see it there?

P: Yes.

ML: I would like for you to draw your hands together, either physically or in your imagination, only so quickly as the two blossoms, and all their aspects, fully integrate. Go ahead and begin that process, and tell me when you have completed that.

P: OK. They're combined.

ML: How does that feel now?

P: Stronger. More complete.

ML: Is there anything else that needs to be done for that blossom now?

P: To live. It doesn't need anything else.

ML: OK. Now I would like for you to go back to that room with the books. What do you notice about that scene now?

P: It's very bright. The sun is shining through the windows.

ML: What else do you notice?

P: The lamp remains. The fog is gone. It's really dusty. Otherwise its normal. Very bright.

ML: Would you like to choose a book?

P: I have no desire to choose a book. I want to open a window.

ML: And then what do you experience?

P: Its cool, clean. Now I'd like a book.

ML: What do you know about the book that you have chosen.

P: It's a book of poetry. It's old and new. It has gilded edges, its carved. Dark green. There is an old colored picture of a child and a mother. The pages have gilded edges.

ML: What is the title of the book?

P: "Mother"

ML: What else do you know about this book?

P: It's very heavy. The gold on the pages is an illusion because the content is heavy, not the book.

ML: What do you notice when you open the book?

P: It's a safe. It's empty. No pages. It has a compartment for storing something. But it's locked. I don't know where the key is.

ML: What would be stored in this book?

P: It's knowledge. Under the door of the safe is all air, laden with stuff. It's not mine to read, but it's mine in the sense that I have to know. The key is the key to some pieces that I need. It's about my mother. She's keeping the key close to her. It's something she's kept all these years. I don't know if it's about her, or about her and me. I sense it's about her, but it affected us both profoundly. The start of it is in the book. But not the manifestation of it.

ML: There is a part of your unconscious mind that is capable of revealing the first piece of this knowledge to you, if this is the appropriate time.   If you are prepared to receive this information at this time, it will begin to unfold for you as I count from 3 to 1. 3-2-1

      From here on the client began to experience an episode from very early childhood.   It involved neglectful abuse from her mother and severe arguments between the parents.   Patty had no previous knowledge of this particular event although it was always a difficult relationship between the family members. Her relationship with her mother continues to be strained.
      In a follow-up call to Patty she said that she was confident that we had gotten to the main issue that had previously been blocking her.   She commented on how powerful the metaphor image had been for her. Being
naturally analytical she had previously had an idea about the nature of the issue, but having experienced it in this fashion, she had an inner sensation that she now had the "ability to be both"....the internal and external beauty.

Lydia's Staircase

Lydia had originally come to my office seeking assistance with depression and panic attacks. We worked for several sessions on her fear of flying which, when on an airplane, would develop into a panic attack. During the year she was able to take several trips by air for both business and pleasure, experiencing a minimum of discomfort. So we moved on to working on her creative talents. You see, Lydia is, among other things, a talented creative writer. For several months during the year, Lydia would come two to four times a month to simply go into trance and create another chapter for her book. When she joined a writing study group her sessions became less frequent, enjoying the challenge and inspiration derived from the class.

Then one day I received a call to schedule an appointment. Lydia had become so depressed that her husband feared she would contemplate suicide. She complained of not being able to sleep, yet not being able to get out of bed. She couldn't go to work regularly and her doctor had her on strong anti-depressants. Her condition had led to irritable bowel syndrome and she frequently experienced an upset stomach, sometimes leading to vomiting.

When she arrived in my office she was solemn, but when we began to discuss her book she became very animated and was delighted to tell me the details of the chapters she had written since our last session. Since most of the book had been dictated to me under trance, she was excited to catch me up on the last few that had been written on her own. She announced that 33 chapters were complete and there were only about

5 to go. The fact that there were only five chapters left to write brought her back to discussing her depression and the reasons for coming to see me.

Upon questioning her about her concerns, she explained that since there are controversial issues presented in the book she is apprehensive about the reception it will receive when published. Will her friends or family disapprove? There is the fear of not being accepted. There is also a fear that there is only one book inside of her. Because of our long-standing association I was able to give her positive feedback about her creativity that she could receive and believe. So that point receded in importance, mostly because her fear of only having one book was only on the surface and not a truly deep-seated fear.

I then asked her, "What would be the worst thing that could happen if your book was published?"

She thought about that for several moments. She replied, "I could get bad reviews and angry people writing to me." As soon as she said that, her demeanor began to relax as though she realized that having given the fear definition, it no longer looked as overwhelming and monstrous.

So I asked her if she was ready to begin hypnosis. She said she was ready. Because of her fertile imagination and creativity, and the fact that we have had so many sessions together, she quickly went into trance. I used a short progressive relaxation, some confusion dialogue and then had her imagine a hallway with doors leading to the information (though not necessarily an event in her past) that will be "most valuable for you today in discovering the root cause, and the means, for healing the depression you have been experiencing. And as I count from 3 to 1 you will find yourself in front of one of those doorways. 3-2-1.

Please describe to me what you observe about where you are."

I have learned with Lydia that she doesn't always go to a doorway. She is so adept at this that she may go right into a scene or see some other imagery. So although I have directed her to a doorway, I only need for her to describe where she is beginning our journey. At this point with Lydia I wasn't sure if the answers we were seeking would come from a metaphor, a past life or a present life experience.

When clients are exploring past lives or metaphors, I have all my clients begin by describing the doorway or wherever they have imagined themselves to be. This allows the client to begin visualizing without the pressure of there being a right or wrong answer. This is only supposed to be their imagination so they feel free to give themselves permission to make it up. However, the door description is frequently so intriguingly symbolic of what the session will later reveal.

Lydia: The door is actually a lattice work, like for roses. It's white, wood, and the tops are pointed, sharp. They would make you bleed if you crawl over them. There are blood red roses growing up the trellis. Roses have thorns. When I look at them I see thorns and not the roses. They seem sharp. I would like to climb the fence and go over, but there is nothing to hold onto but roses. I don't know if there is a gate or
if I can walk around. I feel I have to climb over instead. I stand in front of the vines. I feel small like Alice in Wonderland. The vines are really big.

Mary Lee: Can you imagine yourself bigger and the vines more proportionate?

Lydia: Yes, but I can't stay large. I shrink back down again.

Mary Lee: Why?

Lydia: Because I have to. It's my personal cross to carry. Like the thorns on Christ's head.

ML: Why is it your personal cross to carry?

Lydia: I've grown up with it.

ML: I would like that part of your consciousness that is responsible for carrying this cross to take you now, back through time and space, to the original time that you picked up that cross to carry. As I count from 3
to 1 you will find yourself in a scene, whether metaphor or past life experience, that will show you the origins. 3-2-1. What do you notice around you?

Lydia: I'm in a prison cell, a medieval dungeon. I've been here before. There is a series of spiral stairs. There is no railing. It's frightening. There is nothing to hold onto. It twists and turns - like crossing the bridge over a cavern. There is no way to get across but that bridge. No railings. I can't stand. I can't look down. The only way down the stairs is to crawl. I've always had dreams and fears of having to cross that bridge, and go down the stairs.

ML: Can you take someone or something with you to make you strong?

Lydia: There is never room for 2 people. I need something to hold onto. A railing or a wall.

ML: Can you imagine a wall or railing there?

Lydia: Yes there is a railing.

ML: As you begin to go down the stairs, what do notice next?

Lydia: It is still very dark. I need a flashlight or something.

ML: Would it be helpful if you had one of those flashlights that are attached to a headband?

Lydia: Yes. That would be good.

ML: What happens next?

Lydia: The stairs are sloping so it feels like I could still fall, but not off them.

ML: Would it help if you could imagine them with gritty friction material on them?

Lydia: Yes, there are mats, like shower mats, and I can were tennis shoes so they stick better.

ML: How does that work for you now?

Lydia: I can go down slowly.

ML: What do you experience next?

Lydia: I am holding onto the railing....I am getting vertigo. I can hang on and go a couple of steps at a time. I've reached the bottom.

ML: How do you feel?

Lydia: Relieved. But I am still concerned about what is there. There is something. It's dangerous or frightening. Something that would hurt me. I can't seem to....I have to dwell on the worst thing that could happen....

ML: Let's go back to the top of the stairs again. It may seem silly and redundant, but we will gain more information if we examine it again. Are you at the top of the stairs?

Lydia: Yes. I can put one foot down at a time. I am holding onto the railing. My feet are on the gripping rubber. I can see that it's cold.

ML: Would you like to put a coat on?
Lydia: Yes. That's better.

ML: What do you notice about going down the stairs?

Lydia: They seem shorter. Like driving home and you know where things are in the dark. I'm at the bottom. That wasn't so bad.

ML: Let's go to the top and come down again.

Lydia: OK. I don't have to hold on so tight, I'm more at ease. I know what's going to happen. I'm at the bottom.

ML: How do you feel?

Lydia: I'm home.

ML: Let's start at the top and come down the stairs again. What do you experience this time?

Lydia: I can walk on the rubber. I know where it is. I can just hold on with one hand. I use the other arm for balance. I have my coat. I can turn on the radio. I don't have to totally concentrate on every move I make. It feels more comfortable. I'm at the bottom.

ML: How do you feel?

Lydia: Glad I'm home.

ML: Let's do it again.

Lydia: (I notice she smiles this time) I sit down and think awhile.

ML: What do you find yourself thinking about?

Lydia: About my life. I'm so damned afraid of everything. It keeps me from doing a lot. I'm not always there. Only part of me. Like when it has ascendency, I tend to cower in a corner, afraid of doing things. At other times I can do things. It is something external then internal. It turns a switch. It's

337

been more often as I've gotten older. I don't remember being this afraid when I was younger. Well I was afraid, but I still did things. Now I don't force myself to do the things.

ML: If you could imagine that switch, what would it look like?

Lydia: It would be a big giant electric switch like in Frankenstein - scary.

ML: Where would the switch be located?

Lydia: It's not on me, but it has wires that hit me everywhere - hands, lets, neck, eyes, stomach, knees.

ML: Would you want to remove this switch or change it in some way to function more beneficially to you?

Lydia: I don't want to remove it because you have to experience a degree of pain and anguish to want to express yourself - to be able to. When I see an artist that creates very light frobby (sic) things, cutesy, crowd pleasers - I'm not touched, I'm not moved. I can admire their talent, but I'm not moved. I feel like you have to be able to get in there, in touch with fear, joy, sorrow. By disconnecting I could screw something up. I need to experience.

ML: Instead of disconnecting could you create something like a circuit breaker?

Lydia: Yes, that would be good. To avoid an overload. It sometimes becomes its own monster.

Then I become paralyzed, I can't write or produce. I have to be able to find a way to the boom of the stairs, then be able to come back up. To find them. I don't know when I'm losing them. When I've gone too far. I've been afraid to let go and end it because its......I've experienced such incredible joy, such highs. If it has done this much for you, how can it be wrong. How could it not effect others for the good. I've come out of the darkness. At first my writing was about anguish over what had happened to me. It is becoming lighter. Soul searching, but not a search for reality either. There is a need to be humorous, fun. I turned a corner. It's almost over. I didn't know where to go, afraid to give it up, turn it loose. Do I just finish it and put it in a bottom drawer?

ML: How would you feel if you did finish it and just put it in a bottom drawer?

Lydia: I guess I could do that and then decide later.

ML: OK. So let's go to the bottom of the stairs and go up this time. What do you begin to notice about this?

Lydia: It's different. It's pulling rather than pushing. I have to work harder to get up. There's a concern I could trip and fall back down. When I get to the top there will be the bridge. I've reached the top.

ML: How are you feeling?

Lydia: Tired, tense, but I'm up.

ML: Let's do it again.

Lydia: OK.

ML: What are you experiencing this time?

Lydia: There is a knot in my stomach. Fear. I just hate that fear. Being ruled by it.

ML: What does it prevent you from doing.

Lydia: It prevents me from doing many things. Even getting up in the morning, sleeping, it's too dark. It doesn't let me see daylight.

ML: And what benefit do you receive from it?

Lydia: Benefit?

ML: Yes, what does it allow you to do?

Lydia: I can sleep, that will make it go away for awhile. Then I don't have to be sick. I don't have to go to a stupid job. But it prevents me from getting close to people. I don't want to bring them down. I worry my husband to death.

ML: What would be the benefit in worrying him?

Lydia: I don't think there is a benefit. I suppose I get more attention, but I don't need more attention from him. He gives me enough.

ML: What else happens?

Lydia: I have disturbed sleep. I wake up tired, not relaxed. It puts stress on my body, makes me sicker.

ML: OK, let's go up the stairs again. What do you notice this time?

Lydia: It seems darker and more cavern like. It's closing in on me. But I have no trouble getting up.

ML: How could you make it larger or more comfortable.

Lydia: I could cut a hole in the ceiling, push the walls back.

ML: OK. Do that. How does that feel now?

Lydia: It's lighter. It keeps closing in, I keep pushing back.
ML: What could you do to get it to stay back?

Lydia: I could get strong tape, staples, some tacks. It works a bit.

ML: What else do you notice about this time up the stairs.

Lydia: I can see out windows:

ML: What do you see out the windows?

Lydia: There is grass. It's raining out. Gray. I used to like the rain in the midwest. I enjoyed the storms. It would come hard and then stop. It just goes on and on here. This year has been worse.

ML: How could you perceive the weather here as something interesting or enjoyable?

Lydia: I guess I could listen to it, watch it.

ML: How do you feel when you reach the top of the stairs?

Lydia: I feel weighted down. I want to take all the books off my shoulders. Get rid of all the things, the clutter. Simplify.

ML: If you did that, how would you feel.

Lydia: I would feel freer. Not so many responsibilities. I don't need things. I don't need any more things. I have things at work. Things, things, things. Same at home. I will never have it uncluttered. That's the way I work. But I could get rid of some...but where to start?

ML: Let's go up the stairs once more.

Lydia: This time it is easier. I go faster. No worry about the stairs. I can think of other things. Let myself dream. I'm not afraid to dream. I want big dreams, more stories. Because I have imagination - I just need to let it go. Like when I was a kid. I would tell stories. Writing gives me a great deal of freedom, although its not always easy. I stop halfway. I have to not try so hard. I do everything with a vengeance.

ML: How do you feel when you get to the top?

Lydia: I'm ready to continue. I can go on now without a problem.

Although time could have been spent analyzing the metaphor throughout the session, it was apparent that the unconscious, and perhaps part of the conscious, mind was sufficiently aware of the correlations between the imagery and the real life issues. By having Lydia create tools to help her through each difficulty there was an implication that she was resourceful enough to create a means of managing those events that she perceived as difficult in life.

Having Lydia repeatedly experience each phase of the metaphor provided desensitization to her fears. With each passage she became more familiar with the activity, drew upon additional tools, and became more relaxed. She reacted with a sense of empowerment and capability.

Her fertile, creative mind, which has yielded many imaginative stories, was equally as powerful in conjuring frightening and debilitating perceptions. As her new tools are strengthened, she will learn to discern when this is happening, and how to bring herself back more quickly and efficiently.

Metaphors allow the client to find solutions to problems that they may or may not have found as comfortably with other approaches in hypnotherapy.

15

UFO Experiences:
How to Handle
Extraordinary Cases with Trance
Copyright 1999 Mary Lee LaBay

The subject of E.T.'s (extra-terrestrials) and U.F.O.'s (unidentified flying objects) is at once intriguing and controversial. It is surrounded with speculation, cover ups, zealots and nay-sayers. With the evidence so elusive and often intangible, it is an area that remains an individual opinion. I have my own sense of it, yet here, as in a hypnosis session, one's own personal belief system must stay completely removed.

Some years back a client came to me who speculated that she had experienced alien contact. She wanted to verify her suspicions through hypnosis. During the initial interview she revealed that she had previously sought the help of another hypnotherapist. In that session, and while under hypnosis, she began to describe her experience to him. The therapist abruptly ended the session, telling her that her notion was ridiculous and fictitious. She was so disoriented from the experience that she said she had to sit in her car for about a half an hour before being able to drive away. It had taken her years before she had gathered enough confidence to attempt a session with another counselor, and we had to spend a great deal of additional time establishing rapport and trust in order to even begin our session.

Should you find yourself confronted with a client's issue that you are unable to handle, for whatever reason, it is vital that respect and courtesy is shown to the client. The session can be brought to a close in a gentle, supportive manner, and the client can be referred to an appropriate alternative therapist.

Although the discovery of an E.T. experience during hypnosis is not an everyday occurrence, it certainly has come up in my practice with some regularity. As in any hypnosis session, it is essential that the hypnotherapist remain as neutral and non-leading as possible. The session must be client-centered and non-intrusive.

Frequently these memories will cause great physical and emotional discomfort, terror, anger and a whole range of reactions. Be as encouraging as possible after the session as well, giving them resources for research and support.

UFO experiences to most ring the bell of science fiction and an overactive imagination. But for thousands and thousands of people it is obvious that there are a variety of experiences both seemingly real and seemingly fabricated. We help the client integrate the memory of these events to be comfortable within themselves while making sense of it all. I present two experiencers in this chapter that are very different from each other. Larry is more typical. He has a memory of some bizarre events that need to be explored. Kara is atypical. She is told by someone that she may have had an experience and is coming to the office to find out if indeed she has.

As a hypnotherapist our job is not to judge truth or reality but to help the client gain the understanding and assistance they have come for.

Larry is in his forties, his degree is in the analytical sciences, and his career is in technology. He came for his first appointment filled with curiosity about an experience that he had when he was a teenager. But at the same time, during the intake, he was trying to downplay that experience as a silly dream, or a creation of his imagination.

He told me he had awakened one morning remembering an unexplainable bright light during the night. He was trying to dismiss it as imagination or a dream, when his mother came in to breakfast. She told him that she had noticed a bright light in his room and had gotten up to check on him. When the bright light shone on her she turned around and went back to bed. She thought it was curious that she would react that way. Neither of them had any further information about the incident.

He also vaguely remembered some unusual events that occurred between the ages of 15 and 18, but had no concrete memories of them. So about twenty some years later he was wondering if hypnotherapy could assist him in putting to rest the validity of these memories and perhaps the absurdity of it all.

We began the session with a progressive relaxation technique and then a guided visualization through a hallway with doors.

He describes the hallway as dark with lights coming from beneath the door. He can't move and claims there is a part of his subconscious mind that is protecting him from what's behind the doors. He is apprehensive about the discovery of this information. I ask him to simply describe the hallway and doors, assuring him that we do not need to go anywhere he finds uncomfortable. His environment is described as thatched doors as would be found in a castle and he is aware that there are many, many corridors. It is lit with torches fixed to the walls. He finds himself floating at the level of the torches.

He goes immediately into what is often called an "out of body experience," yet he is still able to communicate the experience to me. He says he is floating in outer space. There are stars, no gravity. He goes around Saturn and sees the rings from all different angles. This makes him feel safe because there are no earthquakes, floods, storms. He claims he can't always feel that way and that he has a fear of the unknown, the uncontrollable.

He realizes that it would be less scary if he had a higher perspective - "that I came from nothing and will return to nothing." I asked him what wisdom he was gaining from this perspective. He replied, "I am temporarily trapped in a body and I can be released to that freedom forever. That's the real existence. This level is an anomaly."

I ask him if he feels safe enough now to return to the hallway and the doors. He says he is ready to do so.

ML: What do you notice now?

L: I can see my body, but it projects up and up.

ML: Where are you?

L: I'm in my bedroom.

ML: Are you lying on your bed?
L: I used to sleep on the floor - I had problems with my back.

ML: What else do you notice this time?

L: I see the pillow, fish tanks, bookcases, stereo, the window, door,
posters, the ceiling, the back steps and yard.   I'm surprised that I remembered some things.

ML: How are you feeling?

L: I was an innocent boy. Something bad happened. I didn't deserve it.

ML: What do you notice happening?

L: There is someone in the room with a black hood, like the grim reaper. It's like there is nothing inside. I'm angry, I feel like swearing. (His body and facial muscles are showing strain.)

ML: Go ahead and swear. What would you like to tell him?

L: "F— Off!"

He then describes floating off again towards the planets and stars. Once again he gains that greater perspective and sense of safety. When he tells me he is ready to experience more, we return to the bedroom scene.

ML: Then what happens?

L: My body floats off. I see a drop of water hitting a body of water creating concentric circles. It's tranquil. Now I see a baby in a dish. It's not right. It's dead. They've experimented on it. It feels like it's my baby. I'm very upset. I'm so angry. I can't do anything. I can't get even. Now I see another baby. It's alive, just born, wet. It's growing to 3 years old, a girl. She's growing up very quickly. I see a chair floating, a cheesy deck chair - it's zero gravity.

ML: What else do you know about where you are?

L: I'm inside something. I can see the huge rim of a planet. Like when you see pictures of sunrise on earth from space. I'm going away from earth. Now I meld into the blackness. The drop of water into the pool. I relax into it. There is nothing to know, forget or learn. Existence for no purpose. Pure being - no doing..........I would like to move on - back to the bedroom.

ML: Moving back to your bedroom on that evening when you noticed the bright light, what do you begin to be aware of?

L: I am aware that there is something big over the house.

ML: What do you know about that something?

L: It's a disk - I'm more aware of it rather than able to see it....It's flying over the house. There's a huge beam of light - 20 feet across. With perfectly perpendicular sides. It's shining down on the house. I float up into it. Like no gravity, slowly. I can almost feel it.

ML: What is floating up?

L: My physical body.

ML: What else do you notice about your physical body?

L: I can see it. I'm naked, lying on something flat. I can see body organs - rotating in front of me. Intestines, liver.....

ML: What are you experiencing?

L: I'm relaxed. I can't move. There are no worries.

ML: When you are finished floating up, what do you notice next about this experience?

L: I'm lying flat with someone at my head. He's hideous. His head is like a prune, skinny neck. I'd love to snap it. It's the diameter of my index finger to thumb.

ML: Is he wearing anything?

L: No clothes. There's no need.

ML: What else do you notice?

L: I'm looking down, all I can see is my skeleton. Someone that looks like Chewbaca in the background. Like in a separate observation room. Behind glass.

ML: What else do you notice about the creature at your head?

L: I can almost see his hand, his long fingers. I can see big black eyes, slightly sunken. I'm surprised by that. From the side I can see a nose ridge.

ML: Does he have hair?

L: No hair. You have called this creature "he". What do you notice that indicates that it is a "he".

L: I'm looking over his body, I don't know. I just know that it's a "he".

ML: Does he have genitals?

L: I can't tell.

ML: Can you float down around where you would normally find genitals? What do you notice in that area?

L: The left side of my chest hurts.

ML: What is happening?

L: He knows I am looking. He knows it now that I am doing this. He turned and is looking at me as I lay here.

ML: He is aware that you are in this room with me?

L: Yes.

ML: How does he know this?

L: He's psychically connected to me. He's always somehow connected to me.

ML: What is his reaction to us doing this?

L: He's shaking his head.

ML: Is he angry?

L: No. He doesn't understand why I am doing it is all. His eyes appear different now. More round with protruding ridges over the eyes.

ML: Now what do you notice?

L: I see an emu, bear, parts - a claw. A rabbit in a field. They are learning from me. They show me pictures, ask me questions. And they are pulling the information out of my brain.

ML: Were these things that you knew about?

L: Yes, I read a lot as a child. I always loved nature and the sciences.

ML: And what happens next?

L: I see the earth rotating slowly. I see a parade of faces - some I know, some not. Some are fictional. I want to look into the future now.

The session continued with a view to the future and then a regression to a past life. And then it ended.

We spoke at length about the experience and he was unsure whether he had imagined the whole episode. I explained that it certainly was possible that he did. It could have been a metaphor, his imagination, a memory of a movie or book, or a reaction to something disagreeable that he had eaten. Or it could be a memory of an event that he had experienced. I suggested that he give it some time to settle in. I encouraged him to allow himself to feel whether the information that he had uncovered "fit" or not. His analytical mind took over rather successfully and rapidly, stating that, although he wasn't sure whether or not it was true, he was OK with the information.

I checked with him some days later. He told me that it all seemed to be pretty fictitious and that he felt it had been a creation of his imagination.

A month or so later we spoke again and he said that he was in complete denial. He felt that none of it was true and that it was pretty much nonsense. I asked him why he would have to be in denial if the information was not true. He admitted that it was because he really did believe it to be true, somewhere deep inside of himself, but that intellectually he wasn't going to acknowledge it.

Five months later he came back for a session that consisted of a few past life regressions. At one point in one of the sessions the following exchange began...

L: I want to go back to my house in (home town). I have some recollection of an experience - it was during the day. Of being in the kitchen and looking out the window and seeing something. And being pulled through the window...and that's all I remember.

ML: OK. Go back to the scene where you remember being in the kitchen. And as I count from 3 to 1 you will return to that day....3-2-1....and how old are you?

L: 16.

ML: And what are you noticing around you?

L: It's weird...it's snippets of anatomy really....like moving x-rays of someone's shoulders and neck and head. This just doesn't make any sense.

ML: There is a part of your mind that is very analytical. I would like to ask that part that is in control of that analytical part if it would like to step aside for a short while so that you can have a pure experience. I promise you that it will be most amusing and that when
the experience is completed, you will have even more information, interesting information, that you will be able to analyze and think about. Would your analytical part be willing to step aside? Say, sit over there by the window and watch what happens?

L: It's willing to step aside, but not that far.

ML: OK, could it just watch say near your shoulder?

L: It's aside.

ML: OK. Thank you. Please back up in time to earlier in your experience in the kitchen. Say half an hour before the scene you were just describing. Are you in the kitchen then?

L: It was ludicrously close to the house. It was huge. A big object. It's solid.

ML: What color was it?

L: The picture is in black and white.

ML: Is the kitchen in black and white as well?

L: Everything is in black and white. It's light colored. It was a blinding light, initially, that attracted my attention. That's what made me look out and see it. I see it has shape and form, it's big, it's....there's something surreal about it. And in a second I just get sucked out the window. One minute I'm there and the next I'm gone.

ML: How do you get through the window?

L: I'm vertical, well, at 45 degrees really. But I'm upright.

ML: So if someone came into the kitchen, they wouldn't see your body? Or would it be there?

L: My body is gone. I'm not there.

ML: OK. Let's back up a bit. Just prior to going into the kitchen, what were you doing?

L: I was watching some TV. I think I was watching baseball. I went out to the fridge to get something to eat. I was making a sandwich at the table and the window was to my left. And there was a big light, like the sun is moving quickly past the window, rising.

And when I look out I see this object. It was always there.

ML: How long has it been there?

L: Minutes. It always knows where to find me. It was waiting for me to come out to the kitchen. And then it reveals itself to me. It made itself visible.

ML: Would it be visible to anyone, or just to you?

L: Probably just to me. It's like it can freeze everything around....it makes sense that when people report seeing flying saucers no one else sees it. They leave no tracks behind. They have a way of giving selective experience. They are not afraid of people missing. They can manipulate things like time and make people forget things.

ML: And so you've come into the kitchen. Tell me again what you are experiencing.

L: I get some food out of the fridge and begin to make a sandwich. There is a blinding light all of a sudden that startles me, catches my attention. I go to the window to see what has happened and I see the object there. It's very large. Battleship gray. But a light tone really. They've come to get me again, those bastards. They're mean.
ML: How do you know that they are mean? Have you had other experiences with them?

L: Yes. When the light hits me, it's like they mark that spot on my brain. It's a marker for my memory so that when I come back that's where my conscious memory will return to. I'll forget everything that happens in between. They've programmed it that way.

ML: What else do you know about this experience?

L: When the light hits and they are marking me, I remember everything that has been hidden by those markers. It's like a light goes on in my brain and all the dark corners are lit up. That's why I can remember bits of it from time to time.

ML: What other information can you now access?

L: It feels really good. Like I am more brilliant. Smarter. I remember all of it, but I can't do anything because when the light goes on it is also when I can't move at all. In that instant I get sucked up in the ship.

ML: Let's take this frame by frame, as if it is in very slow motion. Now you are standing in the kitchen, and you notice the light. At the instant that the light goes on, what is it that you become aware of.

L: I know all the times that this has happened.

ML: How many times have you had this experience?

L: (Pause) Ten times.
ML: How old were you for each of these ten experiences?

L: Four months. And then 16.

ML: You had one experience at 4 months, and then all of the other nine were when you were 16?

L: Yes. They checked on me at 4 months. And then there were many in succession when I was 16.

ML: Why did they come to you so often at 16?

L: They want to know what I know. They take all my intelligence out of me. It's like I was a man then.

ML: Do you remember having any more experiences between the age of 16 and the age that you are now?

L: No. After that they were done. They had taken everything that they wanted from me.

ML: What else do you know?

L: They always know where to find me. It's like I'm marked.

ML: Why do they want to find you? What is their purpose?

L: They are doing some sort of experimentation, but I don't know what it is.

ML: There is a part of your subconscious mind that has been able ˙to understand them telepathically during your encounters. What does that part of you know? 3-2-1

L: They are sfudying our genetic makeup. There is something about our physical bodies - our strength - that they are lacking. They find us banal and stupid, but at the same time there are characteristics we possess that they are seeking to replicate in themselves. We are insignificant to them really. They are so intelligent.   They have allowed their bodies to deteriorate over the millennia. They want to combine a part of our genes with theirs to strengthen their physical bodies, while maintaining their superior minds.   It's not easy and they are performing extensive, intricate experiments.   It is a tedious process. They are patient and meticulous.

ML: What do you remember about their physical bodies?

L: The first thing I always notice is their necks. They are very tiny, like the size of my finger. I want so bad to snap their necks. I hate it that I can't move. I know that I could snap their necks with one hand.

ML: And what else do you notice about their bodies?

L: I described them in my last session.

ML: Could you describe them for me once again?

L: They have large heads and huge flat almond-shaped eyes.   There is a nose ridge.   It is unusual, but I notice the ridge. It doesn't protrude like a human nose, but there is that ridge that starts between the brows.   There are two holes for nostrils, but they are vertical. Our noses point down, but theirs are right there.

ML: Do they have mouths?

L: There is an inch long slit. It appears to have fallen into disuse. Like it is withering. You can see a shadow of what used to be lips. But it really is only a slit anymore.

ML: Do they speak through their mouths?

L: They   don't   speak.   They   communicate telepathically.

ML: Do they use it for eating?

L: (Long pause) I don't want to know about that. It makes me uneasy. There is something about that I don't want to know about.

ML: OK. Do they have facial hair or ears?

L: No hair. They have thick skin, like a prune. They have no breasts, no nipples, or navel. No genitals. The skin looks like it has shriveled, like it's too big for them and it's hanging on them.

ML: How tall are they on an average?
L: I am laying down, but I have seen them many times. They are about 4 ½ feet tall.

ML: If they have no genitals, how do they procreate?

L: (Long pause) I don't know. I know that they have occasionally had sex with humans.

ML: If they have no genitals how does this occur?

L: I am just aware that it has happened. Sometimes they just take babies.

ML: They take human babies?

L: Yes. And fetuses.

ML: How do they acquire fetuses?

L: From the mother.

ML: Yes, but how do they get the fetus from the mother?

L: Sometimes they genetically alter the fetus while it is in the mother.

ML: They operate on the fetus during the pregnancy?

L: Yes.

ML: How do you know this information?

L: I am one of those fetuses.
ML: You are one of the fetuses that have been altered?

L: Yes.

ML: I would like to ask your subconscious mind to take you back to a time when you were in the womb and you had this experience.

L: (I observe some changes in his breathing, his body tension and his facial expression. Also his fingers which were stretched across his prone body now curl up into loose fists.)

ML: As a fetus you are too young to talk, but your adult consciousness that is here will observe your experience and be able to recount it to me. What do you notice about this experience?

L: There is a bright light. It startles me because I have never seen light before.

ML: What do you experience next?

L: I'm being pushed up against a piece of glass. It's as though I am being smashed between two pieces of glass. (At this time his hands and arms move down parallel to his body and his fingers stretch out straight.)

ML: What happens next?

L: It's over.

ML: What do you mean?
L: They are finished. I am back.

ML: You are back in your mother's womb?

L: Yes.

ML: Do you notice anything about yourself that seems to be different than before you had this experience?

L: I seem brighter, more intelligent. I am more conscious. I think I am more aware.

ML: How can you tell?   What gives you that impression?

L: I just sense it. I just know that I am more intelligent now.

ML: And so move ahead in time.

L: I think I need to quit now.

ML: You want to end this session?

L: Yes. I need to stop.

ML: OK.

After the session, I sat down with Larry and asked him how he was feeling about the session. He said that he was fine and that he knew that information all along. I asked him what he meant by having known it all along and he replied that once he became aware of the information it was like he had always known it but had just set it aside. He claims that he has already gone through all the emotions from terror to disgust to anger and now he just wants to have all the information. But he says they don't care and they won't do anything about releasing the memories to him.

Kara's UFO Experience
Copyright 1999 Mary Lee LaBay

Kara came to me because a friend had told her that a particular marking on her hand may have indicated that she experienced an alien abduction. She said she had no prior suspicions of such an occurrence, but was willing to explore the possibility. She also expressed curiosity about experiencing a past life regression. Kara was nervous. She had no idea what we might encounter and we were unable to build an affect bridge. I did not want to influence the possible fabrication of false memories about such an event so I asked Kara's unconscious mind to lead her to an experience or metaphor which would be most appropriate and helpful for her to begin the session.

She went into two past life regressions during the first half hour. These experiences allowed her to relax deeper and become comfortable with the process.. Those memories also reinforced a sense of strength and ability in her by showing her difficult situations that she has come through in the past. At that point her unconscious mind chose to allow her to move to the more difficult issue of an alien abduction.

Kara: I'm sitting on the porch of my house.
ML: What time of day is it?
K: It's dusk.
ML: Is there anyone else around?
K: My cousins were here, but they have left now.
ML: How are you feeling?
K: Quiet, tired.
ML: As you sit there, what are you doing?
K: Thinking about what I have to do. It's Sunday and I have school and work tomorrow.

ML: A little time goes by, until something changes. And then what happens?

K: It's dark.

ML: What else do you notice?

K: I'm sitting in a lounger. I'm not there. It's black, the chair. Like a dentist's chair.

ML: Is it tilted back?

K: Yes.

ML: What else do you notice?

K: My arms are strapped to the chair.

ML: Are your legs restrained?

K: Yeah.

ML: What are you feeling?

K: Terrified.

ML: Who is around you?

K: I can't see anybody.

ML: It's just all black?

K: Well, where I am there is a light.

ML: There's a light over you?

K: Yes, it's bright. Everything else around me is dim.

ML: And what is going on with you now?

K: I'm just nervous. I'm trying to get my arm free.

ML: Do you notice anyone around?

K: Yes, there are creatures around me.

ML: Can you see or describe them?

K: No.

ML: Can you tell what they are doing?

K: No.

ML: Some time goes by until you notice something different. What is it that you notice?

K: The chair is back.

ML: It's flatter?

K: Yeah.

ML: Now what is going on?

K: They are sticking something in my leg.
ML: What is it?
K: It's a needle.
ML: Are they injecting something?
K: They are taking my blood.
ML: OK, they are extracting blood?
K: From my thigh.
ML: Are they taking it from a vein or right out of the flesh?
K: Out of the flesh. (She's wincing in pain and breathing heavier)
ML: They don't know any better?
K: No they want to do that.
ML: Why?
K: Taking it out.....(breathes harder in pain)
ML: Are you in pain?
K: Huh-uh.
ML: Let's move past that until you are more comfortable. What do you notice next?
K: (pause, relaxes) I have a sheet over me.
ML: Over your clothes?
K: They've removed my clothes.
ML: OK. They have you under a sheet. Does it cover your face as well?
K: Just my body. To my neck.
ML: Do you see the creatures yet?
K: I haven't seen them. Gray hands, like gloved.
ML: Do they seem to have 5 digits?
K: Yes.
ML: Do they have opposing thumbs? Do they look like hands?
K: It's a hand.
ML: What kinds of instruments do they have. Do things look familiar or

367

real strange?

K: Familiar.

ML: Like our medical instruments?

K: There's a computer behind. I can hear it. It's as big as the wall.

ML: What do you notice?

K: There are lights. Red and yellow.

ML: What kinds of information does it give them?

K: My vitals. I can't tell the rest.

ML: Is it in a different language, is it very foreign looking?

K: It's beeps.

ML: So instead of visual, it is more auditory?

K: Yeah.

ML: From this perspective can you look now at the creatures?

K: Yeah.

ML: What do you notice about them?

K: They've covered themselves?

ML: In what way?

K: Like a gray sheet, gray flowing afghan type...like a robe. Long and gray.

ML: Do they have holes for eyes or anything?

K: No it's like a gauze screen. They have a nose and a very flat mouth. Their skin is gray.

ML: What are they communicating about?

K: I don't know. They don't talk.

ML: But you know. They don't have to talk. There is a part of your subconscious mind that remembers how to be telepathic. And that part of you can fully understand exactly what they are saying and their intentions of having you here today. Where do they come from?

L: They come back from the future.

ML: Do they come from far away?

K: (Silence)
ML: Have they ever lived on Earth?
K: They do.
ML: They do now or they did?
K: They do now.
ML: So you see pictures:
K: Yes, that's why they have hands like us.
ML: They inhabit humanoid bodies?
K: Yes.
ML: Then how do they get into the gray bodies?
K: They are covering themselves.
ML: Are they energetically possessing these other bodies?
K: They meld their bodies into ours.
ML: While they're here? Do they stay temporarily?
M: As long as they choose.
ML: They can switch bodies?
K: Yes.
ML: What do they typically do while they are here?
K: They are interested in our intellect, what we can do, what we have to offer. They want to understand our muscle structure. They aren't made of the same thing we are.
ML: Do they do this out of curiosity, or is there another motive?
K: I think it is scientific.
ML: They are not here for destructive purposes?
K: No.
ML: Why can't they give you something for the pain?
K: They don't feel the pain. They don't recognize that I do.
ML: They don't know how much pain you are going through?
K: No.
ML: They don't hear you screaming or anything?

K: They're oblivious to it - they don't care.

ML: So they don't have bodies like ours, they don't feel it?

K: No. They don't understand emotion.

ML: So they have come from the future. What year do they live in at their home?

K: 35.....I see 3 5's.

ML: OK. Do they come here from the future and travel back in time?

K: No. It's a different place.

ML: Is it a different planet? Or is it a different plane - described by different dimensions?

K: It's on our plane.

ML: So they are in our three-dimensional...

K: They are in a different stellar....a different solar system than we are.

ML: OK. How did you move from the porch to here.

K: They walked me there.

ML: They came up to the porch and walked away with you?

K: They took me to a van, a regular old van.

ML: And why did you walk with them? Did you think you knew them?

K: I was asleep.

ML: Did they knock you out?

K: No, I had fallen asleep on the porch. I felt comfortable with them it seemed.

ML: Did anyone see you?

K: No one was home.

ML: Which door did you enter the van from?

K: The side door.

ML: How many creatures were there?

K: Three.

ML: And how did they look at that time?

K: Like humans.

ML: And which seat did you sit in?
K: The middle seat.
ML: Was there conversation at all?
K: No talking.
ML: They didn't want to talk? Did you tell you not to talk?
K: They stuck a shot in my arm.
ML: While you were in the van?
K: Yes. I passed out.
ML: At that time you left your body and you could watch your body from that perspective. Where did they take you?
K: In a building.
ML: You drove up to a building?
K: Yes.
ML: What did it look like?
K: White, paneled, glass - sort of an office building.
ML: In a city or out in the country?
K: I've seen the building before. It's at the edge of (town she lived in).
ML: Is it a government building?
K: No, it's an office complex.
ML: Do they just have an office, or the whole building.
K: The whole building.
ML: What do you notice about the outside of the building?
K: There's a number on the outside.
ML: Does it say what kind of building it is?
K: It's a communications company......_____ Communications (name of business).
ML: And where do you enter the building?
K: We go in the side of the building. There's a loading dock on the side of the building.

ML: How do you get out of the van?

K: They carry me.

ML: Were there any other people who were brought there that day?

K: No just me.

ML: Where do they take you?

K: To the basement.

ML: And how many people are there now?

K: Two different people.

ML: Two more? Five altogether?

K: Yes.

ML: And that's when they put you in the chair?

K: Yes. And that's when I woke up.

ML: Did they give you an injection to wake up?

K: No.

ML: What length of time did it seem you were there?

K: 3-4 hours.

ML: After they took the sample from your thigh, what happened next. .

K: They're done.

ML: Why did they take your clothes off?

K: They examined my body. My joints. How I move.

ML: Did they examine any orifices?

K: No. They stuck a tube down my throat. I'm choking.

ML: What was it for?

K: Getting samples of stomach fluids.

ML: How long did that last?

K: Just now.

ML: And they take it out again?

K: Yes.

ML: Anything else they did?

K: No.

ML: Do they put your clothes back on?

K: They left them on the chair. They said I could get dressed.

ML: How is your leg feeling as you get dressed.

K: Sort of numb. Sore.

ML: Do you get dressed OK or are you disoriented?

K: I'm scared. Not very happy.

ML: What happens? How do you get out of there?

K: They walk me back to the van.

ML: Do they drive you back home?

K: That lady is there.

ML: There was a lady?

K: Yeah, there were three that came to the house.

ML: Do you recognize her. Have you ever seen her before or after...on the street.

K: No. I don't believe so.

ML: Do they look like us - like humans?

K: Yes, just like us.

ML: What happens next.

K: They take me to the corner of the street.

ML: What occurs

K: They're laughing....no not laughing, they are talking among themselves.

ML: Can you understand them?

K: I won't remember.

ML: Is that what they are saying?

K: (nods)

ML: What else do they say?

K: They don't have to take me home. I know how to get there myself.

ML: Do they hypnotize you, are they programming you?

K: Yeah, it's all over.

ML: Will they come back again?

K: They will but I won't be there.

ML: Did they arrange for that? Did they tell you to be ready to meet with them again?

K: No, I knew they were coming back.

ML: They planned on seeing you again in (city)

K: Yeah.

ML: Do they have operations in other cities?

K: Not everywhere. They move. From area to area.

ML: The same people?

K: Many different groups.

ML: How many different groups are there.

K: 20....30.

ML: Twenty or 30 around the country? Do they mostly stay in smaller towns?

K: No, in towns where they won't be known.

ML: Larger towns?

K: Yes, they can mold themselves in. I won't do.

ML: Why?

K: They couldn't use me.

ML: Why couldn't they use you?

K: I wasn't willing?

ML: In what way?

K: I guess they can't just do it. They can't just take somebody.

ML: Take them where - to do what they did to you?

K: They can't take their body unless they are willing.

ML: They wanted to take over someone's body?

K: That's what they're doing.

ML: So they possess the person?

K: Exactly

ML: For how long?

K: For as long as necessary. It kills them. It takes all their energy.

ML: What do they do?

K: They aren't particularly hard on the body.

ML: But what do they do, why would they need the body?

K: So they can be here and learn our cultures.

ML: So the bodies that they used when they came to get you were borrowed bodies?

K: Yes. They are projected out of their normal bodies and using humans bodies to do these deeds.

ML: When they dropped you off, do they leave those bodies, or do they keep them.

K: They stay in those bodies.

ML: When you arrived at the examining room, did they leave those bodies and take on the gray bodies?

K: There were two people that were regular alien people - they weren't in bodies.

ML: So they are able to live here and breathe our atmosphere.

K: Yes.

ML: Do they breathe our air or do they use an apparatus?

K: They breathe what we breathe.

ML: So three had taken other bodies. Two didn't take bodies....do they stay in the building?

K: Yes, those two are scientists.

ML: Do they work for a government on their own planet?

K: Everybody does - it's all the same there.

ML: (notice she is scanning her memory for more information) What do you notice?

K: I keep seeing the two men in the basement.

ML: What do you notice about them?

K: They talk with their minds.

ML: Telepathy?

K: Yes.

ML: Why are they so interested in our planet?

K: They like our resources. Where they are from is getting depleted. It's very small.

ML: Are they going to travel back in time as well as space.

K: Possibly.   They are in different times and different places. Not just our planet.

ML: Are they here in different times other than the present on this planet?

K: Yes.

ML: OK. You said that they didn't want your body because you weren't willing. Were they planning to take your body over?

K: That was the idea.

ML: They wanted to use your body?

K: Yes.

ML: How long would they be able to use a body?

K: Months.

ML: Months?

K: Yes, six or eight.

ML: Do they choose people who don't have family ties - or do they turn up missing?

K: They turn up missing.

ML: So some of the people on milk cartons could be these people?

K: Not children. All adults. Teens and up. They pick the smallest bodies they can find.

At this point the client chose to end the session. We concluded with a discussion about what this could possibly mean to her and the implications. She was quite disturbed about the information that was revealed, yet felt that she was no longer in danger of having an encounter with the same creatures again. She felt relieved that she had moved from that town not long after that incident. She felt they would not know how to find her, even though she also was certain that she was not suitable for their purposes.

In all cases such as this where the client experiences extraordinary phenomena, instruct your client to call you if they have any questions or concerns.

16

Your Last Session

If the client you have been seeing has been suffering from a chronic illness, the chances are very good that you will work with the client for months and then say good bye before they are well. In fact you may say goodbye before they have even experienced symptomatic improvement. Every client is different. There are certainly clients that you will see who will be so much better that they will simply tell you that they don't need to come back anymore.

The most common result in dealing with chronic illness is that the client has made some improvement. They will not know if it is time to move on but you will and here is how you will know.

Case Analysis is Complete

A big part of case analysis is listening to your client be frustrated, depressed and angry with their current life. Doing nothing in a session but listening and working through the events of the week is often better than doing high tech hypnosis. Listening to our cilent's difficulties each week is very important to do. You will listen to their problems of the week until they have gone through them all. Then you begin hypnotherapy each week. Hypnotherapy always follows psychotherapy. Do not go back in time, with regression until you have listened to your client share their current time difficulties with you in full. There is no race to begin hypnosis each week.

Regression is Complete

The work you have done in regression was complete if the client actually experienced the causal event(s). This means that they ultimately abreacted as they described the imprinting event to you and then after an hour or two, as they tell the story again and again, it no longer stimulates emotion.

Typically regression work with a client suffering from chronic illness will have multiple causes (ISE's) and will take about 4-7 sessions to uncover and run through these causes.

Ego State Therapy is Complete

The work you have completed in ego state therapy is done when all parts of the person agree that it is in the best interest of the self to get well. This seemingly simple resolution can take hours of work to complete. Typically ego state therapy can be accomplished in one session and there are typically only two or three parts in contention with each other. Creating the resolution to allow healing can be rapid but the implementation of the plan by the physical body can take minutes or months.

Time Track Therapy is Complete

One session is all you will need for Time Track Therapy. You will find this session to be much like that of sewing a patient of a medical doctor. I recommend taping this session so your client has it forever. It is a healing intervention unlike any they will ever experience again.

Suggestion and Maintenance

Whether your client is in trance or just in conversation, keep your suggestions to the client focused on a believable but optimistic future. Many clients will want to see you every month or every other month after having spent so many weeks with you. This maintenance work is just fine and will assure maximum results.

The Last Goodbye

Most clients will not ask you for maintenance sessions after you have completed your 5-10 sessions of therapy. There is no correct answer as to whether you should encourage maintenance sessions, but here is my rule of thumb: If their spouse, significant other or their job plays a significant role in their illness then I strongly recommend seeing the client 30 days after your "last" session. This will ensure that your work is not in vain. Time and again, hypnotherapists watch their clients go home after beginning the process of healing wounds only to have a spouse open the wounds again with unkindness, disrespect, contempt and criticism.

Resolving Difficult Cases and
Answering Tough Questions about Hypnotherapy

1) Why not go straight to the initial sensitizing event? It seems like it would be more efficient than taking the long bridge back to the causal event.

Sometimes bringing a person straight to the initial imprint will work, especially if there is one single initial sensitizing event (ISE). However, this is normally not the case. There are often many causes for one effect. In certification trainings students often get over anxious to get to the ISE and several things can happen.

A) The client will often bounce out of the event and out of trance completely. Once this happens, re-establishing rapport, trust and confidence is not easy.

B) The client will often go to an event which might be *an* initial event but not *the* initial event. It is very common for there to be two or three different triggering events for effects. Most chronic illnesses do not bring just one symptom with them but many. In the case of fibromyalgia, for example, there can be several initial events that need to be abreacted. Therefore, the slower more methodical bridge back to the beginnings of the illness are more powerful than the urging into one specific event too quickly.

C) The client may not get to the event(s) that were causal in nature at all. The unconscious mind is comprised of numerous ego states that will protect the individual from experiencing certain traumas before the ego states are convinced that it is safe to do so. This is why memories are repressed in the first place. The first session with a hypnotherapist is not going to change years of conditioning with the rest of the world.

Be patient with your client. Take your time. Each event that your client brings you back to helps build their confidence in you as a therapist and increases the likelihood of successful therapy.

2)   The client won't go into the initial event, or anywhere past a certain age, or experience anything with a certain person, what do I do?

Always respect the client's boundaries while realizing that without unlocking that door, it is unlikely that healing will happen. Therefore, we must peel the onion from a different direction. If the time period was childhood, age seven, then you may contact an ego state (a set of memories and experiences) related to say, a grandmother or childhood friends, that will allow you to travel that time track back in time to the age where the "work" needs to be done.

For example, if a child was abused by his father at age seven, and the person will not go to any experiences with his father or to the child's early life, then you must begin elsewhere. Begin with an ego state that has memories in the same time period but also has more recent memories. If the child had a grandmother who lived until later in the child's life, say until the person became a man, then you can say, "tell me about a time when you had a really good conversation with your grandmother."

They will tell you about a story or some communication with the grandmother. Then you ask them to tell you about a similar dialogue earlier in the relationship with the grandmother. Keep going back in time until you get to that magical age seven. Then when the client is at age seven with the grandmother you can ask the client, "When you are done talking with gradma, what do you see around you? What other people are around you?"

The client may tell you about the kids next door or other people. This is exactly what you hope for. Eventually the child will go home and will run into Dad. It will not be a pleasant experience. The experience will be ugly but when the adult man realizes that he was abused and that there is nothing for him to feel guilty or shameful for, he will be so much happier after trance that the change will be remarkable.

In cases where there were major "dark spots" in a person's life, the healing that happens from experiencing these tough to get to memories is often amazing.

The unconscious mind will not give you an event or an experience until it trusts you to handle it. In addition because some events or experiences are "state dependent" (only remember when drunk, doing drugs, on anesthesia) it often takes a lot of tinkering to get a person back into the state they were in all those years ago.

3)   When doing ego state therapy should you name the parts or have the client name the parts?

I don't see any benefit in naming parts. I've read about many therapists who do, and I imagine that there is no problem with it, but I don't sense much benefit in doing so.

4)   Are ego states always distinct from each other or do they overlap?

Typically part of one ego state will be part of another ego state. There are literally hundreds of ego states within an individual. An ego state that encompasses age 17 will overlap an ego state that encompasses all dating experiences, for example.

5)   Why not do Time Track Therapy first with a client?

Because instead of getting tears of joy you will get an abreaction and a quick trip to an ISE. When I demonstrate TTT for certification classes typically everyone is in tears after the experience. However, there is almost always someone who is not crying tears of joy but have been en-tranced into an ISE unintentionally. That person then needs to fully abreact the experience they have been unwittingly taken to. Time Track Therapy is a powerful tool but it must be used in it's proper place.

6)   When is the right time to use a script?

Typically the best time to use a script is when the client has had a thorough case analysis, regression work has been completed, parts therapy has been completed and time track therapy has been accomplished. Then you modify a script to the client's specific needs and create an audiocassette tape for the client that they can listen to every day for ego strengthening.

As a rule, scripts are not therapeutic when simply being read by a therapist. Reading causes dissociation in the therapist and therefore is not recommended, except as noted above.

However, on the other side of the coin, you should know that making audio tapes is not an easy task without a script to guide the way. The scripts in this book will give you all the ideas you need to successfully develop tapes to help you help your client.

7)   What are the guidelines for working with clients who are suffering from medical or psychological conditions?

I do not work with any clients who are schizophrenic or suffer from MPD. I do not work with clients who suffer from medical problems if they will not see a medical doctor for a complete diagnostic work up. If someone is suffering from severe depression, I want that person to see a medical doctor for a prescription of an SSRI drug. If someone is suffering from severe anxiety or severe phobias I want them to see a medical doctor and get the appropriate prescriptions. Medication can make my work more difficult as a hypnotherapist but it will almost always make the client's life better. If a client suffers from tinnitus I will not work with them unless they know they do not have a tumor that will kill them. I have had three experiences since 1994 where I suggested clients get an MRI and the medical doctor said, "not necessary." In these three instances, the client's tinnitus got significantly worse, started experiencing headaches, and in all three cases, the client had to have the auditory nerve cut. In two of the cases the seventh nerve (facial) had to be shaved, taking away facial movement and the inability to close the eye on that side of the face. ALWAYS have the client get an MRI if they have tinnitus. These tumors, while rare, will kill the person if left untreated. They can be excised when they are small. When they get bigger, they usually will be so big that the 8th nerve will have to be cut, meaning the person will be deaf for the rest of their life.

Every medical case is to be dealt with the same way: Hypnotherapy is a *complement* to medical care and not an alternative.

8) What if a client doesn't get better after faithfully adhering to the CARPeTS model of therapy?

Be a warrior for your client's health. The CARPeTS model is probably the best model in hypnotherapy, but there is more than hypnotherapy that can be done to help our client. Is the client exercising? Are they eating right? Have they gotten out of the relationships that are keeping them in emotional prison? Have they started a different job that they have wanted?

Hypnotherapy is one factor in a client's healing. Find out what medications and other treatments might be able to help them.

Remember that hypnotherapy is a relationship and that you might not be the best person to help this client even though you may be the best qualified in your community!

Not everyone can be cured, though most can be healed. (Remember that healing is more emotionally based and cure tends to refer to somatic experience.)

9)   How do you know when to use the CARPeTS model and not PLRT?

If someone comes to your office asking for a past life regression then it seems reasonable to help the client have that experience. If a client comes to your office asking for symptomatic improvement in a physical or emotional issue, then I sugggest you use the CARPeTS model.

10)   I don't believe in UFO's. If someone comes to me and wants me to regress them, should I?

Maybe. I'm not a Catholic but I work with an awful lot of wonderful Catholic people. A person's beliefs are for me to empathize with and understand. I am not a person's judge. I do not determine what they should and should not believe in. If you feel that you can be objective and caring with a client who believes he has had a UFO experience then work with them. If not, then definitely, refer them to someone who will be more understanding. We all have our biases and prejudices and part of being a great therapist is recognizing these biases and taking the appropriate action.

11) What makes a truly great therapist?

The best therapists are those that truly care about their cilents. They are warriors for their client's health. They will do whatever it takes to help their client. This special therapist has a great deal of love and empathy for the client. The greatest therapists listen far more than they talk. They take extensive notes and operate within ethical and moral standards at all times.

Commencement means Beginning

This is your beginning. Whether you have been in the hypnotherapy business for 20 years or 20 minutes, this is your chance to begin, or begin again.

The Hypnotherapy Handbook provides you with the information you need to know to have a fundamental understanding about what to do in session work. Many people reading this book have had exposure to hypnotherapy through a certification or college course in hypnosis.

Any handbook can only hope to make a difficult subject understandable. I hope that we have done that for you! Hypnotherapy and hypnoanalysis are interventions that save lives, change lives and help people get well. To be such a big part of so many wonderful people's lives is really quite special and humbling.

The model and techniques employed in this book are not always easy to implement in therapy. It takes a great deal of practice to master this information to the point you become intuitively competent at them. If you have come this far I suggest that you will be able to be one of those people who can really make changes in other people's lives.

I encourage you to contact the Hypnosis Research and Training Center at (612) 616-0732 to get information about learning how to apply the skills you have read about in this book. The master level certification trainings we offer assume you already have a working knowledge of suggestive hypnosis. These trainings will help you move into the top 5% in this field both in income and in the value you provide those you work with.

Welcome to one of the greatest professions on earth. The contributions you make to your client's lives will be dearly appreciated and well worth your hard work and time!

Bibliography

Crasilneck, H.B., and Hall, J.A. 1985. Clinical Hypnosis: Principles and Applications. New York: Grune and Stratton.

Dossey, Larry. Be Careful What You Pray For..., San Francisco, Harper. 1998

Federn, P. (1952) *Ego Psychology and the Psychoses.* New York: Basic Books.

Fielding, J.W.L. "An Interim Report of a Prospective, Randomized, Controlled Study of Adjuvant Chemotherapy in Operable Gastric Cancer: British Stomach Cancer Group." World Journal of Surgery 7 (1983): 390-99

Frank, Jerome. *Persuasion and Healing.* Baltimore, Johns Hopkins, 1993.

Hilgard, E. (1977) *Divided Consciousness: Multiple Controls in Human Thought and Action..* New York: Norton.

Hogan, K. (1998) *Miracles of Hypnosis: Advanced Techniques and Strategies of Hypnotherapy and Hypnoanalysis.* Eagan, MN: Network 3000.

Kluft, R.P. and Fine, C.G. (1993) *Clinical Perspectives on Multiple Personality Disorder.* Washington D.C. American Psychiatric Press.

Meador, C.K. "Hex Death: Voodoo Magic or Persuasion?" Southern Medical Journal 85, no. 3 (1992): 244-47

Phillips, M. and Fredrick, C. (1996) *Healing The Divided Self: Clinical and Ericksonian Hypnotherapy for Post-Traumatic and Dissociative Conditions.* New York: Norton.

Rhein, R.W., Jr. "Placebo: Deception or Potent Therapy?" Medical World News (February 4, 1980), 39-47.

Rossi, E. and Cheek, D. (1984) *Mind Body Therapy.* New York: Norton.

Sinclair-Gieben, A.H.C. 1959. Treatment of Warts by Hypnosis. Lancet 2:480-82.

Stotland, E. 1969. The Psychology of Hope. San Francisco: Jossey-Bass

Voelker, Rebecca. "Nocebo's Contribute to a Host of Ills." Journal of the American Medical Association 275 no. 5 (1996): 345-47.

Watkins, J.G. (1947) *Hypnotherapy of War Neuroses.* New York: Ronald.

Watkins, J.G. (1992) *Hypnoanalytic Techniques: Clinical Hypnosis.* New York: Irvington.

Watkins, J.G. and Watkins, H.H. (1998) *Ego States: Theory and Therapy.* New York: Norton.

Wolf, S. and R.H. Pinsky. "Effects of Placebo Administration and Occurrence of Toxic Reactions." Journal of American Medical Association 155, no. 4 (1954) 339

Author and Contributor Information

Kevin Hogan
http://www.hollys.com/success-dynamics/

Kevin has a Ph.D. in Psychology and is an instructor at the University of St. Thomas Management Center. He is a certified instructor of hypnotherapy and NLP, and is the Director of the Hypnosis Research and Training Center.

The web site is a certification training resource area. Free information about certification trainig, prerequisites, and benefits are available at the site. It includes hundreds of pages of text you can download free. Articles about hypnotherapy, tinnitus, NLP, relationships, communication, non-verbal communication, and a complete catalog of hypnosis products. There are also links to most of the important major websites in the field of hypnosis.

He is the author of several books including:

Tinnitus: Turning the Volume Down
The Psychology of Persuasion
Talk Your Way to the Top
The Gift: A Discovery of Love, Happiness and Fulfillment
Life By Design

Kevin Hogan
Hypnosis Research and Training Center
1960 Cliff Lake Rd. #112-200
Eagan, MN 55123
(612) 616-0732

Mary Lee LaBay
http://www.maryleelabay.com/
Mary Lee is a certified instructor of hypnotherapy and a respected hypnotherapist. She has been practicing hypnotherapy since 1986 and became a Washington State Registered Counselor in 1997. Mary Lee is a member of Mensa, The National Guild of Hypnotists, and The American Board of Hypnotherapy. She teaches continuing education courses at Bellevue Community College, is a dynamic speaker, and has authored numerous articles. She also makes frequent radio appearances. Her website has articles about hypnosis, metaphysics, scheduled appearances, and more. Mary Lee is a world traveler and has lived in places as diverse as Puerto Rico and The Netherlands.

Mary Lee LaBay
9959 Lake Washington Blvd. N.E. #202
Bellevue, WA 98004
(425) 652-1550

Holly Sumner
http://www.hollys.com/
Holly was the 1996 Member of the Year for the National Guild of Hypnotists. She is an Advanced Clinical Certified Hypnotherapist. Holly is a world traveler, leading retreats and workshops throughout the United States and Europe. Her website has information about retreats, her latest textbook on meditation, discussion groups, and dozens of pages of metaphysical interest. She is the author of *The Meditation Sourcebook: Meditation for Mortals.*

Holly Sumner
Box 384
Cape Neddick, Maine 03902
(207) 284-6412

C. Devin Hastings
http://adac-hypnosis.com/
Devin is a certified instructor of hypnotherapy and NLP. He is a licensed massage therapist and a clinical hypnotherapist in the Orlando, Florida area. He specializes in working with people who suffer from diabetes, impotence, and chronic illnesses. He is also a martial artist and a certified fitness instructor. Devin `has produced and authored numerous video and audio programs including *Managing Diabetes with Hypnosis* and *Emergency Hypnosis.* He is a member of the National Guild of Hypnotists and the International Medical and Dental Hypnosis Association.

C. Devin Hastings
1633 S. Kirkman Rd., Ste. 386
Orlando, Florida 32811
(407)-290-3434

Elizabeth J. Nahum
http://members.com/avalonmom/newavaloncentre.htm
Elizabeth is a certified instructor of hypnotherapy and a clinical hypnotherapist through the National Guild of Hypnotists and the Hypnosis Research and Training Center. She is a certified specialist in the reduction of tinnitus symptoms as well as other chronic ailments. Helping pioneer a new integrated effective approach to healing she is a published author in the field of past life regression therapy, with over 15 years of active involvement and practice. Her post graduate work was in crisis intervention and victimology. She is available for private sessions, career training and workshops as well as public speaking. Elizabeth has appeared numerous time on TV and radio.

Elizabeth J. Nahum
1222 Holbcombe Ranch Road
Weaverville, NC 28787   (828) 680-9392

For More Information

Would you like the most recent issue of the Hypnosis Research and Training Center catalog? It's yours free for the asking!

If you would like to receive more information about hypnotherapy, advanced training opportunities and seminars by Kevin Hogan and the other contributors of this book, contact us at the address below.

Kevin Hogan, Ph.D.
Hypnosis Research and Training Center
1960 Cliff. Lake Rd. #112-200
Eagan, MN 55122
(612) 616-0732